Andrew S. Fuller

The nut culturist

A Treatise on the Propagation, Planting and Cultivation of Nut-bearing Trees and Shrubs, adapted to the Climate of the United States

Andrew S. Fuller

The nut culturist
A Treatise on the Propagation, Planting and Cultivation of Nut-bearing Trees and Shrubs, adapted to the Climate of the United States

ISBN/EAN: 9783337185763

Printed in Europe, USA, Canada, Australia, Japan

Cover: Foto ©Andreas Hilbeck / pixelio.de

More available books at **www.hansebooks.com**

THE
NUT CULTURIST

A TREATISE

ON THE

PROPAGATION, PLANTING AND CULTIVATION OF NUT-BEARING TREES AND SHRUBS

ADAPTED TO THE

CLIMATE OF THE UNITED STATES,

WITH THE SCIENTIFIC AND COMMON NAMES OF

THE FRUITS KNOWN

IN COMMERCE AS EDIBLE OR OTHERWISE USEFUL NUTS

By ANDREW S. FULLER,

*Author of the "Grape Culturist," "Small Fruit Culturist," "Practical Forestry,'
"Propagation of Plants," etc., etc.*

ILLUSTRATED

NEW YORK
ORANGE JUDD COMPANY
1896

PREFACE

Believing that the time is opportune for making an effort to cultivate all kinds of edible and otherwise useful nut-bearing trees and shrubs adapted to the soil and climate of the United States, thereby inaugurating a great, permanent and far-reaching industry, the following pages have been penned, and with the hope of encouraging and aiding the farmer to increase his income and enjoyments, without, to any appreciable extent, adding to his expenses or labors. With this idea in mind, I have not advised the general planting of nut orchards on land adapted to the production of grain and other indispensable farm crops, but mainly as roadside trees and where desired for shade, shelter and ornament, being confident that when all such positions are occupied with choice nut-bearing trees, to the exclusion of those yielding nothing of intrinsic value, there will have been added many millions of dollars to the wealth of the country, as well as a vast store of edible and delicious food.

This work has not been written for the edification, or the special approbation, of scientific botanists, but for those who, in the opinion of the writer, are most likely to profit by a treatise of this kind. Unfamiliar terms have been omitted wherever simple common words would answer equally as well in conveying the intended information. There being no work of this kind published in this country that would serve as a guide, I have been compelled to formulate a plan of my own, and to describe all the newer varieties from the best specimens obtainable, and these may not, in all cases, have been perfect. Under such circumstances, this work must necessarily be incomplete, and especially where the possessors of claimed-to-be new and valuable varieties have either refused or failed to give any information in regard to them. On the contrary, however, I must acknowledge my indebtedness to many correspondents, who have so generously placed specimens of both trees and nuts of rare new varieties in my hands for testing and describing, as well as assisting me in tracing their history and origin.

That this treatise may become the pioneer of many other and better works on nut culture is the sincere wish of

THE AUTHOR.

RIDGEWOOD, N. J., 1896.

CONTENTS.

LIST OF ILLUSTRATIONS.

CHAPTER I.

No special amount of prophetic acumen is required to foresee that the time will soon come when the people of this country must necessarily place a much higher value upon all kinds of food than they do at present, or have done in the past. In this we are pre-supposing that in the natural course of events, our population will continue to increase in nearly the same ratio it has since we assumed the responsibilities of an independent nation. The very existence of animal life on this planet depends upon the quantity and quality of available food, and while some sentimentalists may assume to ignore and even attempt to deprecate the animal desires of their race, nature compels us to recognize the fact that there can be no fire without fuel, and the great and useful intellectual powers of man are the emanations of the animal tissues of a well-nourished brain. The brawny arm that rends the rock and hurls the fragments aside, gets its power through the same channel and from the same source as those of other members of society, whatever the nature of their calling; for mankind is built upon one universal and general plan, varied though it may be in some of the minor details of construction. We certainly have no cause to fear that the theories of Malthus, in regard to the overpopulation of the earth as a whole, will ever be verified in the experience of the human race, because with necessity comes industry, also the inventions of devices to enable us to avoid just such dangers, and if these fail to keep pace with our wants and needs, wars, earthquakes, drouths, floods, and contagious, epidemic and other diseases, become the weapons which nature employs to prevent overpopulation. But we cannot deny that nature does sometimes encourage or permit a somewhat redundant population in certain favorable countries and localities, and then follows a struggle for existence, and food becomes the paramount object in life. To ward off danger of this kind and keep the supply in excess of the demand, is a problem which should seriously engage the attention of every one who takes the least interest in the general welfare of his countrymen, even though the day of want or scarcity of food may be very far distant.

Among the various sources of acceptable and nutritious food products heretofore almost entirely neglected in this country, the edible nuts stand preëminently and conspicuously in the foreground, awaiting the skill and attention of all who seek pleasure and profit— to be derived from the products of the soil. For many centuries these nuts have held a prominent position among the desirable and valuable food products of various European and Oriental countries ; not only because they were important and almost indispensable in making up the household supplies of all classes of the people, but often because available for filling a depleted purse, and the thing needful for this purpose has, in the main, been received from far-distant nations, who through indifference and neglect failed to provide themselves with such a simple and valuable article as the edible nuts.

Much as we may boast of our immense natural resources and advantages, we have not, as yet, availed ourselves of one-half of those we possess, and the remainder is still awaiting our attention. We also neglect to avail ourselves of the many superior domestic traits and practices of the foreign nations with whom we are in constant communication. It may be that the absence of incentives has made us careless and indifferent in regard to a day of need, which in all probability will come to us sooner or later; but whatever the cause, the fact remains that we have been spending millions annually on worthless articles and sentimental problems and projects, which have brought us neither riches nor honor; in truth, to use a homely phrase, we have been following the bellwether in nearly all of our rural affairs and pursuits. As a natural result we are spending millions for imported articles of everyday use which might easily and with large profit be produced at home, and in many instances the most humiliating part of the transaction is that we send our money to people who do not purchase any of our productions and almost ignore us in commercial matters. I am not referring to those products ill-adapted to our climate, nor to those which, owing to scarcity and high price of labor, we are unable to produce profitably, but to such nuts as the almond, walnut and chestnut, which we can raise as readily as peaches, apples and pears. There certainly can be no excuse for the neglect of such nut trees on the score of cost of labor in propagation and planting, because our streets and highways are lined and shaded with equally as expensive kinds, although they are absolutely worthless for any other purpose than shade or shelter, yielding nothing in the way of food for either man or beast. Can any one invent a reasonable excuse for planting miles and miles of roadside trees of such kinds as elm, maple, ash, willow, cottonwood, and a hundred other similar kinds, where shellbark hickory, chestnut, walnut, pecan and butternut would thrive just as well, cost no more, and yet yield bushels of delicious and highly prized nuts, and this annually or in alternate years, continuing and increasing in productiveness for one, two or more centuries. Aside from the intrinsic value of such trees, they are, in the way of ornament, just as beautiful as, and in many instances much superior to those yielding nothing in the way of food except, perhaps, something for noxious insects.

I am not attempting to pose as the one wise man engaged in rural affairs, but am merely recounting my personal observation and experience, having in my younger days taken the advice of my elders, and at a time when a hint of the future value of nut trees would have been worth more than a paid-up life insurance policy. But as the hint was not given, I selected for roadside trees ash, maples, tulip, magnolias, and other popular kinds, all of which thrived, and by the time they were twenty years old began to be admired for their beauty, although their roots were spreading into the adjoining field, robbing the soil of the nutriment required for less vigorous-growing plants. Later, however, the discovery was made that I was paying very dearly for a crop of leaves and sentiment, neither of which was salable or available for filling one's purse. When thirty years of age the very best of my roadside trees were probably worth two dollars each for firewood, or one dollar more than the nurseryman's price at the time of planting. The greater part of these trees, however, have since been cremated, a few being left as reminders of the misdirected labors of youth and inexperience.

In this matter of following a leader in tree-planting along the highways, it appears to be a predominant trait of our rural population and as old as the settlement of this country, for nowhere is it more pronounced than in the New England States, where the American elms attracted the attention of the Pilgrims and their contemporaries and descendants, and even continued down to the present day. No one will deny that the American elm is a noble tree in appearance, is easily transplanted and of rapid growth, and yet it is one of the most worthless for any economic purpose. It may

be that its worthlessness for other purposes made it all
the more acceptable for streets and roadsides, the better
kinds being reserved for firewood, fencing, furniture,
and the manufacture of agricultural and other implements. But whatever the cause or object, the elm became the one tree generally selected for planting in
parks, villages, cities, and along roadsides in the country, not only in the older but in many of the newer
States. From present indications, however, the glory
of this much over-praised tree is on the wane, for the
imported elm-leaf beetle (*Galeruca calmariensis*) is
slowly but surely spreading over the country, defoliating
the elms of all species and varieties, and it is a question
whether we should bless this insect for the work it is
doing or look upon it as a pest. Perhaps future generations will sing pæons in its praise, and they certainly
will have reasons for rejoicing if better and more useful
kinds are planted in the places now occupied by the
worthless elms.

In other localities some pioneer or leader in roadside ornamentation selected or recommended some species of maple, linden, catalpa, poplar or willow, but it
made little or no difference as to kind, because, as a rule,
all his neighbors followed without a thought or question
in regard to adaptation to soil, climate, or fitness in the
local or surrounding scenery, or of its future economic
value. The result of this want of taste and forethought
may be seen in whatever direction one travels throughout the older and more thickly settled portions of this
country.

Had the early settlers of the New England States
planted shellbark hickories, or even the native chestnut,
in place of the American elm, they would not only have
had equally as beautiful trees for shade and ornament,
but the nutritious nuts would scarcely have failed to bring
bright cheer to many a household and money to fill oft-

depleted purses, while their descendants would have blessed them for their forethought. Of course there are other valuable kinds of nuts which thrive over the greater part of the New England States, but I refer only to the two, which were so abundant in the forests that one or both could have been obtained for the mere cost of transplanting. But it is not fair to prate about the remissness and follies of our ancestors, unless we can show by our works that wisdom has come down to us through their experience.

What is true of the New England is equally true of all the older States, and is rapidly becoming so in many of the newer, little attention being paid to the intrinsic value of the wood or the product of the trees planted along the highways. There are also millions of acres of wild lands not suitable for cultivation, but well adapted to the growth of trees, whether of the nut-bearing or other kinds. But for the present I will omit further reference to the planting of nut trees except on the line of the highways, just where other kinds have long been in vogue and are still being cultivated for shade and ornament,—with no thought, perhaps, on the part of the planter, that both could be obtained in the nut trees, with something of more intrinsic value added. The nut trees which grow to a large size are as well adapted for planting along roadsides, in the open country, as other kinds that yield nothing in the way of food for either man or beast. They are also fully as beautiful in form and foliage, and in many instances far superior, to the kinds often selected for such purposes.

The only objection I have heard of as being urged against planting fruit and nut trees along the highway is that they tempt boys and girls—as well as persons of larger growth—to become trespassers; but this only applies to where there is such a scarcity that the quantity taken perceptibly lessens the total crop. But where there is an abundance, either the temptation to trespass disappears, or we fail to recognize our loss. As we cannot very well dispense with the small boy and his sister, I am in favor of providing them bountifully with all the good things that climate and circumstance will afford. It is a truism that conscience is never strengthened by an empty stomach.

A mile, in this country, is 5280 feet, and if trees are set 40 feet apart—which is allowing sufficient room for them to grow during an ordinary lifetime—we get 133 per mile in a single row; but where the roads are three to four rods wide, two rows may be planted, one on each side, or 266 per mile. With such kinds as the Persian walnut and American and foreign chestnuts, we can safely estimate the crop, when the trees are twenty years old, at a half bushel per tree, or 66 bushels for a single row, and 133 for a double row per mile. With grafted trees of either kind we may count on double the quantity named, presuming, of course, that the trees are given proper care. But to be on the safe side, let us keep our estimate down to the half-bushel mark per tree, and with this crop, at the moderate price of four dollars per bushel, we would get $264 from the crop on a single row, and double this sum, or $528, for the crop on a double row—with a fair assurance that the yield would increase steadily for the next hundred years or more; while the cost of gathering and marketing the nuts is no greater, and in many instances much less than that of the ordinary grain crops. At the expiration of the first half century, one-half of the trees may be removed, if they begin to crowd, and the timber used for whatever purpose it may best be adapted. The remaining trees would probably improve, on account of having more room for development.

There has been a steady increase in the demand, and a corresponding advance in the price of all kinds of edible nuts, during the past three or four decades, and this is likely to continue for many years to come, because consumers are increasing far more rapidly than producers; besides, the forests, which have long been the only source of supply of the native kinds, are rapidly disappearing, while there has not been, as yet, any special effort to make good the loss, by replanting or otherwise. The dealers in such articles in our larger cities assure me that the demand for our best kinds of edible nuts is far in excess of the supply, and yet not one housewife or cook in a thousand in this country has ever attempted to use nuts of any kind in the preparation of meats and other dishes for the table, as is so generally practiced in European and Oriental countries.

The question may be asked, if the demand is sufficient to warrant the planting of the hardy nut trees extensively along our highways or elsewhere. In answer to such a question it may be said that we not only consume all of the edible nuts raised in this country, but import millions of pounds annually of the very kinds which thrive here as well as in any other part of the world.

I have before me the records of our imports from the year 1790 to 1894, but as I purpose dealing more with the present and future than with the distant past, I will refer here only to the statistics of the four years of the present decade, leaving out all reference to the tropical nuts, which are not supposed to be adapted to our climate.

Of almonds, not shelled, and on which there is a protective duty of three cents per pound, we imported from 1890 to the close of 1893, 12,443,895 pounds, valued at $1,100,477.65. Of almonds, shelled, on which the duty is now five cents, we imported 1,326,633 pounds. The total value of both kinds for the four years, amounted to $1,716,277.32. Whether this high protective duty is to remain or not is uncertain, but it is quite evident that it has had very little effect in stimulating the cultivation of this nut except in circumscribed localities on the Pacific coast.

Of filberts and walnuts, not shelled, and with a duty of two cents per pound, we imported during the same years from eleven to fifteen million pounds annually, or a total for the four years of 54,526,181 pounds, and in addition about two million pounds of the shelled kernels, on which the duty was six cents (now four) per pound. The total value of these importations amounted to $3,176,085.34.

I do not find the European chestnut mentioned in any list of imports, although an immense quantity must be received from France, Italy and Spain every year, and they are probably imported under the head of miscellaneous nuts, not specially provided for, and upon which the duty was two cents per pound in 1890-'91, but was later reduced to one and a half cents.

Under the head "miscellaneous nuts," or all other shelled and unshelled "not specially provided for," there was imported during the period named 6,442,908 pounds, valued at $235,976.05. The total for all kinds of edible nuts imported was $7,124,575.82. These figures are sufficient to prove that we are neglecting an opportunity to largely engage in and extend a most important and profitable industry. It is true that in the Southern States considerable attention has been given, of late, to the preservation of the old pecan nut trees and the planting of young stock, but it will be many years before the increase from this source can overtake the ever-increasing demand for this delicious native nut. Californians are also making an effort to raise several foreign varieties of edible nuts on a somewhat extensive scale, but all these widely scattered experiments are mere drops in the ocean of our wants. Under such conditions I ask, in all seriousness, if it is not about time that our farmers and rural population generally began to count their worthless and unproductive possessions, in the form of roadside and other shade trees—which have probably cost fully as much to secure, plant and care for during the few or many years since they were set out, as would have been expended upon the most beautiful and valuable nut-bearing kinds. If our ancestors were at fault in the selection of trees for planting, we need not expect that posterity will excuse us for continuing and repeating their folly, especially when our dear-bought experience should teach us better.

At the present time there might be some difficulty in procuring, at the nurseries, a choice selection of nut trees in any considerable quantity, suited to roadside planting, because heretofore there has been little demand for such stock; and nurserymen are only human, and conduct their establishments on business principles, propagating the kind of trees in greatest demand, regardless of their intrinsic or future value to purchasers. They will also continue producing such stock just so long as the demand will warrant it, and further, it is but natural that they should sometimes recommend and advise their customers to purchase worthless, and even pestiferous kinds, such as the ailanthus and white poplar, because the profits in raising these trees are large and there is little danger of loss in transplanting. But if purchasers will insist on having better kinds and refuse to accept any other, they will soon be accommodated; and if not, then let everyone who owns a plot of ground become his own propagator of trees. It is not beyond the ability of any moderately intelligent man (or woman, for that matter) to raise nut trees, and as readily as one could potatoes or corn.

Where farmers want a row of trees along the roadside, to be utilized for line fence posts, they cannot possibly find any kinds better adapted for this purpose than chestnut, walnut and hickory; and these will give just as dense a shade, and look as well—besides, in a few years they may yield enough to pay the taxes on the entire farm, the crop increasing in amount and value not only during the lifetime of the planter, but that of many generations of his descendants.

This appeal to the good sense of our rural population is made in all sincerity and with the hope that it will be heeded by every man who has a spark of patriotism in his soul, and who dares show it in his labors, and by setting up a few milestones in the form of nut-bearing trees along the roadsides—if for no other purpose than the present pleasure of anticipating the gratification such monuments will afford the many who are certain to pass along these highways years hence.

It is surely not good policy to enrich other nations at the expense of our own people, as we are now doing in sending millions of dollars annually to foreign countries in payment for such luxuries as edible nuts that could be readily and profitably produced at home. There need be no fear of an overproduction of such things, no matter how many may engage in their cultivation, because in such industries many will resolve to do, and even make an attempt, but a comparatively small number will reach any marked degree of success.

CHAPTER II.

Amygdalus, *Tournefort*. Name supposed to be derived from *amysso*, to lacerate, because of the prominent sharp, knifelike margin of one edge of the deeply pitted, wrinkled nut. Martius, an Italian botanist, suggests that the name came from the Hebrew word *shakad*, signifying vigilant, or to awake, because after the rigors of winter the almond tree is one of the earliest to hail the coming of spring, with its flowers. The common English name is from the Latin *amandola*, corrupted from *amygdala*. In French it is *amandier;* in German, *mandel;* Portuguese, *amendoa;* Spanish, *almendro;* Italian, *amandola, mandalo, mandorla,* etc. ; Dutch, *amendel;* Chinese, *him-ho-gin.*

Under the natural classification of plants the almond belongs to the order *Rosaceæ*, and in the tribe *Drupaceæ*. Linnæus placed the peach and almond in the same genus, and they are now generally considered to be only varieties of one species,—the wild almond tree is probably the parent from which all the cultivated peaches and nectarines have descended. In most of our modern botanical works these fruits are classed as a sub-section of *Prunus*, the plum. They are mainly deciduous shrubs, or small trees. The flowers are variable, both in size and color; but in the almond they are usually somewhat larger than in the peach, almost sessile, and from separate scaly buds on the shoots of the preceding season, appearing in early spring, before or with the unfolding leaves, the latter being folded lengthwise in the bud. Leaves three to four inches long, tapering, finely serrate, with few or no glands at the base of the blade, as seen in many varieties of the common peach. Fruit clothed with a fine dense pubescence in both peach and almond; but in the latter the pulpy envelope becomes dry and fibrous at maturity, cracking open irregularly, allowing the rough and deeply indented nuts to drop out; while in the peach the pulpy part becomes soft, juicy and edible, the reverse of the almond. The nectarine is only a smooth-skinned peach.

History of the Almond.—As with most of our long-cultivated fruits and nut trees, very little is now known of the early history or origin of the almond, and even its native country has not been positively determined, although it is supposed to be indigenous to parts of Northern Africa and the mountainous region of Asia. Theophrastus, who wrote a history of plants about three centuries before the Christian era, mentions the almond as the only tree in Greece that produces blossoms before the leaves. From Greece it was introduced into Italy, where the nuts were called *nuces græcæ*, or Greek nuts.

Columella, about the middle of the first century of our era, was the earliest Roman writer to mention the almond as distinct from the peach. From Italy this nut was slowly disseminated, making its way northward mainly through France, reaching Great Britain as late as 1538 (*Hortus Kewensis*). But its cultivation has never extended in Britain, beyond sheltered gardens and orchard houses, owing to the cool and otherwise uncongenial climate, and the same is true of Northern France and other regions to the eastward in Europe. But in the south of France, also in Italy, Spain, Sicily, and throughout the Mediterranean countries, both in Europe and Africa, the almond thrives, and has long been extensively cultivated. These nuts are an important article of commerce, immense quantities being exported by

Spain, mainly from Valencia, while the so-called Jordan almond comes from Malaga, as very few are raised in the valley of the Jordan. Bitter almonds come principally from Mogador in Morocco.

As for almond culture in the United States, very little is to be said further than that, while we have few experiments to refer to as having been made east of the Rocky mountains, not one of our great pomologists, in their published works, has ever given any reason for the almost entire neglect of this nut. Mr. Wm. H. White, author of "Gardening for the South" (1868), throws no light upon the subject, merely describing a few of the well-known varieties of the almond. Downing's "Fruit and Fruit Trees of America," Thomas' "American Fruit Culturist," Barry's "Fruit Garden," and a score of other standard pomological works may be consulted, without obtaining therefrom any information in regard to the culture of this nut further than to be assured that the hard-shelled varieties are hardy in the North wherever the peach tree thrives, and the thin, or paper shelled, succeed only in warm climates. All these authors agree in saying that the propagation and cultivation of the almond is the same as practiced with the peach.

Coming down to recent years for information in regard to almond culture, we find H. E. Van Deman, pomologist to the Department of Agriculture, dismissing the subject in his report for 1892, as follows:

"I only mention this nut to state to all experimenters that it is useless to try to grow the almond of commerce this side of the Rocky mountains, except, possibly, in New Mexico and southwestern Texas. This is thoroughly established by many reports from those who have tried it in nearly every State and for many years past. It is too tender in the North and does not bear in the South. In California it is an eminent success.

"The flavor of the hard-shelled almond, so far as I have tested it, is little or no better than a peach kernel, and is therefore practically worthless. The tree of this variety is about as hardy as the peach, and bears quite freely. The attention paid to the almond in the Atlantic and Central States might well be given to other nuts."

This is certainly a very easy way of disposing of the cultivation of a nut which has so long figured among our importations from European countries; besides, no experiments are cited, experimenters named, or reasons given why almond culture is a failure in the Southern States. But fortunately there are men in the South who are able and ready to give reasons for their opinions and statements, in regard to the cultivation of crops or plants with which they have become familiar through personal experience. When I asked Mr. P. J. Berckmans, Augusta, Ga., president of the American Pomological Society, for information on this point, he promptly replied as follows:

"The reason that almonds are not cultivated in Georgia and other Southern States is because of their early blooming, as spring frosts usually destroy all the blossoms. We have tried many varieties of the soft-shell without success. The hard-shell will occasionally bear a crop of fruit, as it blooms later, and the blooms seem to resist cold better than the other varieties. In middle Florida soft-shell almonds are sometimes successful, but they have been tried so sparingly that I cannot obtain any satisfactory reports."

Admitting, as we do, that President Berckmans' long experience in the cultivation of nut and fruit trees in the South enables him to speak with authority on this subject, still, we have some encouragement for continuing experiments with the almond in regions known to be favorable for the cultivation of its near relative, the peach. Furthermore, experiments seem to be wanting with the almond in the more elevated regions of the northern line of Southern States, also in Maryland, Delaware and southern New Jersey, near the seacoast, or other large bodies of water, which, as is well known, have considerable influence in retarding the early blooming of fruit trees, as well as warding off late spring and early autumn frosts.

It is scarcely reasonable to suppose that a region of country as extensive as that of one-half of the Middle and all of the Southern States, with a range of climate admitting of the successful cultivation of such hardy fruits as the apple and pear, and from these down to the pineapple and cocoanut, should not yield a locality or localities admirably adapted to the cultivation of the half-hardy almond tree. It is no doubt true that there are extensive regions in the South where late spring frosts are exceedingly troublesome, and sometimes disastrously so, to fruit growers; but even these have their limits, as shown in the vast quantity and variety of fruits annually produced in the Southern States. But great local variations in climate are natural to all countries in the temperate zone, and we frequently find the most favorable and the unfavorable for fruit culture within a few miles of each other.

If there are not thousands and tens of thousands of acres of land located in favorable positions between Virginia and Florida, adapted to produce the commercial almond in some of its varieties, then we must confess that the study of climatology is of little use to the pomologist. Furthermore, all the varieties of the so-called hard-shelled almonds which thrive in our northern States are not worthless, neither are the kernels of all of them "bitter," and even if they were, they would still be worth cultivating, else we would not import such vast quantities from Morocco to supply the demand.

If none of the thin-shelled varieties heretofore tried in the South are successful, it is time that either our experiment stations or individual horticulturists made some attempt to produce those that are adapted to that region of country. But until we have some more definite information than heretofore disseminated, in regard to almond culture in the South, it is safe to conclude that failures in the past have been due mainly to want of judgment, or knowledge of varieties and of positions for the orchard, with, perhaps, some neglect in care and cultivation.

In California almond culture has been pushed with vigor for several decades, but at first with rather indifferent results, because growers depended upon noted European varieties, which, as experience proved, were not adapted to the soil and climate of the country. In a paper read before the American Pomological Society at its session held at Sacramento, Cal., Jan. 16-18, 1895, Prof. E. J. Wickson, of the University of California, alluded to this subject of almond culture in the State as follows: "In no branch of this effort for improved varieties has our success been more marked than in the development of seedling almonds. The achievements of A. T. Hatch in this line are too well known to require but a passing allusion. It is not too much to say that this work rescued almond culture to California. When he began, the almond, because of almost universal failure of the old varieties, was a jest and a byword in our horticulture. Nine-tenths of all the almonds planted during the preceding twenty-five years had gone for firewood or were carrying the foliage of the prune to conceal their hated stems. At the present time, through the dissemination of Mr. Hatch's varieties, the almond, in all regions decently adapted to the tree, is productive and profitable and has a future."

That almond culture in California is rapidly becoming an important and successful industry, we have an

FIG. 1. A CALIFORNIA ALMOND ORCHARD.

ocular demonstration in the tons of these valuable nuts received from there in the past few years, and placed on sale in Eastern markets. If one man, by his individual efforts, can revolutionize or establish a great industry in a region as large as the State of California, it is not too much to expect that something of the kind could be done elsewhere, with the combined efforts of several men. If the varieties heretofore tried in the East are unsuited to the climate, it is certainly within the range of probabilities that others better adapted to surround-ing conditions can be produced. The native grape, raspberry and strawberry have had a history similar to the almond, but now all are extensively and successfully cultivated.

Propagation of the Almond.—The propagation of the almond is identical with that of the peach : that is, from seed to procure new varieties, or by budding the more desirable ones, when obtained, upon seedling almond, peach or plum stocks. The half-wild hard-shelled almond is probably the most congenial and best stock for this purpose, but seedlings of the peach are most generally employed because the most abundant and cheapest. Under certain conditions, such as cold, heavy, moist soils, and where rather dwarfish trees are desired, the plum may be employed with advantage as a stock, but it is not to be recommended for general orchard culture. In mild climates seedlings of the best of the soft-shelled varieties may be raised and planted in orchards without budding, but the nuts from such trees are likely to be somewhat variable in size and quality, although the trees will usually prove to be as healthy and productive as those subjected to artificial modes of propagation. If, however, the grower desires a uniform product, he must resort to the usual means of obtaining it; that is, multiplying superior or distinct varieties by budding, either upon peach, almond or other stocks.

It is advisable, as well as exceedingly important, for all who intend or feel inclined to cultivate almonds in regions where the adaptation of this nut has not been fully established by years of practical experience, that seedlings should be raised in large numbers, and from these a selection be made to meet the requirements of the climate and other conditions under which they are to be propagated and grown. If spring frosts have been heretofore inimical to the cultivation of the almond, then the production of late-blooming varieties would be a remedy. There will also be variations in the season of ripening; some may come on too early, others far too late for special localities, but all these faults or variations may be readily overcome by raising seedlings, and then selecting for propagation those coming nearest fulfilling the requirements of local conditions or circumstances. It is by such experiments and means that fruit culture has reached its present position in this and all other countries, where it is practiced as an art or industrial pursuit. Varieties that have become exceedingly popular and profitable in one locality or country, may not have succeeded elsewhere, and this holds good with all cultivated plants.

In making experiments with the almond in regions where it has not been cultivated, but under conditions which appear to be favorable, I would certainly advise testing the well-known varieties first, and if these fail, then see what can be done in the way of producing new ones adapted to the locality and climate.

Raising Seedlings for Stocks.—In warm or moderately mild climates the nuts, whether peach or almond, may be planted soon after they are gathered in the fall, but should the weather continue warm and moist the nuts will sometimes sprout prematurely and the young sprouts get frosted later in the season, and for this reason it is better to store them in a cool room, packed in dry sand or soil, until the approach of steady cold weather, and then plant. Having lost choice kinds of nuts from being in too great haste in getting them into the ground in the fall, I am prompted to give this warning to those who have had no experience in raising nut trees. If not convenient to plant in the fall, nuts of all kinds may be packed in barrels, boxes, or similar vessels, mixed with or stratified with sharp sand or light soil, then stored in a dry, cool place,—a very cool cellar will answer, but in my experience, out of doors is preferable,—and in the shade of some evergreen tree or on the north side of a building, and there banked over with earth just sufficient to keep the nuts at an equably low temperature. It is advisable to have a few small holes in the bottom of the barrels or boxes, to insure proper drainage, should any considerable amount of water get in at the top; but this will not occur if the vessels are properly covered with boards when placed in position for winter.

It must also be kept in mind that mice, squirrels and chipmunks are fond of almonds and other kinds of edible nuts, and if placed where these little rodents can find them, they are sure to take a share, or perhaps the entire store, before their visits are discovered. I have known field mice to dig down under boxes of nuts, enlarge the holes left for drainage, and spend the winter among the chestnuts which I had put away for planting in spring. The safest way is to place fine wire netting on the bottom of the box, and then cover it with the same. Owing to the abundance of mice and other little nut-eating animals, I have never dared to plant out nuts in the fall, and so have always stored them in sand, but out of doors during the winter, and well covered with earth. In other lacalities it may be safe to sow in autumn, and if protection from vermin is required, coat the nuts with gas tar, the same as practiced by farmers in protecting seed corn against the attacks of crows and other corn-pulling birds. One pint of warm tar will be sufficient for a bushel of nuts, and the application is readily made by placing the nuts in a barrel, pouring the tar on them, and stirring with a stick until every nut is coated. To prevent the tar sticking to the hands in planting, dust the nuts with dry wood ashes, land plaster, or fine dry sand.

If peach stones are to be planted for stocks they may be put into the ground as soon as ready in autumn, because they are rarely disturbed by vermin; or if more convenient, mix with common soil, and in heaps, in the open ground, and leave in this position until spring, then pick out as they begin to sprout, and plant. The hard-shelled almond may be treated in the same way, only they are not to be handled quite as roughly as peach stones, and for protection it is best to put them in barrels or boxes, as described above.

When ready for planting take out the nuts and drop them in shallow drills, one every ten or twelve inches, then cover with about two inches of soil. It is to be supposed, of course, that a seed bed has been prepared, by thorough working over and enriching, if necessary, in advance of planting. The distance between the drills or rows should be sufficient to admit of cultivating the plants with a horse or mule, and cultivator, during the summer, and if this is done and the soil stirred often enough to keep down all weeds, the stocks should become large enough to admit of budding the first season; if not, then this operation must be deferred until the following year. But in case the seedlings are raised from choice varieties and to be left in their natural condition for fruiting, they may be lifted when one or two seasons old and set where they are to remain permanently.

The Season for Budding.—So much depends upon climate, location, and variation of seasons, that no special date or time can be given for budding trees of any kind, but it is always to be done while the stocks are in active growth, because the bark must part freely from the wood underneath, in order to admit of inserting the bud under it. If the buds are set too early in the season there is danger of a premature growth; that is, of pushing out a shoot in the fall instead of remaining dormant until the following spring. Under certain conditions, however, and for special purposes, it may be advisable to force the buds as soon as they have formed a union with the stock, but as a rule, in the propagation of hardy and half-hardy trees, it is better to keep the buds dormant during the cool or cold winter months.

Here in the Northern States we usually begin to look over our stocks during the latter part of July or first week in August, and note their progress and condition. Should they show the least signs of cessation of growth, we begin budding them, and push the work as rapidly as possible. If the season is a wet one the stocks may continue to grow and remain in good condition for budding until the middle of September; but in a dry season they may cease to grow in August, and it is these variable conditions which gives to the close observer and man of experience such an advantage over the novice in the propagation of plants. It is better to begin budding too early than to be a few days too late.

The operation called budding consists in taking a bud, with a small portion of the bark adjoining, from one plant, and inserting it in another, or in some other part of the same plant from which it was taken. The physiological principles which govern the operation are, that there must exist an affinity between the plant from which the bud is taken and the one upon which it is to be placed, and the nearer the relationship the more readily will it unite and the more perfect the union. For instance, the cultivated peach and almond are supposed to be of the same origin, and descendants of one original species; consequently there is a close relationship between the varieties of both sections, and their seedlings may be employed indiscriminately for stocks. The next nearest relatives in the family line are the plums (*Prunus*), some of which answer very well as stocks for the almond, although very rarely used for

FIG. 2. BUDDING KNIFE.

this purpose. The next group in the line of botanical relationship are the cherries (*Prunus cerasus*), but these are too far removed to be employed as stocks for either the peach or almond.

For budding are necessary a small knife for preparing the buds for insertion and making an incision in the bark of the stock to admit them; and a quantity of some material to tie around the stock, so as to hold the

FIG. 3. YANKEE BUDDING KNIFE.

bud in place. Budding knives are made after various patterns; one that is commonly used has an ivory or bone handle, made very thin at the end, that is used to peel the bark from the stock where the bud is to be inserted (Fig. 2). Another form of budding knife is made with a horn handle, and a small tapering piece of ivory fastened in the end. These knives, of various shapes and sizes, can be had at the seed stores; but another and quite a different form of budding knife is shown in Fig. 3, and is known as the "Yankee budding knife." It is merely a small one-bladed pocket knife with a thin blade, round at the end. The cutting portion extends about one-third around the end of the blade and two-thirds of its length, leaving the lower part dull. Although this form of budding knife has been in constant use in some of the older nurseries in this country for nearly a century, it does not appear to have been manufactured for the general trade, but only on special orders for nurserymen. It is so simple a knife, however, that with a little grinding almost any small one-bladed pocket knife can be transformed into one of these handy budding knives. The rounded end of the blade is used for lifting the bark, and for rapid work it is far more convenient than any form of knife that must be reversed in the hand every time a bud is inserted. In addition, a polished bit of steel is smoother and far less likely to lacerate the alburnous matter between the bark and wood than the best piece of bone or ivory. It may be said, however, that it is immaterial what form of knife is employed, provided it has a keen edge and is dexterously used.

The material most commonly used in times past for tying in the bud is the inner bark of the linden or basswood tree, usually called bass, and always to be procured in the form of mats, or as prepared from our indigenous basswoods and kept on sale at the seed stores. Recently, however, another excellent tying material has come into use, known in the trade as raffia or roffia. It is the cuticle of the Jupati palms. One species (*Raphia tœdigera*) is a native of the lower valley of the Amazon and Orinoco, and another (*R. Ruffia*) of Madagascar and adjacent islands. Raffia is somewhat softer and more pliable than the ordinary bass, although it does not hold its form quite as well ; but it is so cheap, soft and strong, that it has become very popular, and is extensively used for budding and many other purposes. But if none of these tying materials are at hand, the inner bark of the persimmon, corn husks, cotton twine, woolen yarn, or even strips of old muslin and calico may be employed with equally as good results, although not as handy and convenient for such purposes. The amateur, with only a few stocks to bud, can readily improvise implements and materials for doing the work, even if they are not of the regulation type. In selecting buds, the young shoots of the present season's growth are preferred, and these should be taken from the most healthy and vigorous branches of bearing trees, if possible. The leaves should be immediately removed, not by breaking or pulling off with the hand, but by severing the leaf-stalks with a knife, as shown in Fig. 4. If the leaves have fallen from the twig, the buds may be too ripe, with some kinds of plants, but with the almond, and where only a few leaves near the base have dropped, all may be used with fair success. If there are any soft and immature buds on the upper part of the shoot, or any undeveloped ones at the base, they should be rejected. Success

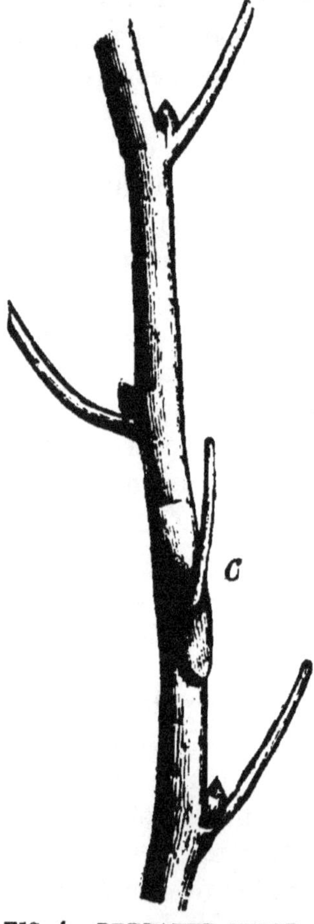

FIG. 4. PREPARED SHOOT. in budding depends very largely upon the condition of the stocks at the time the operation is performed. Unless the sap is flowing and in sufficient abundance to allow the bark to part or peel readily from the wood underneath, the bud is certain to fail. If the buds used should happen to be a little over-

ripe or wholly dormant when placed in direct contact with the living tissues and the juices of the stock, they will absorb moisture and nutriment, and be as likely to unite and live as under opposite conditions.

In performing the operation of budding, the following rules may be observed : Take the twig from which the buds are to be removed, in the left hand, with the small end pointing under the left arm ; insert the knife-blade half an inch, or a little more, below the bud, cutting through the bark and a little into the wood ; pass the knife under the bud, and bring it out about the same distance above it, taking off the bud with the bark, and a thin slice of wood attached, as at *c*, Fig. 4. Then, if using the Yankee budding knife, or one of similar form, let the forefinger clasp the lower part of the blade, make the horizontal incision in the stock first, and from this an incision downward about an inch long,— or it may be twice this length without doing any harm,—being careful not to cut too deep. Lift up the edge of the bark by passing the back of the end of the blade (without removing it) up to the horizontal inci-

FIG. 5. INCISION FOR BUD.

sion. Lift the bark on the other side in the same manner, the two incisions making a wound in the stock resembling the letter T, as shown in Fig. 5. If other forms of budding knives are used, the thin end of the ivory handle is thrust under the bark, raising it sufficiently to admit the bud. The budder holds the bud between the thumb and forefinger of his left hand while making the incision in the stock ; and as the knife leaves it he places the lower point of the bark attached to the bud under the bark of the stock before this falls back into place, and thrusts it down into position. If the upper end of the bark attached to the bud does not pass completely under the bark of the stock, it must be cut across, so as to allow that which remains with the bud to fall into place and rest firmly on the wood of the stock, as shown in Fig. 6.

When the bud is in position and fitted to the stock, as shown, wind the raffia, or other material used, around the stock, both above and below, covering the entire incision, leaving only the bud and part of leafstalk uncovered. Of course experienced propagators have their own individual systems and modes of operation, but the

FIG. 6. BUD IN POSITION.

above may be taken as a safe guide for the amateur budder. The ligatures should be loosened or removed as soon as the bud has become firmly united with the stock, which will usually be in ten or fifteen days, if at all. When the buds have failed, others may be inserted, provided, of course, the stocks are in condition to admit of the operation. Exceptions, however, may be made where the budding has been done so late in the season that the stock has ceased to grow by the time the buds have taken, and in such cases the ligatures may be left on later and removed any time before winter. In cold climates the snow, ice and water are likely to get in around the bud if the ligatures are not removed. But where the stocks are vigorous and the buds set early, there will be danger of the ligatures cutting into the bark as the stocks swell or increase in diameter, unless they are loosened or entirely removed.

Under ordinary circumstances budded stocks should not be headed back until the following spring, and then should be cut off two or three inches above the inserted bud; and when this pushes into growth, all suckers and sprouts below and above it should be rubbed off as they appear, for the object is to throw the entire strength of the stock into this one bud, and when this has made a growth of two or three feet the short stump of the stock above the base of the shoot may be carefully removed with a sharp knife. This is usually done the last of July or first of August, which gives time for the healing of the wound before the close of the growing season. Sometimes it may be necessary to place small stakes by the side of these shoots for their support and to prevent breaking at the point of union with the stock; but this will rarely be necessary, except in very exposed situations.

If the young trees make a fairly good growth they will be ready for planting out in the orchard the following spring, and one-year-old almond trees are usually preferable for transplanting than older. It is not advisable to prune these young trees during the growing season the first summer, but allow all the side shoots or branches to grow unchecked, for by so doing we secure a more stocky plant, if not as tall a one, than we would if trimming up was practiced. But when the trees are taken up for transplanting, in the late fall or early spring, then they may be pruned and the lateral branches cut off close to the main stem, leaving a naked rod, and if low-headed trees are desired (and they usually are), cut back the main stem to about three feet from the ground. If the young trees have made a growth of from four to six feet, then prune away the lateral branches to a hight of three feet or a little more, and cut in all branches above this point to within four to six inches of the main stem, leaving the buds on these stumps to form the head of the tree. Four or five branches at the top of the stem will be sufficient for the foundation for an open, round-headed tree, or in what may be termed a vase form, which is the best for almonds.

Soil and Exposure for Almonds.—The almond requires a warm, rather light and well-drained soil. Cold, heavy clays, and low, moist soils, whether light or heavy, are always to be avoided for the almond and closely allied trees. That the soil should be moderately rich is, of course, a condition required with all cultivated nut and fruit trees, but over-stimulation may result in excessive and immature growth late in the season, this leaving the twigs in such a state that they will be unable to resist even a few degrees of frost, to which they may be subjected the ensuing winter. In what are generally termed mild climates, or where the temperature seldom goes more than four to six degrees below the freezing point, hardy trees, if they have made a late growth, are often injured more than they would have been in a colder climate, with early matured wood. There are many kinds of what we consider very hardy trees and shrubs here in the North, that are very likely to be winterkilled or severely frosted when grown at the South, simply because the conditions are such that they do not ripen up in time to resist the cold.

In touching upon the subject of location for an almond orchard east of the Mississippi, I should be inclined to relegate this valuable nut to semi-tropical Florida, were it not for the fact that almost a score of ornamental species and varieties of the same genus,—to say nothing of the widely cultivated peach,—flourish over a very wide range of country and climate, and nowhere better than near the Atlantic ocean in the Middle and some of the Northern States. It is also generally conceded that several of what are called hard-shelled varieties thrive and bear fruit in nearly all of our best peach-growing regions. From all that I have been able to learn of almond culture, and with my own limited experience with this nut, experiments are wanting to prove that it cannot be successfully cultivated in the peach-growing region of the Eastern States. I will not say "profitably" cultivated, for this is a rather vague. term when applied to horticultural operations of any kind. Success is not synonymous with profit; in fact, it is frequently quite the opposite, and an abundant crop may mean glutted markets and a corresponding loss to the producer. But, to return to location, the principal cause of failure in almond culture, where it has been tried in the older States, seems to be the early blooming of the trees and subsequent destruction of the embryo fruit by frosts. To avoid this, high, open, airy situations, and even the north side of hills, would certainly be preferable to southern slopes and protected locations, especially in the South or where the temperature in winter does not go low enough to kill the wood of the previous season's growth. Theoretically, we might suppose that there are many locations favorable to almond culture in the elevated regions of North Carolina and Tennessee, as well as in the northern tier of counties in Alabama and Georgia. But in the absence of carefully conducted experiments in these regions, we have only to wait for their consummation at some future time, to prove the truth or falsity of our theory.

In the rich, warm valleys of New Mexico, Arizona and California, congenial locations are plentiful, inasmuch as almost every variety of climate is at hand, with a temperature ranging from that of perpetual summer to the opposite extreme, and all to be found within a few miles, and frequently to be found in the same county. Under such conditions, it rests with the would-be cultivator to decide upon the kinds of fruits desired, then to seek a location best adapted to his purpose.

If, as claimed,—but not proven,—there are no limited or extended areas fitted for almond culture east of the Mississippi river, there are certainly plenty of such west of it, awaiting the industrious and intelligent nut culturist. Almond orchards have been planted in California and Arizona, and the quality of the nuts, as well as the quantity, is very satisfactory; but a greater number and more extensive orchards are needed to meet the home demand.

Planting and Pruning.—In planting and pruning the almond tree the same system should be adopted as with its near relative, the peach. One-year-old budded trees are preferred for planting in an orchard, to older, except in the case of seedlings, then two-year-old may be selected, because these are seldom larger than one-year budded trees. The trees should be set fifteen to eighteen feet apart, varying the distance according to variety, soil, and other local conditions, and it is best to place them in rows and at right angles, in order to admit of cultivating both ways, as it is termed, thereby saving as much hand labor as possible. For the first two or three years after planting, all weeds and grass should be kept away from the stems and over the roots, either by frequent hoeing, or covering with a mulch. The best way, perhaps, to prevent the growth of weeds, is to use the land among the trees for some low-growing crops, such as beans, tomatoes, melons or potatoes, then see that the workmen, when hoeing these crops, hoe up the weeds and grass about the trees at the same time. We might reasonably suppose that the most careless cultivator of trees would think of this, but, unfortunately, extended observation proves quite the contrary, and it is scarcely possible to go through any very extensive fruit-growing region without seeing many such instances of neglect. A square yard or more of tough sward is frequently left for years undisturbed about the stems of all the trees in an orchard, while the little annual plants growing near by, and not worth, at an extreme valuation, five cents each, are cultivated with the greatest care.

The first pruning of the trees should be done at the time of transplanting from the nursery rows, as directed on a preceding page, and from the top of the stem only three or four shoots allowed to grow the first season, all others being rubbed off as soon as they appear, or when they have made a growth of two or three inches. These three or four upper branches are to become the foundation of the future head of the tree, and should be allowed to grow unchecked the first season ; the next spring cut back one-half to two-thirds of their original length. This pruning will force out strong side or lateral shoots near the base, thus giving a sturdy foundation to build upon later, the pruner keeping in mind that the weaker the growth the more severe should be the pruning. Better leave a few strong buds, from which vigorous shoots will be produced, than a great number succeeded by many feeble twigs. If blossoms and fruit appear on the young two-year-old trees, a limited number may be left to mature, although no considerable crop ought to be gathered before the third year.

In after years a somewhat different system of pruning may be adopted, keeping in view the fact that the fruit buds and fruit are always produced on the young shoots of the previous season's growth, and for this reason an annual renewal of such parts of the tree is absolutely required, in order to secure a good crop on trees of any age. In some localities and countries it may be possible that almond trees produce a crop every year ; but this is scarcely to be expected anywhere. Consequently a system of pruning should be followed which will conform to the variations of circumstances and conditions ; and this brings us to the consideration of—

The Proper Time to Prune.—If the growth of the trees and their fruiting were always uniform, then we might readily adopt some invariable system and season for pruning ; but as we are dealing with uncertainties, our rules must be equally flexible and variable. If the season is favorable, and the trees bloom freely and fruit sets abundantly, we may proceed to prune as soon as the embryo nuts are as large as peas,—but only cutting back some of the largest bearing shoots, and thinning out others here and there, just enough to equalize and evenly distribute the crop through the head of the tree. But in case the frost or cold of winter has destroyed the crop for the season, then as soon as this is discovered, prune and cut back all the shoots and branches sufficient to insure a vigorous growth of young bearing wood for the ensuing year. Under this system of pruning we fix the time as after blooming in the spring, in order to have our work correspond to circumstances and conditions, and where there is a crop in prospect the pruning is comparatively light; but if there is to be no fruit, or but little, then one should aim to produce an abundance of bearing shoots for the following season. In other words, we prune severely in non-bearing years, whether they occur alternately or otherwise; but this system is only applicable to trees like the almond and peach, which produce their fruit on the shoots of the preceding year's growth.

VARIETIES OF THE ALMOND.

Almonds are usually divided into three groups, viz. : Bitter, hard-shelled, and soft, or paper-shelled. In each there are many varieties, although they are rarely known in market except by the general name of the group to which they belong. If they are soft, hard or bitter, this is sufficient designation for commer-cial purposes, with, perhaps, the addition of the name of country in which they were grown, or that of the city or seaport from whence exported.

Bitter Almond, *Amygdalus communis amara.*— The varieties of this group are not specifically distinct, and some have soft, thin shells, while others are thick and hard; but the kernels are very bitter, hence the name. But in the countries where these almonds are most extensively cultivated, as in the South of France, Austria, Spain and Greece, the trees are generally raised from the nut, and, as might be expected, the crop produced under such conditions is exceedingly variable, the nuts being large or small, and the shells of various degrees of hardness, with an occasional tree producing both bitter and sweet kerneled nuts. These wilding trees are, in the main, more hardy than the improved varieties, hence are largely employed as stocks for the better sorts, as well as for the plum and apricot. It is also claimed that, as a rule, the bitter almond trees bloom later in the spring than those of the other two groups, and for this reason are not so liable to be injured by spring frosts. The trees are hardy in all of our most favorable peach-growing regions of the Middle and Northern States, but some of the varieties ripen rather too late for localities north of the latitude of New York city. All this, however, and other obstacles, will soon disappear, whenever the time arrives for our horticulturists to take up almond culture and pursue it with half the zeal they have the cultivation of the peach and many other kinds of fruits.

Hard-Shelled Almond, *A. c. dulcis,* or sweet-kerneled almond.—The varieties of this group, as a whole, differ from those of the next only in the firmness of their shells, which are moderately firm, with a slightly rough and deeply pitted surface, as shown in Fig. 7. Varieties of this group are fully as large as, and perhaps a little longer than the thin-shelled, and the kernels are fully as valuable when removed and sold as shelled almonds. It may require a little more labor to crack and remove the kernels for market, but the difference is scarcely worth taking into consideration by the grower,

The common sweet, hard-shelled almond thrives in peach-growing regions as far north as Central New York, and I well remember of seeing trees loaded with these nuts, in my boyhood days, in the western part of the State. The late Patrick Barry, in the Fruit Garden, when referring to this nut, says: "This is a hardy and productive tree, succeeding well in the climate of Western New York, and still farther north. Nut very large, with a hard shell and a large sweet kernel; ripe here (Rochester) about the first of October. The tree is very vigorous, has mooth, glaucous leaves, and when in bloom in the spring is more brilliant and showy than any other fruit tree."

FIG. 7. HARD-SHELLED ALMOND.

Nearly every one of our noted horticulturists who have said anything about almond culture in the North, agree with Mr. Barry in regard to the beauty of this tree and its productiveness; but it is well to keep in mind that it is no more to be depended upon than the peach, and the barren years will far outnumber the bearing ones. But the almond is probably as certain here as in France, where it is cultivated extensively as an article of commerce, although a full crop once in about five years is about all that is expected. We can probably do much better than this, especially if proper attention is given to the production of new varieties adapted to our climate, as has been done in California with the almond, and here in the East with the peach and many other kinds of fruits; and when such have been secured, proceed to multiply them in the usual mode of budding upon seedling stocks.

Soft, or Brittle-Shelled, *A. c. fragilis.*—In this group we have many distinct varieties, besides others which are known by local names, but have no permanent and pronounced distinguishing characteristics that would aid in separating them, should this be desired. The most common form, widely known as the sweet-kerneled thin-shelled (Fig. 8), is one of the oldest in cultivation in European countries. The flowers usually appear with the leaves, or before they unfold, and are large and of a pale rose color. The tree is rather tender for latitudes north of Philadelphia, but succeeds southward, and westward to the Pacific, if late frosts do not come to destroy the flowers or embryo nuts.

FIG. 8. THIN-SHELLED ALMOND.

Large Fruited Almond, *A. c. macrocarpa.*—This is an old French variety, and perhaps most widely known as the Sultana, although the latter name is often applied in market to almost every variety of sweet almond. The leaves of the genuine variety are much broader than those of the preceding groups, and are smooth and deep green. Flowers very large and showy, of a pale rose color, and always appear in spring before the leaves, and for this reason it has long been cultivated in England as an ornamental tree. Fruit large, depressed or flattened at the base, but pointed at the top. Shell rather hard and firm, and will withstand rough handling and transportation long distances. Kernel very sweet and tender, hence highly prized everywhere. There are several sub-varieties; one, known as the Pistache almond, is highly esteemed for the table, on account of its delicate flavor, although it is very small and not popular for commercial purposes.

The Peach Almond, *A. c. persicoides.*—This is another old variety, described by Du Hamel about the middle of the last century, under the name of *Amandier-*

Pecher, or peach-leaved almond. Leaves similar to those of the common peach. Fruit ovate, obtuse; husk slightly succulent; shell of a yellowish color, and the kernel sweet-flavored and excellent. Du Hamel says the fruit varies widely, even upon the same tree or branch, some having a dry, thin husk, while on others it is soft and fleshy, somewhat like that of the peach. As the almond and peach are of the same species, it would not be at all strange if an occasional variety raised from the seed of either class should diverge towards, or even pass completely over to a closely allied group.

From the varieties found in the forementioned groups we must seek to find, or produce therefrom, those which will succeed in this country wherever it may be thought desirable to attempt the cultivation of this nut. So far as my knowledge extends, no attempts have, as yet, been made to produce distinct American varieties in the Eastern States, as with its near relative, the peach, but all the almonds thus far cultivated here are of well-known foreign varieties. Perhaps the demand for almond trees has not been sufficient heretofore to encourage very extended experiments in this direction, but I cannot believe that our people will continue for another century to import millions of pounds annually of almonds if it is possible to raise them in this country. That it is possible on the Pacific coast has already been fully demonstrated, but we want to see the field greatly enlarged, and give the people of the Eastern States a share in what is evidently soon to become a large and profitable industry.

Ornamental Varieties of the Almond.—These are only referred to because some of the many in cultivation belong to the groups producing the most valuable nuts, but the greater part of the purely ornamental varieties are worthless for other purposes. *Amygdalus cochinchinensis* grows to quite a large tree in its native country, or thirty to forty feet high; flowers small, white, produced in long racemes; tender. *A. orientalis*, a small shrub, with grayish or hoary leaves, and small rose-colored flowers; sometimes cultivated under the name of *argentea*, or Silvery almond. *A. incana* (hoary) is another dwarf species, from the Caucasus, with solitary red flowers. *A. nana* and *A. pumila* are oriental species of very dwarf shrubs, with either red or white flowers. The double-flowering varieties of these have long been inhabitants of our gardens.

Properties and Uses.—For domestic purposes the almond is highly esteemed wherever it is known, and is employed in hundreds of different ways in the preparation of appetizing dishes and dainties for the table. In countries where this nut is in cultivation, it is brought to the table in the half-opened green husk, for at this time the kernels are just passing from the milky stage, and are considered more readily digested than later, or when fully ripe. But it is only when they are fully mature that they are gathered for market, and after thorough drying they are placed in strong sacks and distributed among dealers in all parts of the world. But only certain varieties are exported in this condition, and principally those with very thin shells, because these are most in demand, for the table and dessert, where the almond is not a home product. Other sweet varieties, whether with very hard or very tender shells, are cracked and only the kernels exported. The importation of shelled almonds into this country is somewhat in excess of the unshelled, and as they are of greater value per pound, the duty levied is proportionally higher. There is also a great saving to the importer and consumer,—not only in freight, but the extraction of the kernels is done in countries where labor is abundant and cheap. Whether the almond shells are used for any purpose in European countries, or are considered as wholly a waste product, I have been unable to learn, but it is asserted, and by men whose word is worthy of credence, that almond shells ground into a fine golden colored flour, is much used in this country for adulterating red pepper, cinnamon and other spices.

Almonds are not only used extensively at all times and seasons, by persons of all ages and sexes, at table and elsewhere, but they are employed largely in the making of fancy confectionery with sugar, or in the form of salted almonds, the kernels having been first thoroughly steamed or scalded, to remove the skin, and then rolled or dusted with fine salt. Prepared in this way they are usually considered more readily digestible and healthful than in their natural state.

Sweet almonds are also valued in the form of emulsions, as a medicine in pulmonary disorders, and the oil of almonds is a common standard article in the stock of druggists everywhere, as it enters into the composition of cosmetics, syrups, pastes and powders of various kinds.

The kernels of the wild bitter almond contain a poisonous principle known as hydrocyanic or Prussic acid, which does not exist in the sweet varieties, although found in their leaves and the bark of their twigs. But as bitter almonds are not palatable, there is little danger of anyone being poisoned from eating them, should these nuts ever be cultivated here for any special purpose, as in other countries.

Insects and Diseases.—Whenever the almond tree becomes common here in orchards it will doubtless suffer from the attacks of the same kinds of natural enemies as affect the peach. One of the most widely distributed of these pests is the common peach-tree borer. The parents of these borers are small, slender-bodied, bluish, transparent-winged moths, the male somewhat smaller than the female. These moths usually appear in this latitude during the month of June, and the female deposits her eggs on the stems of the trees near the surface of the ground, or a little below it if she can find a convenient opening to suit her purpose. The eggs deposited soon hatch, and the young larvæ bore through the tender bark at this point, and when fairly under it, branch off, cutting galleries through the soft alburnum underneath. When a number of these borers are at work on the same tree they sometimes girdle and kill it the first season, especially if it is young or a small specimen. But if the tree is not killed outright it will show, by the check to its growth, that borers are at work. The borers continue feeding throughout the remainder of the season, and up to the time freezing weather sets in for the winter, and if not full grown at this time they will finish their growth early in spring, then crawl to near the outside, or just under the old bark, and there spin a thin cocoon, in which they are transformed to the pupal stage, remaining in this form for a few weeks, then issuing in the winged or moth stage.

In the line of preventives and remedies there is nothing better than clean cultivation about the trees, and annual examination of each tree early in summer and the crushing of every borer found. The next best thing, in the way of a preventive, is to wrap the stems from a little below the surface of the ground to a foot or more above it with heavy paper, cloth, or bark of some kind, to keep the moth from laying her eggs on the bark of the tree. I have used common tar paper for this purpose, not only because it is very cheap and does not decay when exposed to the weather, but the exhalation or odor of tar seems to be offensive to the moths. In the use of this material I have never found that it was in the least injurious to the bark underneath. Painting the stems with soap, cement, clay, or even common mineral paints, will answer very well if a little care is given to keeping down the number of insects by removing the larger part of the borers with knife or gouge.

In recent years a pest known as the "shot-hole borer" (*Scolytus rugulosus*) has appeared in many and widely separated localities, in both the Eastern and Western States, attacking the almond, peach and plum tree. It is supposed to have been introduced from Europe with imported nursery stock, and thence rapidly distributed, by similar means, through the country. In its perfect stages it is a minute brown beetle, about one-twelfth of an inch long and one-thirtieth of an inch in diameter. This pest appears about midsummer, boring numerous minute holes through the bark and into the sapwood underneath, and in this the female deposits her eggs, and from these are hatched the little grubs found later feeding on the soft inner bark and alburnous matter beneath it. From every hole made in the bark a small globule of gum will soon appear, drying upon the surface—thence onward until autumn—and glistening in the sun, an immutable sign of the presence of a minute but destructive enemy.

When the beetles and their eggs are once in possession there is no practical way known of removing them, and the best thing to be done is to cut down and burn every infested tree, and just as soon as it is known to be in this condition. There are also several indigenous species of bark beetles, which will very likely attack almond trees as soon as they are as abundant as peach trees, but all may be destroyed with the same, or very similar weapons and materials.

What are called preventives consist mainly of substances to be applied to the stems in a semi-liquid form, and of such a nature as to be offensive to the beetles because of their odor, taste, or because so hard that the insects cannot cut through them with their mandibles.

Common lime whitewash, soft soap, whale-oil soap, or a thin mineral paint made of pure linseed oil, will answer very well for this purpose if applied often enough to keep the bark constantly coated.

Of the fungous diseases affecting the almond in this country, very little is as yet known, although we may safely include under this head all those that have been inimical to the peach, for the transition from this tree to the almond would only be a natural sequence. The peach-leaf curl (*Taphrina deformans*) would not be far from home on the almond leaf, neither could we expect that almond orchards would be wholly exempt from that mysteriously distributed and uncontrollable disease known as "peach yellows."

In California an almond-leaf blight has already appeared and seriously affected the trees in some of the orchards. It is caused by a fungus known as *Cercospora circumscissa* Sacc. This fungus attacks the leaves and young twigs, causing the former to fall off early in the season, thereby checking the growth of the tree and preventing the maturing of the fruit. It is thought that remedies may be applied to check this disease, and there will probably be some form of copper solution employed for destroying it, as with various species of fungi on other kinds of fruit trees.

CHAPTER III.

THE BEECHNUT.

Fagus, *Linn.* The Beech. The Latin name of the genus (*Fagus*) supposed to be an equivalent of the Greek *phegos*, an oak, or it may be derived from *phago*, to eat; the nuts of this tree having been used as food by man in all ages and countries where it is a native. The modern English name, beech, was probably derived from the Anglo-Saxon *bece* or *boc;* in Dutch it is *beuk;* French, *hetre;* Icelandic, *beyk;* Danish, *bog;* Swedish, *bok;* German, *buche* or *buoche;* Russian, *buk;* Italian, *faggio;* Armenian, *fao;* and in Welsh *ffawydd.*

The beech belongs to the order *Cupuliferæ,* or oak family. The genus contains about fifteen species of handsome deciduous and evergreen trees, or shrubs, very widely distributed throughout the temperate and colder regions of both the northern and southern hemispheres. Male flowers are bell-shaped, in long-stalked drooping heads; calyx five to seven cleft, containing numerous stamens. Female flowers two to four in a cluster on the summit of the scaly-bracted peduncle; the inside scales uniting, forming a four-lobed involucre of imbricated bracts, the whole becoming at maturity a somewhat prickly, scaly bur, within which are found a pair of sharp-edged triangular nuts, containing a tender and sweet-flavored kernel.

History of the Beech.—The common beeches of both Europe and North America are so closely related that the two species may be considered as one for all practical purposes, such as propagation, cultivation, and

value of the wood and nuts. It is true, however, that
our native beech is not environed with ancient myths
and stories of love and war, neither is it celebrated in
poetry and song, yet it has, doubtless, played just as
noble a part in human affairs among the pre-historic
races of America as those recorded of its European con-
temporary. As the beech in Europe is found in the
forests of Great Britain, Norway, Sweden, France, Germany, and southward to Constantinople, Palestine, Asia
Minor and Armenia, it was well known and highly appreciated by all the early inhabitants of these countries,
and is frequently referred to by the earlier writers of
Greece and Rome who touch upon the rural affairs of
their times. It is supposed that Theophrastus refers to
the beech under the name of *Oxua*, and Dioscorides
as *Phegos*, and the latter author places it among the
oaks, in which he was not far out of the way, because
the beech is a member of the oak family in our modern
classification. Virgil and Pliny speak highly of the
little triangular nuts, and the people of their times set
considerable value upon beechnuts as an article of food.
Pliny also assures us that at the siege of Chios, the be-
sieged inhabitants lived for some time entirely on these
nuts. We are inclined to think, however, that both
Virgil and Pliny are in error when they tell us that
the beech was propagated by being grafted on the
chestnut. They were probably led astray in this by
some romancing gardener of their time, for we even
have some of the same ilk with us at this day. Pliny
refers to the beech several times in his writings, and
places a much higher value upon this nut than he does
upon the chestnut; in fact, speaks rather contemptu-
ously of the latter, and seems to be surprised that nature
should have taken such care of the nuts, which he calls
"*vilissima*," as to enclose them with a prickly involucre
or bur.

But my limited space will not allow of tracing the history of the beech from ancient to modern times, although it has always been esteemed as food for man, as well as for wild and domesticated animals. Swine fattened on beech and oak mast have for ages been noted for their excellent flesh, and the value of many an old estate in Great Britain was determined more upon the mast the forest produced, than the area or number of square miles they contained.

As a monumental tree the beech has no rival, for its smooth gray bark, perennial and almost unchangeable, has ever been a convenient place to register challenges to enemies, epitaphs, epithets, and probably more frequently than all, the initials of the name of some loved one, who might possibly pass that way and find her name engraved on the beechen tree. I doubt much if there is a beech grove in all Europe or in America, within a convenient distance of a city, country village or schoolhouse, on which the bark of the trees is not scarified by the knives of boys in recording the initials of their own names, and those of their favorites of the opposite sex. These living registers were long ago recognized by the poets, and more than eighteen centuries ago Virgil admits it in these lines :

> " Or shall I rather the sad verse repeat,
> Which on the beech's bark I lately writ."

In more modern times Tasso hints of the same habit, in *Jerusalem Delivered*, to wit :

> " On the smooth beechen rind, the pensive dame
> Carves in a thousand forms her Tancred's name."

That the Spanish youths were not oblivious to their opportunities for recording the names of their favorites we must assume to be true, from the lines of Don Luis de Gongora, who tells us that :

> " Not a beech but bears some cipher,
> Tender word, or amorous text.
> If one vale sounds Angelinu,
> Angelina sounds the next."

Propagation of the Beech.—The beech, in all its species and varieties, may be propagated by the usual modes, viz. : By seed, layers, budding and grafting. The seeds, when gathered, should be mixed with clean, sharp, moist sand, placed in boxes, and then stored in a cool or cold place and carefully protected from mice, until the time arrives for sowing in spring. They may also be sown in the fall and lightly covered with leaf mold or other light soil, but unless coated with tar or some offensive poisonous substance, vermin of some form will be very likely to find them and leave few to grow. Seedlings are used for stocks upon which to work the many varieties in cultivation; but as I am not writing this for the encouragement of propagators of purely ornamental trees, I will omit giving any very extended description of the different modes of propagating the beech, further than to say that should remarkably fine varieties with extra-sized nuts be discovered or produced, they can be perpetuated and multiplied by the same processes adopted for other kinds of nut trees.

Soil and Location.—The beeches of Northern countries, in their many varieties, thrive best in a cool, moist soil, for their roots rarely penetrate very deeply, but spread out widely and near the surface, forming an intricate network, which will try the patience of the woodman who attempts to clear away a forest of beech and break up the ground. In this country, as well as in Europe, the beech thrives in calcareous soils, or what is usually termed limestone regions; consequently, when transplanted or raised in sandy soils, or on the red sandstore formation, light applications of lime are usually found very beneficial; but more than all, the beech requires moisture, and if not planted in a moist soil the surface over the roots should be kept constantly covered with some kind of mulch.

Species and Varieties of the Beech.—In the Dictionary of Gardening, edited by George Nicholson, of the Royal Botanic Gardens, Kew, England, the following species of Fagus are briefly described, viz:

F. antarctica.—Leaves ovate, blunt, glabrous, attenuated at the base, doubly dentate, alternate, petiolate, one and a half inches long. A small deciduous tree or shrub, with rugged, tortuous branches. Native of Tierra del Fuego, S. A.

F. betuloides (birch-like). Evergreen beech.—Leaves ovate, elliptic, obtuse crenulate, leathery, shining glabrous, round at the base or short footstalks. An evergreen tree, native of Tierra del Fuego, S. A.

F. ferruginea (rusty). American beech.—Leaves ovate, acuminate, thickly toothed, downy beneath, ciliate on the margin. A large deciduous tree, very closely resembling the common European species, from which it is distinguished by its longer, thinner and less shining leaves.

F. obliqua (oblique). Chile beech.—Leaves ovate, oblong, oblique, somewhat rhomboid, blunt, doubly serrated, entire at the base, attenuated into the petiole, and somewhat downy. A hardy deciduous tree, native of the cooler elevated regions of Chile, S. A.

F. sylvatica (sylvan). European beech.—Leaves oblong, ovate, obscurely toothed; margin ciliate. A well-known large deciduous tree, widely distributed in Europe from Norway southward to Asia Minor. From this species a large number of ornamental varieties have been produced, many of them merely accidental variations of the wild forms of the forests, while others have originated in the seedbeds of nurserymen. But so far as I am aware, no variety has ever been introduced bearing superior or improved forms of nuts.

Our American beech (*F. ferruginea*) is a widely distributed tree, extending from Nova Scotia in the north, south to Florida, and westward to Wisconsin and Missouri. Formerly it was exceedingly abundant, but like many other of our most valuable forest trees, it is disappearing before the axe of the woodman, who has always found a ready sale for beech timber. It is used in the manufacture of plane stocks, shoe lasts, handles for paring chisels, and hundreds of similar articles. Beech wood is hard, firm, and takes a good polish, but is not very flexible. It makes excellent fuel, and ranks next in value to hard maple and hickory for this purpose. In the more northern States and where the beech grows to its largest size, the heartwood is usually of a reddish color; but here in New Jersey and farther south, the wood is usually white almost to the center of the tree, no matter how large it may be. The color of the wood, however, does not in any way detract from its value, for fuel and many other purposes, although some European dendrologists have been deceived into supposing that the white beech was almost or quite worthless. Loudon, in *Arboretum et Fruticetum Britannicum*, Vol. III, in referring to our beech, says: "The wood of the white beech is little valued in America, even for fuel; and the bark is used for tanning, but is little esteemed," etc. But if any one, in these later years, has had occasion to purchase beech timber for any purpose, he has probably learned, from the price charged, that it is esteemed, even for such base purposes as firewood.

I am not, however, attempting to extol the American beech as a timber tree, but ask that it be given a place among the select ornamental nut-bearing kinds. And I think every farmer who has a pasture lot could afford a place for at least one beech tree, and if there is a low, moist spot in the field, or a stony corner, this will be a suitable place for such a tree; and the horses, cattle or sheep out in pasture during hot days in summer will be very grateful for the shade which a wide-spreading specimen will give them. It may be that the owner of said pasture may recall the lines of Garcilaso :

> " But in calm idlesse laid,
> Supine in the cool shade
> Of oak or ilex, beech or pendant pine,
> Sees his flocks feeding stray,
> Whitening a length of way,
> Or numbers up his homeward-tending kine."

He may be sure of one thing, and that is, the beech-nuts produced by one or many trees will always be acceptable to the children, and of these hungry mortals there is likely to be a few, at least, roaming about in ages to come, as in times past.

The beech is not really a desirable tree to plant on a lawn or near one's dwelling, because of its persistent foliage, which clings to the twigs very late in winter, and the rustling of the wind through the dry leaves is not soothing to one's nerves, although not quite as dismal as the moaning pines. In summer, and until late in autumn, the American beech is a noble and graceful tree,—and if I may be allowed the expression, one of the cleanest of trees ; its large, thin, bright-green and glossy leaves retain none of the dust and cast-off material of other trees which may be floating through the air, but are ever bright and pure. The tree has naturally wide-spreading and somewhat drooping branches, and should be given plenty of room for development when planted for the nuts or as an ornamental tree. Its leaves and the small slender branchlets (Fig. 9) are eaten with avidity by all kinds of farm animals ; consequently, protection may be required until the trees have reached a hight to be safe from such depredators.

Beech seedlings do not usually come into bearing in less than twenty to thirty years, but as no one in this country has ever attempted to cultivate this tree for its nuts, or search our forests for precocious and superior varieties, we have to admit that the field remains unexplored, and as barren of results as it was when our ancestors first discovered America. Every hunter, woodman, farmer and botanist who has roamed through forests where the beech trees grow, is well aware of the fact that distinct varieties are not at all rare, some having nuts twice the size of others in the same woods or groves, and it is possible and probable that some nut culturist in the near future will find time to select these choice wild varieties for cultivation and propagation. It would not, in my opinion, be beneath the dignity of our national department of agriculture, or some of its numerous costly annexes, to occasionally take into consideration the natural products of this great country, and determine, by a series of experiments, whether or no they were not worthy of attention.

FIG. 9. BEECHNUT LEAF, BUR AND NUT.

Insects Injurious to the Beech.—No disease has, as yet, been known to seriously affect the beech, and as for insect enemies, it probably has a less number than any other denizen of our forests. It is true that transplanted trees, and those left exposed by cutting away protecting neighbors, are sometimes attacked by borers in the stem, branches and twigs, but these enemies naturally follow in the train of debility, it being one of the immutable economic laws of nature to hasten the demise and decomposition of the half-starved or otherwise enfeebled members of both the animal and vegetable kingdom.

Isolated beech trees growing by the roadsides in parks and fields are occasionally attacked by a large grayish, long-horn beetle, the *Goes pulverulenta*. It is about one inch long, and a rather sturdy beetle of a light grayish color, and usually infests the branches, but may occasionally attack the main stem. It is not abundant, and has seldom been found infesting the beech. There are also two or three borers of the Buprestis family of beetles which occasionally attack beech trees. They are distinguished by the broad heads and flattened bodies of the grubs, and they work just beneath the bark in the sapwood, causing dead patches, mainly on the south side of the stem and larger branches. If the dead bark is removed and the wounds painted they will soon heal over, unless the tree is suffering for moisture and nutrients at the roots. A few twig borers, with an occasional colony of caterpillars on the leaves, embody about all the insect enemies of the beech calling for any special attention, but there are a host of different species and kinds ever ready to pounce upon a sickly or dead tree, whether found in the field or forest.

Properties and Uses.—The beechnut has been so long and favorably known that very little need be said here in regard to its properties and uses. In the forests it affords food for many kinds of birds, such as the wild turkey, partridge or grouse, and especially the pigeon, and immense flocks of these collect in the beech forests in autumn to feed upon the nuts. Deer are very fond of these nuts, and so are all of the squirrel family, and the little ground squirrel or chipmunk, *Tamias striatus*, of our Northern States, gives us a good practical lesson in the way of preserving the nuts over winter. These little rodents pack away the nuts in small pockets in their burrows and from two to three feet below the surface, where they are protected from excessive moisture and any considerable change of temperature. The chipmunk always stores the nuts in the ground, and not in hollow logs, as is sometimes asserted. The deer-mouse (*Hesperomys leucopus*), however, does select such places for putting away his winter's supply, but more frequently he chooses a hollow in the stem of some old tree, and several feet from the ground. Unlike the chipmunk, this mouse cleans the shells from the kernels, storing only the latter, and I have often found a quart or more when cutting down trees in winter. These kernels are usually so clean, bright, and free from odor, that it is to be feared the finder always confiscates them for his own use.

As the beechnut contains considerable oil, many schemes have been set on foot, in European countries, for its extraction and use as a salad oil. Early in the last century (1721) Aaron Hill, an English poet, proposed to pay off the national debt from the profits to be derived from the manufacture of beechnut oil; but his scheme fell through, like many others of its kind. It is also stated that Henry Fielding, so well known by his delightful stories of English society, once speculated rather largely on the manufacture of beechnut oil. In France, however, beechnut oil was formerly made in considerable quantities, and used in cooking fish and as

a salad oil.   In Silesia it is used by the country people
instead of butter, and the cakes which remain from the
pressure are given to fatten swine, oxen and poultry.
The forests of Eu and of Crécy, in the department of
the Oise, it is stated by Duhamel du Monceau, have
yielded, in a single season, more than 2,000,000 bushels
of mast, but probably this referred to all kinds of nuts,
and not beechnuts alone.   Years later, or in 1779,
Michaux states that the forests of Compiègne, near the
Verberie department of the Somme, afforded oil enough
to supply the wants of the district for more than half a
century.   In some parts of France beechnuts are roasted
and served as a substitute for coffee.   Many of these old
forests have disappeared, but other kinds of nut trees
are still being planted in France, and the product is
simply enormous, and a source of wealth to the peasant,
as well as the owners of extensive forests and orchards.

The beechnut has never been an article of commerce
in this country, and it is rarely seen on sale in either
country villages or our larger cities, not because of its
scarcity or want of demand, but all that the country
boys and girls find time to gather are wanted for their
own pleasure and use.   Picking up beechnuts among
the leaves in a forest, or even after raking off the leaves
and then whipping the trees, is, at best, slow and rather
tedious work, as I know full well from experience, and
only once do I remember of having secured a rounded
half bushel as the sum total of many raids on the beech
trees in the neighborhood.   But as the beechnut is the
diamond among the larger and less precious gems of our
forests, we should set a higher value upon it because
small and rather difficult to obtain.

CHAPTER IV.

California chestnut. Western chinquapin. Evergreen chestnut.

Castanopsis, Spach. Name derived from *Castanea*, the chestnut. Order, *Cupuliferæ*. A genus of evergreen shrubs and trees, intermediate between the oaks (*Quercus*) and the chestnuts (*Castanea*). There are about a dozen species indigenous to Eastern Asia and the adjacent islands. Blume, in "Flora Javae," Vol. II, 1828-36, describes three species under *Castanea*, which he found in the mountains and more elevated regions of the Javanese islands. Very little, however, is known of these oriental evergreen chestnuts outside of the herbariums of professional botanists, and they are rarely referred to, even in standard botanical dictionaries, or dictionaries of gardening, and when mentioned they are usually placed in the genus *Castanea*. Edouard Spach, a half-century or more ago, gave a synopsis of the genus, for which he proposed the name of *Castanopsis*, and although not recognized by botanists in general for a number of years, it is now accepted by botanical authorities everywhere. We have but one indigenous species, and this on the Pacific coast, viz :

Castanopsis chrysophylla, A. de Candolle. *Castanea chrysophylla*, Douglas. *Castanea sempervirens*, Kellogg.

"Leaves coriaceous, evergreen, lanceolate or oblong, one to four inches long, acuminate or only acutish (Fig. 10), cuneate at base and shortly petioled, entire green and glabrous above or somewhat scurfy, densely scurfy beneath, with none or few yellow scales; male aments one to three inches long, densely pubescent; styles three, stout, glabrous, divergent; fruiting involucre with stout divergent spines (Fig. 11) one-half to one inch long,

FIG. 10. LEAVES AND NUT OF CASTANOPSIS CHRYSOPHYLLA.

subverticillately many branched; nut usually solitary, obversely triangular, six lines long."—"Geological Survey of California," Botany, Vol. II, p. 100.

"This handsome broad-leaved evergreen tree is indigenous to the elevated regions, from Monterey, California, northward to the Columbia river in Oregon. It is also common in the Sierra Nevadas at elevations of six thousand feet, but in its southern limits rarely below ten thousand feet elevation."—C. S. Sargent ("Woods of the United States").

In the warmer and drier regions of California it is a mere shrub two to six feet high, and these dwarf forms have, in some instances, been described as varieties. As, for instance, *Castanea chrysophylla*, var. *minor*, Bentham; *C. chrysophylla*, var. *minor*, A. de Candolle; and *C. chrysophylla*, var. *pumila*, Vasey. But northward, where the climate is more moist, it becomes a large tree fifty to one hundred and twenty feet high, with a stem two to three feet in diameter. In its wide variation in habit of growth, this western chinquapin is similar to our Eastern dwarf chestnut, which is mainly a low shrub in the more Southern States,

FIG. 11. CASTANOPSIS BUR.

but becomes a fair-sized tree in the Middle States, or near its northern limits.

I have introduced the Western chinquapin here among the nut-bearing trees, not with the idea that it will ever be extensively cultivated for its edible nuts, but because it is a beautiful broad-leaved evergreen tree, and of which we have far too few kinds in cultivation to give warmth and a cheerful aspect to our gardens and pleasure grounds in winter. It is true that, so far as can be learned at this time, no extended experiments have ever been made to introduce or cultivate the Castanopsis in the Atlantic States, consequently nothing pos-

itive is known as to whether it will succeed here or not.
In its northernmost range it thrives in forests among
many kinds of trees and shrubs that are already common
in our gardens, and this leads me to think that specimens or seeds of this tree procured from the mountains
of northern Oregon will withstand the rigors of our
climate.

Mr. S. B. Parsons writes me that he first saw *Castanopsis chrysophylla* in Kew Gardens (Eng.) thirty-five
years ago, and procured specimens, which were planted
in his gardens at Flushing, N. Y., but they failed, presumably because not hardy. It may be that his specimens were raised from nuts procured in the warmer part
of California, and, as with many other Pacific coast
plants, proved to be tender, while later introductions of
the same species collected in colder localities have proved
hardy here. In my experience I have found a great difference in the hardiness of trees and plants obtained
from the higher and lower levels of the mountains from
Colorado westward to the Coast range, for in those regions acclimation extending over thousands of years has
developed and fixed certain physiological attributes,
which enables them to readily adapt themselves to similar conditions elsewhere, especially in the line of temperature. It may make no difference to those who want
plants for warm climates, whether they are obtained
from mountain or valley, but it certainly does to those
who value hardiness above all other merits.

In horticultural matters we are supposed to confine
ourselves within certain natural lines in making experiments, but if we fail in one, or one hundred, it proves
little beyond the bare fact that we have not been successful. I have experimented enough to have become
somewhat wary of deciding that a thing cannot be done,
or is impossible, because of my own and others' failures.
Every practical horticulturist can call to mind many

productions which had evaded the pursuit of experimenters for decades and even centuries.

For specimens of the nuts, burs and plants of this handsome nut-bearing tree I am indebted to Mr. J. J. Harden, of Stayton, Oregon, who informs me that it grows in the mountains near by to a very large size, and among such well-known kinds of shrubs and trees as *Rhamnus Purshianus, Cornus Nuttalli, Corylus rostrata,* and various species of conifers which are now more or less common in our Eastern gardens and parks. The twigs and leaves are shown in Fig. 10, and below a nut, and in Fig. 11 a bur, all of natural size. The small conical nut is slightly triangular, with a rather firm, brittle shell, not fibrous as in the acorn and chestnut. The burs are produced singly, but sometimes several on a twig, and when mature, instead of opening by valves, as in the true chestnut, they break up irregularly. The kernels are sweet and excellent flavored, and are sought for by various kinds of birds, as well as by all the squirrel tribe, and for this reason it is very difficult to procure specimens, unless gathered before they are fully ripe. The nuts do not mature the first season, but pass the winter in a partly developed stage, usually ripening the second year about midsummer or, in northern Oregon, in July.

It is quite probable that this Castanopsis, when planted in the Atlantic States, will require a little shade or protection, like the American holly and similar broad-leaved evergreens, and while it may not thrive anywhere north of Delaware and Maryland, it is worth trying, as the sole native representative of a genus containing several species of noble evergreen trees.

CHAPTER V.

THE CHESTNUT.

Castanea, *Tournefort.* The ancient classical name derived either from Castanis, a town in Thessaly, or one in Pontius, as historians disagree in regard to its derivation. The genus belongs to the order *Cupuliferæ.*

Male flowers irregularly clustered in long, naked, cylindrical catkins from the axils of the leaves and on the new shoots of the season. Calyx five or six parted; stamens or pollen-bearing organs seven to fifteen; anther two-celled. On old, mature trees, the male catkins are usually crowded near the end of the short new twigs, as shown in Fig. 12, the terminal one productive; but on young thrifty trees, wide apart. Female flowers always on and near the base of a late-developed male catkin, sometimes two or three together,—or even six or eight on the chinquapins,—oval or ovoid, scaly, prickly, two- to four-valved involucre or bur; calyx usually with a four- to six-lobed border crowning the three- to seven-celled ovary; stigmas bristle-shaped, and as many in number as there are cells in the ovary. Shell of the nut leathery, not brittle, ovoid, two or more together in the larger species, in others solitary, or only one in a bur. Kernel very thick, fleshy, and somewhat plaited, sweet and edible.

Both male and female flowers appear late in spring, the males usually exceedingly so, exhaling a slightly nauseating odor. The productive male catkins appear the latest, their base becoming the rachis or stalk supporting the burs, this rather anomalous arrangement appear-

FIG. 12. CHESTNUT FLOWERS.

ing to be a natural provision to secure fertilization in case the earlier catkins failed.

The genus *Castanea*, as now restricted, contains shrubs and large trees, with simple, alternate deciduous leaves, coarsely serrate, with pointed spiny teeth. Indigenous, and widely distributed over northern Africa, southern Europe, Asia and the eastern half of the United States.

The common English name of this nut is supposed to be derived from the Anglo-Saxon *cystel*, chestnut, and *cyst-beam* or *cisten-beam*, chestnut tree; Old English, *chastein* or *chesten;* Old German, *chestinna* or *kestinna;* Modern German, *kestene* or *kastanie;* French, *castaigne* or *chataigne;* Provencal, *castanha;* Spanish, *castana;* Italian, *castagna*, from the Latin *castanea*.

History of the Chestnut.—The so-called European chestnut is supposed to be indigenous to Asia Minor, Armenia, Caucasus and northern Africa, and from these countries it was introduced and became naturalized throughout the greater part of temperate Europe, where it has been cultivated from time immemorial. The Romans are supposed to have distributed it northward through France and Great Britain, and in the latter country there were trees centuries ago of such large size that many of the early English authors claimed this tree was indigenous. But in the absence of any natural forests of chestnut, the claim had to be abandoned. In parts of France, Italy and Spain, the chestnut has become thoroughly naturalized and, as we may say, run wild, but as one of the early investigators says, in speaking of the abundance of old chestnut trees on the Apennines, they are generally scattered over the surface like trees on a well-arranged lawn, and not crowded and massed, as they would be in a state of nature or in a forest. On the south side of the Alps the trees grow up to an altitude of twenty-five hundred feet, and on the Pyrenees some two or three hundred feet higher.

There are old trees of immense size almost everywhere in the milder regions of Europe, and the celebrated monarchs of Etna have been many times described by travelers. The largest measure one hundred and eighty feet in circumference near the root. All the early Roman writers who have anything to say about rural affairs, mention the chestnut as one of their valuable trees, producing nuts used for various purposes. Pliny enumerates eight varieties, but Columella appears to place more value upon the timber, especially the sprouts, for stakes, than he does on the nuts. But long before the Romans began to cultivate the chestnut, the Greeks held it in high esteem under the name of *Sardianos Balanos* or Sardis nut, and still later it was called *Dios Balanos Lopimon.*

The European chestnut has been so frequently and extensively referred to by ancient and modern authors that it would not be at all difficult to fill a large volume with brief extracts from their works, but my aim is not so much to show what has been done with this nut in other countries as what we may do with it here. All nations who have any experience with it admit its value as food for many wild and domesticated animals, as well as for the human race, and we know, from our long experience with the native species, that it is highly esteemed wherever known, although it must be admitted that our sparse population and the abundance of other kinds of food, have tended to make us careless and neglectful of the indigenous chestnut.

It may be well, before dismissing this brief history of the chestnut, to add that while nearly all the ancient authors, in referring to it, employed its present scientific name of *Castanea,* still, when botanists first attempted what has since been recognized as the scientific

classification of plants, many of them placed the chestnut in the same genus as the beech, retaining the generic name of *Fagus* for both.

Linnæus, in his *Systema Naturæ*, 1766, Vol. II,
p. 630, describes two species of the chestnut and one of
beech in the genus *Fagus*, although Tournefort, in his
"History of Plants Growing About Paris," published
seventy years before that of Linnæus, had recognized
the distinctive characteristics of these two groups of nut
trees, and he adopted the present name of *Castanea* for
the generic name of the chestnut, and *Fagus* for that of
the beech. But nearly all of the English and earlier
American botanists adopted and followed Linnæus in
his classification, ignoring the works of the earlier as
well as contemporaneous continental botanists. I merely
refer to this matter of botanical nomenclature because
some of my readers may have occasion to consult the
earlier authors who describe American plants, as, for
instance, such works as John Clayton's "Flora of Virginia," 1739, Thomas Walter's "Flora Caroliniana,"
1787, or Humphrey Marshall's "American Grove," 1785.
In all of these, and others, the chestnut is described as a
species of beech (*Fagus*).

Propagation of the Chestnut.—The usual mode
of propagating the chestnut is from seed, when trees are
wanted for general planting or for stocks upon which
to graft improved and rare varieties. Under some conditions and circumstances, it is best to plant the nuts
soon after they are ripe in autumn, and this appears to
be the most natural method; in fact, it is the way in
which forests have been produced and are constantly
renewed and perpetuated, when man does not interfere
to prevent it. But nature is in no hurry in such matters, while man always is, because his time is limited;
consequently, in our attempts at the multiplication and
cultivation of plants we aim to save both time and mate-

rial, therefore cannot afford to adopt nature's slow and wasteful processes.

The principal objection to planting chestnuts in the fall is the danger of having them destroyed by vermin, which abound almost everywhere. There is also danger of the nuts sprouting prematurely in the autumn, and of the young growth being killed by cold or by excessive moisture during late fall rains. But these natural enemies and obstacles prevent an excess in number and the overcrowding of trees in our forests. It is, no doubt, possible and practicable to smear the nuts with poisonous substances, or those sufficiently offensive to prevent the depredations of vermin, but taking all things into consideration, I am decidedly in favor of preserving the nuts in bulk and in a dormant state until the season arrives for insuring a rapid and continuous growth, and then planting them. To do this in our cold northern climate, as well as in the South, requires more care and attention with chestnuts than with the harder-shelled kinds, like the walnut and hickory nut. As a rule, it may be said that all the hardy kinds of nuts sprout at a rather low temperature and a few degrees above the freezing point, and for this reason it is well to select as cool a spot in the open ground as possible for their winter quarters, and then examine them as early as can be done conveniently in the spring.

In this matter of manipulating and preserving chestnuts for planting, as well as what follows in regard to transplanting, pruning and grafting, I shall give my own practice, with results; and while it may differ from that of other propagators, it is one evolved from long experience, many successes, and a few failures.

Gathering and Assorting Nuts.—When the nuts begin to ripen and fall, gather as soon as possible, and if the trees are on your own grounds and will admit of such an operation, thrash them and secure the entire crop at once. The object of this early gathering is to collect the false and weevil-infested specimens and destroy them. But in whatever way the nuts are collected, they should be stored in the shade and in shallow boxes, or spread out on a tight floor; but the better way would be on screens over a floor, and then when the grubs worked their way downward through the nuts and screen, they would fall upon the floor, from which they could be taken up and burned or otherwise destroyed. The nuts, while on the screen or other receptacle, should be stirred over daily for two or three weeks, and by that time they will be in good condition for either planting or packing away for the winter. But before finally disposing of the nuts in either way, they should be carefully looked over, and every shrunken specimen, as well as all with punctured shells from which the grubs have escaped, removed from among the sound stock, because these damaged nuts are not only useless, but are very likely to decay and affect all with which they come in contact. It is not to be expected that by such means or handling we can get rid of all the grubs enclosed in the nuts when gathered, for there will always be a few not more than half grown at the time, and these will remain hidden in the nuts until midwinter, or later, but the greater part of the brood will reach maturity within two or three weeks after the nuts are ripe. Of course, what is said here about chestnut weevils is only applicable to chestnuts grown in this country, but all species and varieties, when planted here, are subject to the attacks of this pest—at least, everywhere in the Eastern and Southern States.

Having assorted the nuts carefully, the sound ones should be reserved for planting; these should be mixed with or stratified with moist, sharp sand, and stored in boxes of convenient size for handling and examination, whenever this is required. In preparing the boxes, bore a number of small holes through the bottom, and over each of these lay a piece of a broken flower-pot, brick or stone, then cover the bottom one inch deep with the moist sand, and on this place a single layer of nuts, then fill in all interstices with sand, and also use enough more to fairly cover the layer; and proceed in this way until all the nuts are disposed of or the box is full, covering the top layer one or two inches deep, because the sand will settle some after the work seems complete. The boxes may be covered with fine wire netting or with narrow strips of boards, fitting these so that mice cannot get in, but should not be air-tight. They may then be buried in the open ground, selecting some knoll or dry spot for this purpose, for the nuts should not be placed where they will be submerged, or even be watersoaked, at any time during the fall, winter or early spring. If no such spot is conveniently near, then set the boxes on the top of the ground, and on the north side of some building or in the shade of an evergreen tree, and bank over with soil, covering the boxes a foot deep. If the spot selected is under the eaves of a building, place boards over the heap of soil, to carry off the water, for the object is to keep the nuts moderately moist, cool, and where they will not be subjected to frequent changes of temperature. In our Northern States the nuts, under such conditions, usually become frozen during the coldest weather, but this does not injure them if the sand is moist and they remain frozen, as there will be no danger of germination; while if kept too warm, they may start to grow before the seedbed is ready, in spring, for their reception. I have tried keeping the nuts mixed with sand in a cool cellar, also in outbuildings, but have not found any other place so certain as pits in the open ground.

Seedbed and Soil.—It is well to have the seedbed prepared the previous autumn, but it is not absolutely necessary. The soil for the bed should be light, either sandy or loamy, and if not rich, made so by adding very old and fine stable manure, or leaf mold from the forest —I prefer the latter, as it is the most natural for all kinds of seedling nut trees. Whatever fertilizing materials are used, they should be placed on or near the surface, and never worked in deeply, for our aim should be the production of side or lateral fibers, and not coarse perpendicular roots. Furthermore, seedling nut trees grown on light, sandy soils or in pure leaf mold, produce a far greater number of small fibrous roots than on heavy soils, and this is a decided advantage with those which are to be transplanted.

Planting the Nuts.—When the time arrives for planting, take the nuts from their winter quarters, and after sifting out the sand, sow or drop them in drills, covering about two inches deep with fine soil. With the small native varieties my practice has been to sow in wide drills; that is, those made with the blade of a common garden hoe, and of the same width, the nuts being scattered along the bottom two to three inches apart.

The soil is then drawn in over them and pressed down with the back of the hoe, or by passing a light garden roller over the surface. If the size of the seed-bed is not limited, or only a small quantity of nuts are to be sown, then the single row would be preferable, because less hand weeding will be needed to subdue the weeds, and for all the larger varieties I should certainly recommend it, because they are of a more stocky growth. The distance allowed between the drills will depend somewhat upon the implements to be employed in cultivation, as well as how long the seedlings are to remain in the seedbed before transplanting, but from two to three feet will be found convenient for the ordinary modes of cultivation.

If the seedlings make a fair average growth the first season they will be from one to three feet high in the autumn, and as soon as the leaves have fallen they may be taken up, or allowed to remain until the following spring and then lifted. But if, from any cause, they have made a feeble growth, it is better to let them remain in the seedbed another year. Where large quantities of seedlings are raised they are usually taken up with a tree-digger drawn by a span of horses or mules, but with only a few hundred or a thousand to dig, a common spade will answer every purpose; and if, when removed from the seedbed, they are found to have produced long perpendicular taproots, these should be shortened to about one-half their original length. For instance, if these taproots are taken up entire and are eighteen to twenty inches long, cut away the lower half, whether it consists of one or more long perpendicular roots, as this pruning will force the plants to produce a greater number of lateral roots, and it is upon these we depend mainly for keeping our trees alive and vigorous if transplanted when larger and older. All side branches should be pruned off close to the main stem, for we aim to favor the latter in its growth upward until it reaches the required hight for either grafting or forming the future head of the tree.

In taking up seedlings, it is not safe to leave them for any considerable time exposed to the sun and drying winds, and they should be carried either to a shed or other building while being pruned, and also covered with blankets in the field, except during moist, cloudy days. A very little drying of the small fibers on such plants is always more or less injurious.

Planting in Nursery Rows.—After the seedlings have been taken from the seedbed and pruned, they should be set out in nursery rows, four feet apart, and the plants about eighteen inches in the row. Trenches should be opened for the reception of the plants, and wide enough to allow all the roots to be spread out in a natural position; and it is well to set a little deeper than the seedlings were in the seedbed, because newly plowed ground will settle some after the planting is finished, although the soil should always be packed firmly about the stems of newly set trees, whether large or small. The more frequent and thorough the cultivation during the ensuing summer, the more rapid will be the growth of the trees.

If the transplanted seedlings have produced any considerable number of side branches,—and especially, low down,—these may be pruned off at any time during the summer, for our object is usually to secure straight, upright stems for grafting the following spring, if they are large and tall enough; if not, we may delay this operation for another year. Of course, small chestnut stocks may be grafted close to the ground, but there is nothing really gained by this, for a good strong stock will push a cion forward more in one season than a weak stock in two or three seasons. But when the stocks have reached a diameter of from three-eighths to one-half an inch three or four feet from the ground, they may be grafted, but I would prefer to have them a little over than under these sizes.

Stocks From the Forests.—It is not necessary for a man who may need a few chestnut stocks for experimental or other purposes, to wait until they can be grown from the nut, because these can always be purchased at the nurseries; but if one does not wish to incur even this small outlay, it may be avoided by obtaining a supply from the forests, provided there are any in the neighborhood where chestnut seedlings are to be found, and the owner will permit their removal. The best wild stocks are usually to be found in recent clearings, or where the larger trees have been cut off for timber, and the underbrush, composed of seedlings and sprouts, is left to grow up again into a forest. There are many thousands of acres in New Jersey, New York, and other Eastern States, from which the timber is cut every twenty or thirty years, and no further attention paid to the land or what it produces. Wherever such clearings are found containing chestnut trees, good stocks can usually be procured by selecting those varying from one to two inches in diameter at the ground, and if the soil in which they are growing is rather poor and stony they will usually have pretty good roots, if carefully taken up. They should be pruned to a single stem, and this cut off at a hight of from five to six feet or less, then planted where they are to remain permanently. Such stocks, if carefully taken up and planted, will throw out numerous sprouts from their stems during the summer, but all should be rubbed off while small and tender, except three or four at the top, and the following spring, if wanted for this purpose, they may be grafted in the same way as the young stocks growing in the nursery, thereby saving three or four years of time in securing bearing trees. Having often employed such wildings for stocks with just as good results as with those raised from the nuts in nursery rows, I am inclined to recommend them, where obtainable, knowing that there are thousands of farmers and owners of small places in the country who can do likewise, but may have never thought it practicable to transplant nut trees from the forest, although well aware of the fact that elms, maples, and similar kinds were obtained there, and in immense numbers, for planting in the streets of villages and alongside country highways.

The Season for Grafting.—The proper time for grafting the chestnut is in early spring, just as the buds begin to swell, but not until all danger of freezing weather is past, although light frosts will not seriously injure newly set cions. The grafting may be continued while the leaves are unfolding, provided the cions were cut early and stored in a cool place, where they remain in a dormant state until used. I usually cut the shoots wanted for this purpose during the late fall or winter, and then pack them away in a cool cellar between layers of damp moss (*sphagnum*) to be obtained in almost any swamp. Cions may be taken from the tree on the same day that they are used, but there is some risk in this, because we cannot control the weather, and a week of warm rain in spring may delay us in grafting, while it is pushing our stocks into leaf; and then, our dormant cions are available, while those on the trees are not, owing to their expanded and tender buds.

The shoots used for cions are those of the previous season's growth, or as usually termed, one-year-old ·wood; and in selecting these, endeavor to get such as are plump, well ripened and firm. If taken from young and very thrifty chestnut trees, there is likely to be a considerable portion of the upper end of the shoot that is rather soft, spongy and immature, and this should be discarded, as it would be a waste of time to use it. Of course, I am supposing that the grafter is so fortunate as to be able to make his own selection of the wood desired; if not, then he may be compelled to do the best he can with that obtained elsewhere.

Grafting Materials.—The really essential materials and implements required in grafting nut trees are few in number. Grafting wax must be provided, and while there are many different compositions used for this purpose, I much prefer, for ordinary work in the open air, a wax made after the old formula, and as follows: Take one pound of common rosin, one-half pound of beeswax, and one-quarter of a pound of beef tallow; melt together and stir enough to insure the thorough intermingling of the ingredients, and then set away to cool, or pour into cold water and work up into cakes or rolls and wrap in paper until wanted for use. Larger quantities may be made if required, preserving the same proportions of the materials used. If to be used immediately in grafting chestnuts and similar trees, then procure some sheets of tough manilla paper of only moderate thickness, and cut this up into sheets about six inches wide and a foot long. While the fresh-made wax is melted, take an old and rather stiff paint brush, dip it into the hot wax and coat the papers thinly with it, and then spread them out on shelves or elsewhere to cool, and let them remain undisturbed until wanted for use. Any thin kind of cloth may be used instead of paper, but I prefer the latter because it will yield to the pressure of the enlarging stock and cion when growth begins, and it will not be necessary to examine the grafted stock so frequently during the summer to prevent girdling, as is usually the case when a tougher material is employed for wrappers. Before these waxed sheets are taken into the field for use, lay each one separately on a piece of board with the waxed side up, and with the point of a sharp knife cut them crossways into narrow strips of from one-half to three-fourths of an inch wide. But for convenience in handling, insert the point of the knife a half-inch from one edge, but cut the other clean through, so that the whole sheet of strips can be lifted together.

In early spring there is usually more or less windy weather, and if waxed sheets of paper are taken out into the field unprotected they are very likely to become tangled up and useless. To prevent this, procure a number of large but very shallow paper boxes, such as can usually be had at the stores and groceries of almost any village, and in these place a single layer of the cut waxed sheets, where they will be protected from wind and dust until removed for immediate use.

Other kinds of grafting wax can, of course, be used, and are usually procurable at the seed stores or made at home, and I have given their composition and the formulas for their manufacture in my work, "The Propagation of Plants;" but, as I have already said, this old standard kind of wax is just as good as any other, although a little more troublesome to use on account of its sticky consistency. Raffia or bass may be employed as ligatures for holding the cions in place, then covered with Leport's or other kinds of liquid grafting wax; but when these are employed it will be necessary to examine the grafted trees frequently, in order to cut the ligatures to prevent girdling.

The best implement for grafting is a common broad-blade pocket knife. One with a blade three to three and a half inches long and three-fourths of an inch wide, is a handy size. It should be of the best material for grafting chestnuts, because the wood of this tree is coarse-grained, and so filled with siliceous matter that it soon dulls the keenest blade, and the grafter will, of necessity, have to use his whetstone frequently. In grinding the knife-blade have the sides a true level, from the back to the edge, especially the underside when to be held in the right hand with the edge towards the body. The importance of having a blade of this form will soon become apparent when the grafter attempts to make a true sloping cut on either stock or cion, and it would be well for the novice to practice for an hour or two in splicing some worthless twigs before commencing upon more valuable material, for even an expert workman is very likely to make some awkward dissections and joints when out of practice. The professional propagator of plants may think such details are unimportant, but I wish to impress upon the amateur that in grafting nut trees we are dealing with kinds that will not respond satisfactorily to such free manipulations as the apple and pear; consequently, better and more careful handling is required to insure success.

When ready to begin operations in the field, take out a quantity of the shoots to be used for cions, and keep them wrapped in damp cloth or packed in a box, basket or other receptacle with wet moss, to prevent drying. If any considerable number of stocks are to be grafted, then an assistant or two will be required, for the grafter cannot be alternately handling the knife and cions and wax, and do good work, but if he only inserts the cions and his assistant applies the waxed ligatures, the operation will proceed more rapidly and satisfactorily.

Modes of Grafting.— The only two modes of grafting that I shall recommend for the chestnut are the splice or whip graft, and the cleft or wedge graft. In the splice graft, the cion and stock should be of about the same diameter, but if there is any difference let it be in favor of the stock, and this the largest. In this mode of grafting, the stock is cut off with an upward slope, exposing two or three inches of wood; and about midway on this slope a small cleft or incision is made, forming what is called a "tongue." The cion is then cut in the same way from the upper end downward, with a corresponding incision, as seen in Fig. 13. Then the two are

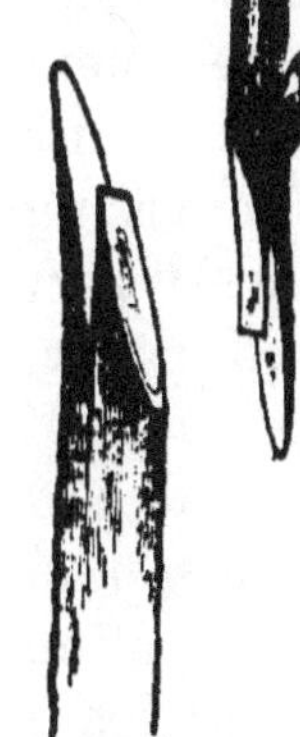

FIG. 13. SPLICE GRAFT.

FIG. 14. SPLICE GRAFT INSERTED.

neatly fitted together, the tongue on one entering the cleft on the other, making a close joint, as shown in Fig. 14. The bark of the cion and stock should be exactly even on one side at least; and if they are of the same size, so much the better, for then they will be even on both sides; but we cannot expect to secure such perfect joints on every stock, or any considerable number, although we aim to do so as frequently as possible. When the cion is fitted, the waxed paper is applied by placing one end of the strip at or near the base of the splice, then wind it spirally and firmly upward until the entire wound is covered. If one of the waxed strips is not enough use another, for it will do no harm if they are double on a part or all over the joint. The cion should not be much over four inches long, and a less length is preferable, but not so convenient for handling. One good prominent bud on each cion is sufficient, and this left near the upper end, but on short-jointed wood we may use cions with two or more buds without greatly increasing their length. After the cion is in place and every part of the splice is carefully sealed with the waxed paper, place a small piece or a little wax on the upper end of the cion, just enough to cover the exposed wound and prevent evaporation of the natural moisture or sap in the wood. I have found, in practice, that this sealing the end of the cion is time well spent; in fact, to leave any of the wood cells exposed to the air endangers the success of the operation.

Young shoots from a quarter of an inch in diameter up to five-eighths may be used for cions, in splice grafting; and with a little care in the selection of stocks, or by cutting them off a few inches higher or lower, we may readily manage to have them nearly of the same diameter to match our cions, whether they are large or small, and such unions will soon heal over, leaving no scar at the point where the two have been joined.

If the new growth or shoot to be employed as a cion
is slender and feeble, then the base of the cion may be of
two-year-old wood, leaving just a bud or two on the
upper end of the one-year shoot. But it will seldom be
necessary to employ such cions in grafting the chestnut,
although it may occur when seeking to secure wood for
propagation, from very old trees which have made only
a feeble annual growth.

Cleft Grafting.—This method is employed principally upon stocks or branches of trees too large for splic-

FIG. 15.
STOCK.

ing. The stock is first cut off at the
point where it is desirable to insert the
cion; then split with a knife, being
careful to divide it, so that the edges
will be kept smooth, and not rough
and ragged (Fig. 15). When the knife
blade is withdrawn, the cleft may be
kept open with a hard wood wedge,
if the stock is too large to admit of
opening it with the point of the knife

FIG. 16.
CION.

when ready to insert the cion. The cion may be three
or four inches long, containing two or more buds; the
lower end is cut wedge-shape, as shown in Fig. 16, and
slightly the thickest on the side to be set
against the bark of the stock. In stocks
of an inch or more in diameter, two cions,
one on each side, may be inserted (Fig.
17), and if both grow one should be cut
away, else the tree, in later years, will be
very likely to divide or break apart at this
point. In stocks of an inch or less in diameter, one cion is sufficient, the top of
the stock to be cut off with an upward
slope, as shown in Fig. 18. After the cions are inserted,
the entire exposed surface of the wood must be covered
with grafting wax or waxed paper, and usually both may

FIG. 17. FIG. 18.

be employed with benefit. All the various forms of grafting in the open air, as described in my work on the "Propagation of Plants," may be employed on the chestnut, but the two here given will probably answer just as well as others for those who may have occasion to propagate this tree.

Success in Grafting.—The question has been asked many times, and will, no doubt, be frequently repeated, "What percentage of cions should one accustomed to grafting make grow?" As there are no statistics upon which to base an answer to the question, I can only give my own personal experience, and this leads me to say that seventy-five per cent may be considered an excellent, if not a high average. In some seasons this has been exceeded by at least ten per cent, while in others it has fallen as much or more below, with no apparent reason for the difference. Ninety-five per cent of the cions may push their buds, or even make a growth of several inches, then begin to die off; consequently, the time to count your successfully grafted trees is in the autumn, and not in spring or midsummer, as it is to be feared some are in the habit of doing when making a report upon what they call success in grafting nut trees.

Growth of Cions.—Cions set in strong stocks usually make a very rapid and vigorous growth, and if left unchecked, there is danger of loss by being broken or blown off by strong winds during the summer and autumn. To prevent this as much as possible, it has been my practice to pinch off the ends of the young shoots when they are about two feet long. Lateral shoots will then push out freely, and in some seasons it may be necessary to check their growth in the same way later. On feeble stocks, or those quite small, and with the less vigorous growing varieties, no summer pinching or pruning will be required. My experimental grounds are well protected upon the north and west, not only by rising ground, but by Norway spruce and American arbor vitæ hedges twice as high as the grafted chestnut trees in the nursery rows, and yet almost every season some of the stronger-growing grafts are blown out or broken off by the wind. After the first season there is little danger of injury, probably because the union between cion and stock has become stronger.

Grafting Chestnut Sprouts.—In grafting the vigorous sprouts that always spring up from the stumps of old trees that have been recently cut down, we may reasonably expect a prodigious growth of the cion the first season, as well as in succeeding ones, and if all goes well with them we will secure large bearing trees in a very few years, but such stocks are only available where old trees are sacrificed for their timber or other purposes. Having a few such sprouts on my place, they have been utilized from time to time in testing some of the newer varieties. In one instance I allowed the cion, set on a sprout about one inch in diameter, six feet from the base, to grow unchecked throughout the season, as it was in a protected position, and in the fall the entire length of the main stem and lateral branches was sixty-five feet, and all from one bud on a cion set early in the spring. The third year this tree bore about a peck of very large nuts, to which I shall have occasion to refer again under "Injurious Insects."

Grafting Large Trees.—Grafting large chestnut trees with stems of six inches or more in diameter, and with large spreading heads, is possible, but far from being economical or practicable, especially if the trees stand out where they will get the full sweep of prevailing winds. By cutting off and grafting a few of the branches at a time for several seasons in succession, one may, in a few years, succeed in getting the entire head grafted, but there is constant danger of some of the cions being broken out if they make a vigorous growth, leaving a distorted and ill-shapen tree. Having experimented somewhat in this line with variable success, I am not inclined to recommend it, because ten trees can be raised to a bearing age on moderate-sized stocks with less labor, and the results will be more satisfactory.

Budding Chestnuts.—I have frequently tried budding chestnut stocks as described for the almond, and extensively employed with other kinds of fruit trees. But the results of my experiments have been unsatisfactory, although buds were set from very early in summer until late in the fall, also on young and old wood; but so few have taken and remained alive over winter that my personal experience in this mode of propagation will not justify its recommendation to others. Perhaps there is some secret connected with the operation that I have not yet discovered, but which is known to other propagators. Of course, budding with semi-dormant wood and buds in spring, as soon as the bark will peel from the wood, is practicable, but there is really nothing to be gained by this mode of propagation over that of grafting.

Transplanting and Pruning.—There is no tree that will bear or withstand more severe pruning than the chestnut. If trees of one or five hundred years of age are cut down, the stumps are sure to throw up an immense number of sprouts from adventitious buds, as these are readily produced at almost any point on the sapwood or alburnum under the bark; and yet, with this inherent vitality and faculty of recuperation, the chestnut tree does not naturally, like many other deciduous kinds, throw up suckers from the roots. Keeping this peculiarity in mind, the cultivator has only to use his pruning knife freely upon the trees to secure almost any form desired. But after the trees have become well established, very little pruning will be required, except to occasionally thin out or remove a rambling branch, to secure a well-balanced and shapely head to the tree.

In transplanting from the nursery rows, after grafting, and especially if the trees are of some considerable size and large enough to set where they are to remain permanently, there is sure to be a loss of roots, and those that are preserved are likely to remain for a short time inactive and incapable of absorbing nutrients from the soil to which they are transferred, or until new rootlets are produced. Under these conditions we aim to favor the roots by removing or cutting back the greater part of the branches. No matter how carefully such trees are lifted and their roots protected during the operation of transplanting, it will check the growth, and the best and most practical restorative is severe pruning of the top, and every young shoot of the previous season's growth should be cut back to within three or four inches of its base. I am presuming that the trees have been grafted only one year, but if older, and the cions were set high enough to begin the formation of the head of the tree, then the entire young growth may be cut away and some of the older wood, but of course not below the graft. All broken roots must be cut off; and the ends of the larger ones, roughly severed with the spade or other implements employed in digging, should have their wounds smoothed with a sharp knife.

Frequent transplanting and root-pruning young nursery stock tends to keep up a proper root system, and an abundance of small fibrous roots near the main stem, and trees so treated are worth much more, if to be transplanted later, than those left undisturbed; but while the latter may be twice the size of the former when of the same age, they are not worth half as much to the purchaser, or for transplanting in our own grounds.

Staking Transplanted Trees.—This is always necessary for recently planted trees, if they are of any considerable size, or from six feet high and upwards.

If not supported by stakes they are sure to be swayed about, if not thrown over, by strong winds in summer. A strong stake, two or three inches in diameter, would better be set at the time of planting the tree, thereby avoiding breaking off or crushing the roots, as frequently happens when stakes are driven down among them later in the season. Set the stakes or drive into the subsoil six inches from the stem, then use strips of cloth, sacks, carpet, or some similar material, for tying, because hard cord or twine will be very likely to cut through the tender bark from the constant swaying about of the stems. Wind the strips around the stem, and then cross between it and the stake once or twice, to prevent the tree from pressing against or coming in contact with the stake. Renew the stakes and tying materials, if necessary, until the trees become firmly established, and provided with lateral roots large enough to keep them in an upright position.

Mulching.—Placing a few forkfuls of coarse stable manure, half-rotted straw, leaves, or any similar material, on the surface about the stems of recently planted trees, will prove very beneficial, in not only keeping down the weeds, but aiding greatly in retaining moisture in the soil about the roots. The application of some such material as a mulch is all the more important with the chestnut, because these trees are always to be planted in a naturally dry and well drained soil.

Distance Between Trees.—How far apart chestnut trees should be planted will depend very much upon the species and varieties, some growing to immense trees, while others are only fair-sized shrubs at maturity. But for the larger-growing varieties, forty to fifty feet between the trees is none too much space, when planted for their nuts and not for timber. If set in a single row along the public highways, farm lanes or around the outbuildings, to serve as shade or ornament, and for their nuts, then about forty feet will answer very well for the larger-growing species ; and I will add that, in my opinion, all the larger kinds of nut trees will give better returns if placed in such positions, than when set in orchards or in compact masses. When set in single rows or widely scattered, they are less liable to be attacked by insects and diseases, while they will still serve the double purpose of being both ornamental and useful. I must admit, however, that in my experimental grounds. the trees are planted only twenty feet apart, but with the expectation of soon cutting out every alternate specimen.

Soil and Climate.—The chestnut thrives best in light, well-drained soils, and those containing a large proportion of sand or decomposed quartz, slate, or volcanic scoria ; but it is rarely found, nor does it succeed, in heavy clays, limestone soils, or on the rich western prairies, where we might think it would grow most luxuriantly. That limestone soils are inimical to the chestnut has often been disputed, but my own observations, which have been somewhat extensive in years and range of country, rather confirm the impression that this tree avoids land containing any considerable percentage of lime. It is true that chestnut groves, and sometimes extensive forests, are found on hills and ridges overlying limestone, but a careful examination of the soil among the trees will show that it is a drift deposit containing little or no lime. Such groves can be found in all the southern tier of counties of New York, also among the hills of northern and western parts of New Jersey, and thence west and south along the Blue Ridge and Alleghany mountains to the Carolinas, and westward in Tennessee and Kentucky. The chestnut is sometimes found in New Jersey and other northern Atlantic States growing in considerable abundance near streams only a few feet above sea level, but when found in such situations the subsoil is invariably sand, gravel or porous shale.

The range of climate in which the native sweet chestnut thrives is quite extensive, as it is found sparingly in Maine in latitude 44°, extending westward,—but not very abundant on this line,—through New England and New York, crossing the Niagara river, skirting the north shore of Lake Erie in Canada, and thence into southern Michigan, but does not reach Illinois. From this line southward it increases in abundance in Virginia, western North Carolina and eastern Tennessee and Kentucky. But in following this tree southward we meet another indigenous species, widely known as the chinquapin (*Castanea pumila*). This species is indigenous to southern New Jersey, and sparingly in parts of Pennsylvania, becoming more plentiful as we proceed southward, the two species named overlapping and in part occcupying the same region; but the chinquapin extends further south, and also to the westward, near its northern limits crossing the Mississippi into southern Missouri, then extends south again, becoming quite abundant in Arkansas.

The European chestnut, in its many varieties, extends over about the same number of degrees of latitude in Europe as our species do here, although reaching a higher latitude in countries bordering on the Atlantic, as shown in the old chestnut trees of England. The Oriental chestnut has also a very wide range, but the limits are not so well known as those of the European and American species; but a study of its geographical distribution is of considerable importance, now that we are importing these nuts for cultivation. The same is also true of the European varieties, and the cultivator who neglects to take this matter into consideration will fail to secure whatever advantages may have accrued from acclimation, an agency which, undoubtedly, has been active and continuous in modifying and changing the primary characteristics of these plants during unknown ages.

To more fully impress upon the reader the importance of care in the selection of materials to be employed in any pursuit with which he is not perfectly familiar, I am prompted to relate the story of my first personal experience in chestnut culture, as it may serve as a warning to others who may attempt to raise these nuts in a cold climate.

At the time of purchasing the farm which has been my home for the past thirty years, nut trees of various kinds were on my list of things wanted, and the chestnut occupied a leading position, probably because there were already many old and large native trees on the place. My first planting consisted of a number of imported seedlings, obtained from a well-known French nursery. The trees were three or four years old, very stocky and vigorous, and they made a good growth the first season; but the following winter the young shoots were all frozen down to old wood, with the exception of one tree, and thinking that this might prove hardy, cions were taken from it and set in thrifty sprouts growing in a grove near by. The cions made rapid growth, and from one of these I soon had a large tree, which remained in good health for twenty years, but during all that time it produced but one bur, containing two half-developed nuts. Why it was unfruitful I do not pretend to know, but it was certainly not for want of company, for it had large native chestnut trees all about it, and these bearing heavy crops. The seedling trees planted in the orchard also failed to be fruitful, and were finally dug up and burned. Thus ended my first experiment in the cultivation of the European chestnut. Had my location been farther south and in a milder climate, the experiment might have ended differently, but I am relating experience, and not attempting to guess what might have been the results under more favorable conditions. In the meantime, however, I had seen a few trees of the Japan chestnut bearing on Long Island, and had received specimens of the Numbo and Paragon, two now well-known and superior varieties of the European species, although raised in this country. These varieties were secured, and succeeded so well that I have continued to add others from time to time, or as soon as trees or cions were obtainable.

The success which appears to have attended the propagation and dissemination of these two varieties of European parentage has awakened considerable interest in chestnut culture, besides attracting the attention of those interested in such matters to the fact that there are many old trees of the same or similar origin scattered about the country, awaiting the coming nut culturist to propagate them and make known their merits.

It may be well, before leaving this subject, to remind the novice in chestnut culture that seedlings of these hardy and productive descendants of the European species will not come true from the nut or seed, and while it will be admitted that the chances are somewhat better for procuring a hardy variety from such nuts than from those imported, still, there is no certainty of any considerable number being equal in hardiness or other respects to the parent tree. There is an inherent tendency, in tree seedlings of all kinds, to revert to the wild form or type, and the chestnut is no exception to this rule.

Species of Chestnut.—What is called a " species," among plants, is a particular form or type supposed to have descended from one original stock, whether this was composed of one or more individuals. But variations doubtless occurred at the first inception or multiplication of the original, but so long as the offsprings do not differ so widely as to be untraceable to the proemial types, they are held to be varieties of one species.

Whether all the chestnuts found in the various countries of the world are descendants of one original tree or group of trees is now beyond our ability to determine; consequently, what are now termed species rests very much upon the opinions of botanists, as may readily be demonstrated by consulting the works of hundreds of authors who have essayed to describe and classify the plants of any locality or country, and this, too, without reaching an absolute finality acceptable to their contemporaries, or at all likely to share a better fate with posterity.

For many years after botany began to be recognized as a science, the common American sweet chestnut was considered a distinct species, but in recent years it has been relegated to the position of a widely distributed variety of the European chestnut, and it is so described and classified in most of the botanical works of the present time, and under such names as *Castanea vesca*, variety *Americana*; *Castanea sativa*, variety *Americana*; *Castanea vulgaris*, variety *Americana*, etc.

The Asiatic species or varieties—under whichever cognomen we may find them described in botanical works—have fared little better than our American kinds, for some botanists have described the Japan chestnut as a distinct species, while others only as a widely divergent variety of the common European chestnut.

I regret that there should be any need of giving so much space to this matter of species and varieties, yet presuming that far the larger number of my readers will not be professional botanists, nor persons with a botanical library at hand to consult for unfamiliar terms, I have thought this explanation in regard to classification might assist them in making clear the apparent confusion of names which, in the main, are only synonyms. Furthermore, I purpose retaining some of the older specific names of the distinct groups of varieties, whether it be strictly in accord with the ideas of eminent authorities or otherwise, because it will be more convenient to do so, and certain phases will thus be made clearer to the practical cultivators of nut trees, for whom this work is written. My wish is to assist those who do not know, but want to learn how to obtain, plant and make nut trees grow and bear remunerative crops.

CASTANEA AMERICANA (*American sweet chestnut*).—Leaves oblong-lanceolate, serrate, with rather coarse teeth, each terminated with a feeble prickle or spine; smooth on both sides (Fig. 19). Burs thickly covered with sharp, branching spines a half inch long or less, from a fleshy green envelope, becoming hard and somewhat woody; opening by four valves or divisions when mature. Usually three nuts in each bur, the center one flattened by compression, the two outer ones plano-convex. Shell tough and leathery, dark

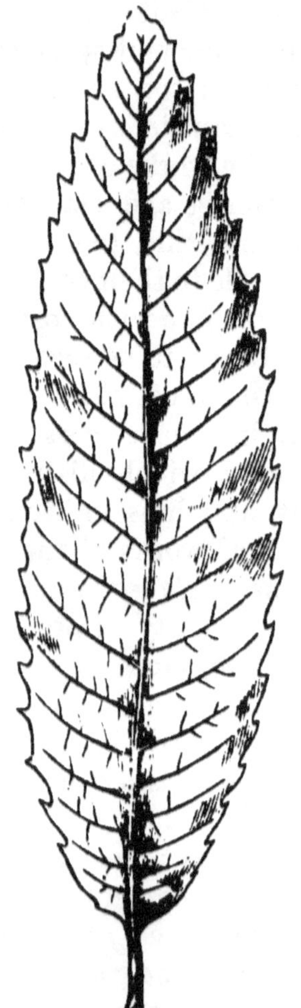

FIG. 19. AMERICAN CHESTNUT LEAF.

brown, smooth, or more or less inverted, with a silvery pubescence from the point downward; variable in size from five-eighths to an inch in diameter. Kernel sweet and fine-grained. A very large and common tree in the Middle and Northern States, living to a great age.

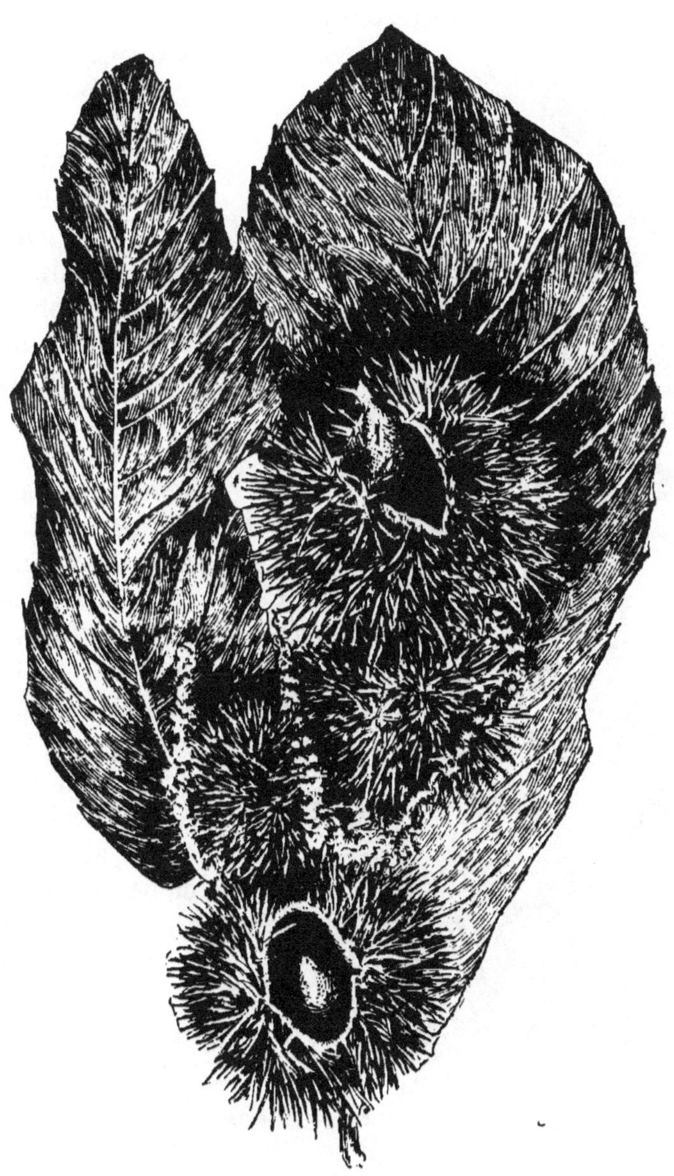

FIG. 20. SPIKE OF BURS OF BUSH CHINQUAPIN. *C. nand.*

CASTANEA NANA (*bush chinquapin*).—Leaves oval-lanceolate, serrate, with feeble prickles on teeth and often wanting; pale green above and white tomentose underneath. Burs in racemes, small; husk thin, opening by two divisions or lobes, instead of four, as in the last species; spines short, somewhat scattering, sessile or very short-stalked; nuts small, pointed, brown, smooth, thin-shelled, solitary or only one in a our. Kernel fine-grained, sweet and delicious. Common from North Carolina southward to Florida, in dry soils and barrens. A medium-sized shrub or low-spreading bush, rarely reaching a hight of ten feet, the slender twigs usually tomentose. A spike of burs and leaves of this species are seen in Fig. 20.

FIG. 21. SPIKE OF CHINQUAPIN CHESTNUT BUR.
C. pumila.

CASTANEA PUMILA (*chinquapin chestnut*).—Leaves oblong-lanceolate, short or acutely pointed, coarsely serrate, with incurved pointed teeth, green above, tomentose underneath. Burs in racemes (Fig. 21), two-valved. Sometimes the burs are single, as shown in Fig. 22. Spines branching from a short stalk; nuts solitary, ovoid, pointed, with dark-brown polished shell. Kernel fine-grained, sweet and excellent. A medium-sized tree twenty to forty feet high; in rich soils from New Jersey, Southern Pennsylvania and southward, to Georgia, and sparingly westward to Arkansas.

CASTANEA SATIVA OR VESCA (*European chestnut*).—Leaves oblong-lanceolate,

FIG. 22. SINGLE BUR, NUT AND LEAF OF CHINQUAPIN CHESTNUT. *C. pumila.*

pointed, coarsely serrate, with rather long incurved spines on the teeth; smooth on both sides, but glossy

FIG. 23. JAPAN CHESTNUT LEAF.

and dark green above; thicker and of more substance than in any other species. Burs very large, with thick husk, and long, stout, branching spines, from a woody stem at the base; shell of nut thick, tough and leathery, of a dark mahogany brown; kernel enclosed in a rather tough but thin skin that is usually intensely bitter, a characteristic that readily distinguishes this from any of our species. Trees of large size, rather stocky; young shoots coarse, with smooth bark; buds prominent, glossy, and of a light yellowish-brown color.

CASTANEA JAPONICA (*Japan chestnut*). —Leaves lanceolate-oblong (Fig. 23), finely serrate, indentations shallow, and the teeth slender pointed; pale green above and silvery or rusty white underneath. Burs with a very thin husk; spines short, widely branching from a short stem. Nuts large to very large, usually three in a bur; shell thin, and of a light brown color; the inner skin thin, fibrous, but not as bitter as in the European varieties, and the kernel somewhat finer grained and sweeter. Trees of moderate growth and are said to rarely exceed fifty feet high in Japan. The growth is slender in comparison with the European or American chestnut, and the habit is decidedly bushy, the new growth of the season usually producing a number of lateral twigs late in summer. The leaves here seem to be more persistent, probably because the season is not long enough to insure thorough ripening.

The reader will please bear in mind that this description of the Japan chestnut is drawn from the introduced varieties or those raised from the imported nuts, and not from the trees growing in their native habitats. All the varieties that I have seen appear to belong to one type or species, and they come from the warmer parts of that country; but Prof. Sargent, in his "Forest Flora of Japan," says that while the largest nuts appear in the markets of Kobe and Osaka, from whence they come to this country, there are varieties offered for sale in the markets of Aomori, which is much further north, and these, he thinks, would produce a more hardy race of varieties than those we have already received from that country. As a race, all the Japan chestnuts are very precocious, the trees coming into bearing early whether raised from the nut or propagated by grafting.

Native Varieties. (Group One).—While it is well known that our American sweet chestnut varies widely in the size, flavor, form, color and general appearance of the nuts, no special effort has been made to select and perpetuate the most distinct and valuable varieties. This is to be regretted, inasmuch as the opportunities for making such selections, and preserving and propagating those most worthy of it, are rapidly passing away with the destruction of our chestnut forests; but there is still time to do something in this direction, and perhaps save a few varieties as valuable as those already destroyed. It is to be hoped that every man who knows of a large variety, will either propagate it himself, or point it out to some one who is sufficiently interested to do so. If proper attention was given to the raising of seedlings, we might soon secure many improved native varieties, and I would urge this mode of propagation upon all whose circumstances and surroundings will admit of it, and especially upon the young men who possess the talent and inclination to make such experiments; for there is a wide and fertile field open to them, and they can scarcely fail to reap a rich reward for their labors, if applied with earnestness and a moderate amount of intelligence.

BURLESS CHESTNUT.—This is a peculiar variety or freak, in which the burs are merely shallow cups upon which the nuts rest, and at no stage of their growth are they enclosed in a husk or bur. The nuts are small and usually perfect, but being unprotected they are preyed upon by birds and squirrels as soon as the kernels are well formed, few escaping to reach maturity, This chestnut is of no economic value, but is worth preserving as an illustration of extremes in variation. The original tree was found in the forest near Freehold, Green Co., N. Y., by Mr. Harry Bagley, to whom I am indebted for cions sent me in the spring of 1885. Another and very similar variety was found about the same time on Staten Island, N. Y., and this also has been propagated, to a limited extent, as a curiosity.

HATHAWAY.—A very large and handsome native variety, and one of the very best. A strong and vigorous grower, and productive. Raised by Mr. B. Hathaway, the veteran and widely known pomologist of Little Prairie Ronde, Mich. Some thirty years ago Mr. Hathaway purchased a half bushel of native chestnuts of a dealer in Ohio, and from these raised a large number of trees for sale; but a few were reserved for planting out on his own grounds, and when these came into bearing the one named here was selected for propagation, because of its large size and productiveness.

PHILLIPS.—A large and handsome variety of excellent flavor, with a very smooth, dark-brown shell. Grafted trees exceedingly vigorous, upright growth, as well as precocious and productive. The original tree is growing in the grounds of the late Whitman Phillips, at Ridgewood, N. J. Several years ago my attention was called to a number of large varieties of the chestnut growing in and near the village, and from these I obtained cions for propagation; but I name only one at this time, reserving the others until more fully tested.

This is rather an insignificant number of varieties to be named among the many hundreds that are to be found in almost every town or neighborhood where the chestnut is a native, and yet I have been able to find only one named in nurserymen's catalogues as being propagated by grafting. It is true that nearly all dealers in trees offer seedling American chestnuts, which may mean good, bad or indifferent varieties when the trees come into bearing. Among all of the many thousands that have been raised and planted in the East and West, beyond the natural range of the chestnut, as, for instance, in Missouri, Kansas and Iowa, there must be some distinct and valuable varieties worthy of names and propagation. There are not only distinct varieties to be found in every forest, but in some instances the entire product of an extended area of country are distinct in their color, size, and general appearance of the nuts produced; as, for instance, in the woolly chestnuts of the Piedmont district of Virginia, these being so nearly covered with a white down that they remind one of popcorn. Hundreds of bushels of these woolly chestnuts come to our markets, and among them I have often found very large specimens, but so far as known, no effort has been made to perpetuate them.

So far as can now be determined, the wild or original European chestnut was much inferior in its flavor, and little, if any, larger than our American sweet chestnut; but by continued selections of the largest for planting, and propagation by grafting, it has attained to its present size and excellence; but this system of improving our native varieties has scarcely, as yet, been attempted, a fact which does not, in the least, redound to our credit.

Bush chinquapin (*C. nana.* Muhlenberg).— Of this I do not know of any named varieties in cultivation. Plants are occasionally seen in cultivated grounds, and I have one in my garden growing in a sheltered position, where it has fruited for several years. It is a pretty, round-headed, silvery-leaved bush, about six feet high; ornamental, if not specially valuable for other purposes, although the little sweet nuts are always acceptable. As a rule, the seedlings of this species are not hardy in the Northern States, but an occasional one will survive if planted in a light, porous soil and a protected situation.

COMMON CHINQUAPIN (*C. pumila.* Miller).—This is a small tree, sometimes thirty to forty feet high; found sparingly as far north as central New Jersey, and on Long Island. It is more common in cultivation than the bush chinquapin, probably because more hardy and better known, but I do not know of any improved varieties that have been disseminated under distinct names except the one hereinafter described.

Among many seedlings raised, of this species, I have selected one which good judges of such things have thought worthy of propagation, and as I do not raise plants for sale, no one will be likely to accuse me of having any selfish motives, f u r t h e r than a pardonable pride in producing something worthy of perpetuation. Furthermore, a s an earnest of my confidence in its merits, I have distributed it under my own name.

FULLER'S

CHINQUAPIN.— Leaves large,

FIG. 24. BURS OF FULLER'S CHINQUAPIN. ONE-HALF NATURAL SIZE.

broadly oval, pointed, coarsely serrate, pale green above, clear silvery white below. Bark on main stem; branches and twigs smooth, light gray, with numerous white dots. The young twigs thick and stocky, cylindrical,

7

with moderately prominent, grayish buds. Burs in long racemes (Fig. 24), very large for this species; spines long, strong, branching and sharp. Nuts only one in each bur, rather short, broad, top-shaped, with blunt point; shell very smooth, glossy, almost black; kernel fine-grained and sweet. Ripens early, or with the earliest of the native sweet chestnuts. The original tree is

FIG. 25. FULLER'S CHINQUAPIN. FIVE YEARS OLD FROM NUT.

only six years old, twice transplanted, and is now ten feet high, with a head fully as broad, and as shown in Fig. 25. Although growing in a rather exposed position, it has never been injured by low temperature in winter or a high one in summer. It has thus far been the most rapid-growing chestnut tree in my grounds, although given no special care. Whether it will eventually become a large tree, or soon cease to extend, is, of course, a question to be answered at some future time, but from present indications this tree will be well worthy of cultivation as an ornamental shade tree, even if we leave out of the account its rapid growth, productiveness, and delicious little nuts, which will be very acceptable for home use, if not possessing any great commercial value.

European Varieties.—In the use of this term I wish it understood that the varieties named and described in this group are all of American origin ; that is, raised in this country from seed. At the same time they are descendants of the European species. They are, in other words, "Survivals of the fittests," the few that have survived the many being raised from imported nuts (perhaps one out of a thousand) that tests and time have shown were adapted to our climate. There may be many other varieties scattered about the country which are worthy of a name and of propagation, but I can speak only of those I have been able to procure, or that have been brought to my notice.

In describing the following varieties, and in seeking to get at the facts relating to their origin, name and history, the reader will please bear in mind that there has been no previous attempt to arrange or classify these semi-American varieties. Furthermore, there is much confusion in regard to the true names of a number of them, and the most I can say is that I have endeavored, under the circumstances, to get as near the truth as possible. Could I defer writing this chapter ten years, some moot points might be cleared up, but as this is out of the question I must follow the light already in my possession.

To Mr. John R. Parry, of Parry, N. J., I am greatly indebted, not only for specimens of new and rare varieties, but also notes relating to the history of several of the older ones.

COMFORT.—Burs very large, broad, somewhat flattened; spines very strong and long, branching; nuts very broad, with short point, and shell covered from base to point with scattering silky hairs, thicker at upper end. In quality, about the same as in the ordinary varieties of the species, but to some persons' taste it is better, having less astringency in the skin surrounding the kernel. Origin uncertain, but said to have been grown for many years at Germantown, a suburb of Philadelphia, Pa., where the Paragon chestnut was discovered. The Comfort certainly closely resembles the Paragon, but I have not had an opportunity of fruiting trees under the two names side by side, as would be necessary to determine their identity or difference, if they are really distinct.

COOPER.—A very large variety; has been in cultivation for several years in Camden Co., N. J., but up to the present time the trees have not been propagated for sale, although I am informed by Mr. John R. Parry that there are a large number under cultivation. The tree is described as of a broad spreading habit, with enormously large leaves, and immensely productive. Nuts very large, smooth and glossy, with little fuzz near the top. In quality they may be considered excellent for a variety of this class. The burs are very large, and this is its greatest or only fault; for when nearly mature they absorb and retain such a quantity of water during heavy rains, in addition to the original weight and the enclosed nuts, that the trees are liable to be broken down by strong winds.

CORSON.—Burs of immense size; spines an inch or more in length, from a stout, woody, irregularly branching stem, resting on the moderately thin husk. Nuts extra large, usually three in a bur; shell dark brown, somewhat ridged; the upper end or point of the shell densely covered with a white, almost woolly, pubescence, or fuzz as it is usually termed. This is a remarkably large and fine variety and of good quality. Originated with Mr. Walter H. Corson, Plymouth Meeting, Montgomery Co., Pa.

DAGER.—A large variety originated near Wyoming, Delaware, from seed of the Ridgely. My specimen trees are good vigorous growers, and hardy, but have not, as

FIG. 26. BUR OF NUMBO CHESTNUT.

yet, produced fruit. It is said that the nuts are of fair quality, but not as good as the best of its class.

MONCUR.—Another seedling of the Ridgely, raised on the farm of Mr. Frank Moncur, near Dover, Del. The original tree is about thirty years old. Described as smaller than its parent, but of better quality.

Numbo.—Burs medium, and distinctly long pointed before opening, as shown in Fig. 26, the four divisions of the burs extending an inch or more beyond the nut as

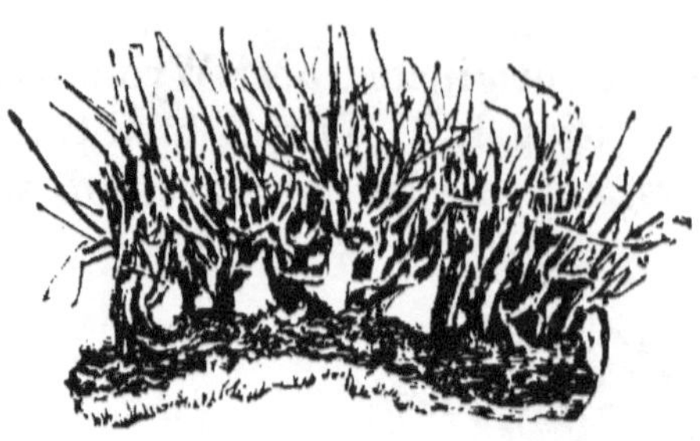
FIG. 27. SPINES OF NUMBO CHESTNUT.

they open. This is an exceptional form of the bur, and will enable almost any person to recognize the variety with bearing trees. Spines only medium in length (Fig. 27), and not as strong as in most other varieties of this species. Nuts very large (Fig. 28), smooth, decidedly pointed, light brown when first mature, and of good flavor. Tree hardy and a vigorous, free grower, and is very productive even when young. The original tree is now some forty years old, and is one of a large number raised from imported nuts, by the late Mahlon Moon, of Morrisville, Pa.

Miller's Dupont.— Burs large, spines long and

FIG. 28. NUMBO CHESTNUT.

strong but not as stout as in some of the closely related varieties. Nut medium, and kernel of fair quality. A promising variety. Origin unknown. Received from Jos. Evans, Delaware Co., Pa.

Paragon.—Burs of immense size, often five inches and more in lateral diameter; distinctly flattened on the top, or cushion shape (Fig. 29); spines an inch in length, widely and irregularly branching from a stout stem springing from a thick, fleshy husk, as shown in Fig. 30, the whole making an involucre or bur out of proportion to the nuts within. Nuts of large size, slightly depressed at the top (Fig. 31), and they are

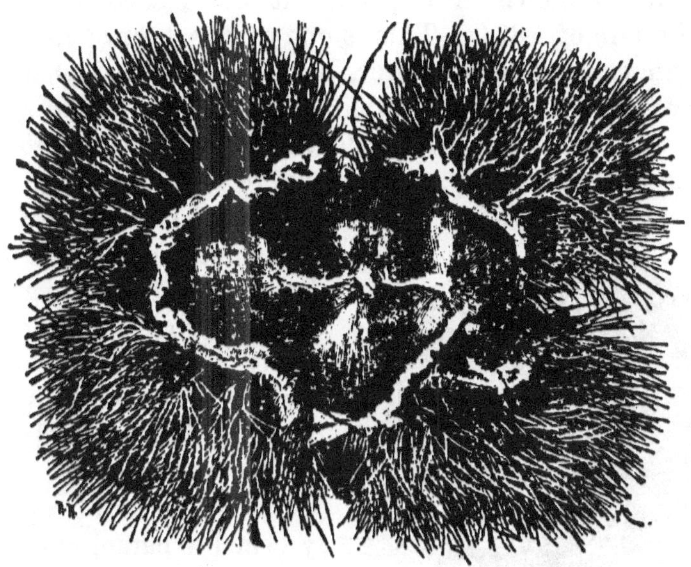

FIG. 29. PARAGON CHESTNUT BUR. (*One-half natural size.*)

usually broader than long; shell very dark brown, slightly ridged, and covered with a fine but not very

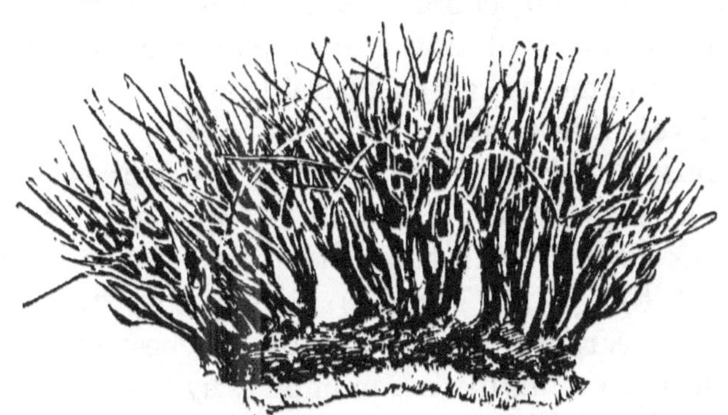

FIG. 30. SPINES OF PARAGON CHESTNUT BUR.

conspicuous pubescence. Kernel sweet, fine-grained, and of superior flavor for one of this species. Tree hardy, exceedingly precocious and productive when grafted on strong, healthy stock. A four-year-old tree on my grounds is shown in Fig. 32. It was loaded with nuts in the fall of 1894. This is one of the best of its class. Origin somewhat in doubt, but it is claimed that the late W. L. Shaffer, of Philadelphia, raised it from a foreign nut planted in his garden, and who, some eighteen years or more ago, gave cions to W. H. Engle, of Marietta, Pa. Mr. Engle has since propagated and disseminated this variety quite extensively under its present name, but should further investigation prove it to be distinct and that it was raised by Mr. Shaffer, then it should certainly bear his name, and Paragon become a synonym.

FIG. 31.   PARAGON CHESTNUT.

No more appropriate monument could possibly be erected in honor of a distinguished horticulturist like the late Mr. Shaffer, than a chestnut tree, nor could his memory be perpetuated under more pleasant and agreeable surroundings than to have his name linked inseparably with such an excellent and valuable variety.

RIDGELY.—Burs large, with dense spines, but not as long as those of the Paragon. Nuts large, pointed ; shell dark brown, with very little pubescence, and this mainly at the point (Fig. 33). In quality this variety ranks very near, if not the equal of, the best of its class, and it has been highly commended, by those who have been acquainted with it, for many years.

The origin of the Ridgely, as recorded, leaves the question of name a debatable one. Some sixty years ago a Mr. Dupont, of Wilmington, Del., gave or sent to

Mr. D. M. Ridgely, of Dover, Del., a sprouted chestnut, and this was planted and became the original tree
of the variety under consideration. It has been called
Dupont, because he raised the nut and kept it over winter and until it sprouted ; then it passed into the care of

FIG. 32. FOUR YEAR OLD PARAGON CHESTNUT TREE.

Mr. Ridgely, who thenceforward gave it his attention.
The tree is now of immense size, and some seasons has
produced more than five bushels of nuts, selling at eleven
dollars per bushel. It is quite probable that the Dupont

family were the first to raise European chestnut trees to a bearing size in this country, for some of its members were settled in Delaware before the war of the Revolution. Pierre Samuel Dupont de Nemours, during the French ministry of Vergennes, was employed in forming the treaty of 1783, in which the independence of the United States was formally recognized by England. In

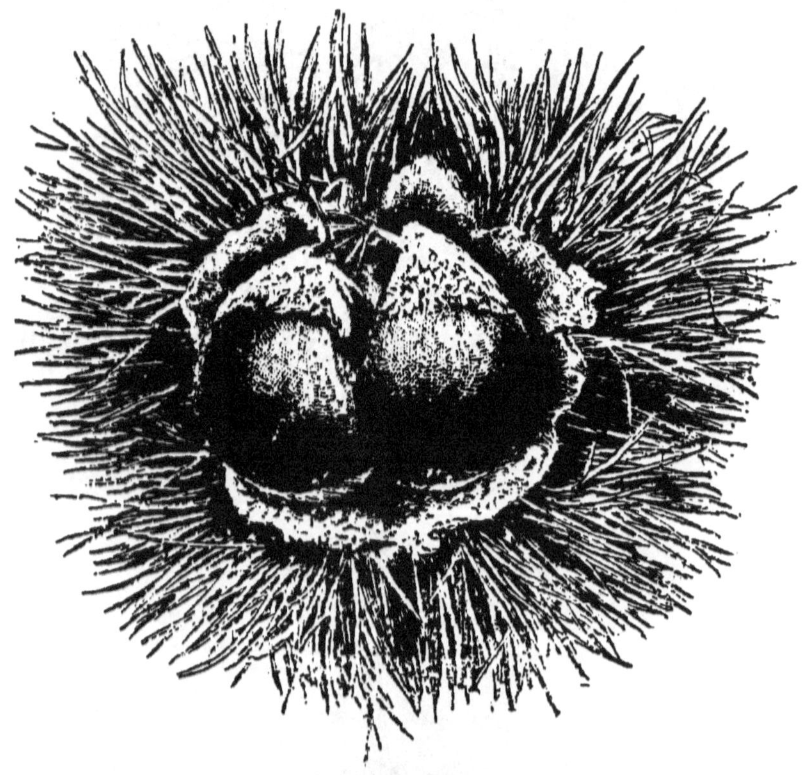

FIG. 33. OPEN BUR OF THE RIDGELY CHESTNUT.

1795 (Am. encyclopedia) he came to this country and joined his sons, who had become successful manufacturers of gunpowder at or near Wilmington, Del., where their descendants, or at least some of them, are still engaged in the same business. If any of the old and original chestnut trees have escaped the numerous "powder mill explosions" which have frequently occurred in that neighborhood, they are probably much older than the Ridgely. I am also inclined to believe that a very large majority of all the hardy chestnut trees of the European species scattered about the country are the direct descendants of the old Dupont stock.

SCOTT.—Burs large, with long branching spines. Nuts from the original tree, as received the past season, are only of medium size, but said to be much larger on younger trees. Shell dark brown, smooth, with a little fuzz around the point. As my specimen tree has not, as yet, fruited, I am unable to say anything of its productiveness from personal experience, but in a note from Mr. William Parry, under date of Oct. 15, 1894, he says: "I send specimens of the Scott chestnuts, grown by Judge Scott, of Burlington, N. J. The crop is about gone and it was with difficulty I could get these, which are about the average size; earlier in the season many are larger. Judge Scott has grown these nuts for market several years. The original tree was bought by his father many years ago from the nursery of Thomas Hancock. He bought three trees for Spanish chestnuts, planted them in a row about thirty feet apart, and the one from which these nuts were obtained happened to be in the middle. It is now a large tree, the trunk about five feet in diameter. It is a regular and heavy bearer. Judge Scott has propagated and planted an orchard from this variety, and claims among its important features, large size and early bearing,—two-year grafts generally produce nuts; immense productiveness and good quality; beautiful, glossy, mahogany color; freedom from fuzz, and an almost entire exemption from the attacks of the chestnut weevil. While the crop of two trees standing on either side of the Scott is badly damaged by worms, it is the exception to find a wormy nut among the Scott.

"The crop ·sells readily at ten to twelve dollars per bushel. This year (1894) some sold as low as eight dollars, the lowest ever known for this variety."

STYER.—Burs large, round ; spines long, branching, but not as coarse as those of Comfort. Nuts medium to large, decidedly pointed, and the point fuzzy. Shell dark brown, with a few longitudinal stripes, but not ridged. A handsome nut of good quality. This variety has been distributed under the name of Hannum. The original tree, which is a mammoth in size, is still standing on the farm of a Mr. Hannum, near Concordville, Delaware Co., Penn. But Mr. T. Walter Styer, of the same place, is propagating and introducing it as the Styer.

Some of the varieties in this group may not prove to be distinct, and later they will be relegated to their proper place as synonyms, but 1 have thought it best to record them by the names under which they have been received. In writing these descriptions I have had the nuts and leaves before me, but there may be characters overlooked which will become more conspicuous as the grafted trees become older and more mature. The Dager chestnut, from Delaware, is a promising variety, disseminated through the Department of Agriculture, but as I have not seen the nuts at this writing, a description is necessarily omitted.

Among the French varieties of this species which are said to succeed admirably in California, a large proportion would probably do equally well in Delaware and further south. Among those worthy of trial I may name the *Avant Chataigne, Comale, Exalade, Green of Lemousin, Grosse Précoce, Jaune Rousse, Lyons, Merle, Nouzillard, Quercy*, etc. I have tried some of these, but with such indifferent results that they were abandoned. Cultivators of nut trees located in a milder climate, should take advantage of whatever improvements there have been made in Europe, by importing grafted trees or cions. There are a few ornamental varieties of the European chestnut, but none worthy of any special attention.

JAPAN CHESTNUTS.—The first authentic account I have been able to find of the introduction of the Japan chestnut into this country, is of a number of trees received by S. B. Parsons & Co., Flushing, N. Y., 1876, from the late Thos. Hogg, who, as is well known to all horticulturists, spent several years in Japan collecting many rare kinds of trees and shrubs, which were shipped direct to Parsons & Co. The chestnut trees received in 1876 fruited two years later, or in 1878, and soon attracted attention, on account of the large size and excellent quality of the nuts and the precocious habits of the trees.

The success of this typical variety of the Japanese species, as I have assumed to designate it, proved that there were oriental chestnuts—heretofore untested in this country—that were certainly worthy of an attempt to obtain. This variety, introduced by the Messrs. Parsons & Co., does not appear to have been disseminated under any distinct varietal name, but merely bears the rather meaningless one of Japan chestnut, and for the purpose of giving it a position where it may be recognized—by name at least—from other varieties more recently introduced, I shall take the liberty of calling it "Parsons' Japan."

Soon after it became known that the oriental chestnuts would succeed in this country, the fruit growers and nurserymen of California began to import and plant these nuts, shipping an occasional lot to their customers in the Eastern States, and from these hundreds of seedlings have been raised and distributed, under the general name of Japan chestnut. Among the nuts imported there are some of extraordinary size, even larger than anything of the kind obtained from Europe, as shown in Fig. 34, natural size, and from a specimen received direct from Japan. Some of the nurserymen who have secured these very large nuts for planting, offer the

FIG. 34. JAPAN GIANT CHESTNUT.

seedlings raised therefrom under such names as Mammoth and Giant Japan, but as there is no certainty, and scarcely a probability, that such seedlings will produce nuts as large as those planted, the names are rather misleading, although proper enough if given to grafted varieties of large size. When an extra-fine variety is produced from the nut, it should, of course, be preserved and propagated in the usual way.

The late Wm. Parry, of Parry, N. J., was one of the first nurserymen to attempt to produce new varieties of the Japan chestnut in this country, and his sons have continued his experiments in this direction. Others may have been equally successful, but I have been unable to obtain any satisfactory reports from those to whom I have applied for

FIG. 35. SPINES OF JAPAN CHESTNUT.

information; consequently, I can only say that the following, with few exceptions, originated at the Wm. Parry nurseries:

ADVANCE (Parry).—Burs medium, slightly flattened on top; spines medium, short, almost sessile, as shown in Fig. 35, and this is a characteristic of all the Japan chestnuts; branching and widely separated on a very thin husk. Nuts very large; shell a light yellowish brown, with a few slight darker streaks from base to apex. Quality excellent for one of this species. Ripens early, and long before touched by frost.

ALPHA (Parry).—Very similar to the last, but ripens earlier, which would be an advantage in some localities. Tree vigorous and productive.

BETA (Parry).—Bur medium; spines rather long and thin for one of this group, set on a thin husk. Nut large; shell light brown, smooth, with a slight trace of pubescence near the tip. The leaves are shallow and coarsely serrate, and on some the teeth or serratures are entirely wanting. Ripens a little later than the Alpha, or about the first of October in northern New Jersey.

EARLY RELIANCE (Parry).—Burs medium, with short, almost deflexed spines, on an exceedingly thin husk. Nuts large, more pointed than in the last, and of a lighter color the past season, but this may not be constant, and may be due to the long and severe drouth of the summer of 1894. Usually three nuts in a bur, and sometimes four or five, but I do not consider this increase in number a merit in any variety, for where there are more than three they are likely to be of small size and very much deformed. The original tree of the Reliance is enormously productive, and a regular bearer.

FELTON.—A seedling of the common Japanese chestnut, raised by J. W. Killen, of Felton, Delaware.

GIANT JAPAN (Parry).—Burs large to extra large for a variety of this species, with medium low branching spines on a very thin, parchment-like husk. Nuts extra large, usually only two in a bur, often only one, and about two inches broad, much depressed at the top, with a short point set in an irregular depression or basin. Shell dark mahogany color, more or less ribbed; kernel coarse grained, as is usual in the extra large varieties of nearly all species of the chestnut. This is probably the largest variety of the Japanese chestnut raised in this country, of which grafted trees are obtainable at this time. There may be others equally as large, but if so they are unknown to the writer.

KILLEN.—Of the Japan species, and described as very large, the nuts over two inches in diameter and of fair quality. Raised by J. W. Killen, of Felton, Del.

PARSONS' JAPAN.—Burs medium, with rather thick-set and long spines. Nuts large, one inch and a half broad, curving regularly to a point; shell smooth, almost glossy, brown, with faint stripes of a darker shade extending from base to apex. In quality the kernel is far better than most of the European varieties, being finer grained and sweeter. When grafted on strong stocks the trees come into bearing early, or in two or three years. This is the best known, and probably the most widely distributed variety, of the Japanese species in this country, having been introduced, as I have stated elsewhere, in 1876.

PARRY'S SUPERB (Parry).—Burs broad, cushion-shaped, or much flattened on top, with extra long, widely branching spines from single or multiple stems, very much as in the European varieties. But the thin husk, the nuts, and the growth of tree, wood and leaves, stamp it as a pure Japanese variety. Nuts large, broader than long, with a decided sharp woody point; almost entirely destitute of even a sign of pubescence. A very promising and distinct variety.

SUCCESS (Parry).—Burs very large, broad, with only a few short, scattering, branching spines on the top, thicker toward the base; on a thin, parchment-like husk, and this is so thin that it sometimes cracks open and exposes the nuts within before they are fully ripe. Nuts extra large, nearly equal to the Giant, but of a more regular and symmetrical form, being nearly as long as broad, tapering to a point. Shell smooth, dark brown, with a slight pubescence about the point. Usually three nuts in a bur; an ideal variety in every respect.

There is a variety of the Japan chestnut recently much lauded under the name of Mammoth or Burbank, which is said to be of immense size, and as sweet as the common American chestnut.

Injurious Insects.—The chestnut tree is rarely attacked by insects. It is true that grubs may occasionally be found boring into the wood or cutting sinuous burrows under the bark, but this is mainly in trees weakened by exposure, in removing protecting companions, as when removing forests, or by plowing up and destroying the roots, in cultivating the land about them; but the attacks of insects upon such specimens is nature's way of getting rid of the feeble and least valuable, making room for the healthy and strong. But my thirty years' residence in a chestnut grove leads me to think that this nut tree is exceedingly free from wood borers of any kind.

Entomologists, however, have noted several instances of insect depredations upon individual trees, by a few species of the longhorn beetles, three or four in all, but these occur so rarely that they are scarcely worthy of notice as pests of the chestnut. There are also several species of caterpillars occasionally found feeding on the leaves of this tree, also some sucking bugs or tree hoppers, and two or three kinds of plant lice, but none of these have, as yet, become at all formidable enemies, or likely to become so later. But the chestnut has one enemy which is so abundant and destructive to the nuts as to call for an extended notice. I refer to the common native chestnut weevil (*Balaninus carytripes*, Boheman). The little fat, white, round, legless grubs, nearly or quite a half-inch long, must be familiar to every person who

8

has handled or eaten chestnuts raised in this country, whether of the exotic or native varieties. The parents of this grub are oval-shaped beetles about one-half inch long or less; wing covers, body and legs densely covered with a short yellow down, and from the front or thorax there extends a long, slightly curved, slender snout (Fig. 36), sometimes nearly an inch in length in the females, but usually less in the males. The mouth parts are at the extreme end of this snout or proboscis, and the female, with her mandibles, it is claimed, reaches down among the chestnut spines and gnaws a hole in the husk, into which she drops an egg; and when this hatches, the minute grub cuts its way through the green husk and into the nut, the hole made in its progress closing up behind, leaving no mark or scar. Although I have taken hundreds of these weevils on chestnut trees, I never have been so fortunate as to take one in the act of ovipositing, but have come so near it as to find the ovipositor still extended as the insect crawled out from among the spines.

FIG. 36. CHEST-NUT WEEVIL.

The chestnut weevil usually appears in great numbers soon after the trees bloom in spring, but they continue to come out all through the summer; I have occasionally found them late in September, which probably accounts for finding small and half-grown grubs in the nuts as they ripen and fall from the trees. These late grubs often remain in the nuts all winter, but the greater part escape earlier, or very soon after the crop is ripe. The grubs crawl out of the nuts and work their way into the ground to a depth of from a few inches to two feet, much depending upon the nature of the soil. Having very powerful jaws, they readily cut through a layer of leaves or soft wood, and I have known them to cut holes in sheets of dry cork. These grubs remain in

the ground until the following season, then come forth
in their winged or weevil stage, except the belated
broods, or those that have not reached full size in the
autumn; these remain in the ground the entire summer,
coming out late in the fall, or pass over until the second
year, as I have proved by burying the grubs in a barrel
sunk in the ground, covering the top with fine wire netting, to prevent the escape of the weevils as they emerged
from time to time during the season.

As a rule, we find only one grub in a nut, of the
American sweet chestnut, but in the larger varieties of
the European and Japanese, two or more is not unusual,
which rather favors the idea that the female weevil does
possess something akin to reason, which guides her in
locating stores of food available for her progeny. I have
never observed that the weevils had any choice among
varieties, all being subject to their attacks alike, provided all were growing in equally favorable positions.
But if the trees are of different sizes, some tall and
others short, some exposed to the winds and others protected, then the ravages of this pest will, no doubt, be
as variable as the surrounding conditions. As the
weevils emerge from the ground in spring or early summer, they will naturally seek the nuts most convenient
and on the small trees, then those on the lower branches
of the larger ones, while those on the upper part of the
tree, where they are fully exposed to the winds, may
wholly escape the attacks of these pests. This leads me
to think that whoever attempts to cut off native chestnut forests, with the expectation of renewal with the
larger varieties, by grafting the sprouts, will find the
chestnut weevil a rather formidable enemy. I have
found it so on a limited number of trees in my own
grounds, that are grown from grafted sprouts near large
native specimens, the weevils destroying nearly every
nut; but out in the field, away from the woods, and

where the young trees are scattered and exposed to the full sweep of the winds, the nuts are sound and free from insect enemies. The only remedy is to collect and destroy the weevils, which is not a serious matter where only the larger varieties are cultivated.

Diseases of the Chestnut.—I have never noticed any special disease among chestnuts, neither do I find any mentioned in European works on forestry. The nearest approach to any such malady being recorded as having appeared in this country, is found in a paragraph in Hough's "Report on Forestry," 1877, p. 470, where the author copies from Prof. W. C. Kerr, State Geologist, North Carolina, as follows: "The chestnut was formerly abundant in the Piedmont region, down to the country between the Catawba and Yadkin rivers, but within the last thirty years they have mostly perished. They are now found east of the Blue Ridge only, on higher ridges and spurs of the mountains. They have suffered injury here, and are dying out both here and beyond the Blue Ridge. They are much less fruitful than they were a generation ago, and the crop is much more uncertain."

While there is nothing said about any chestnut disease in the paragraph quoted, we only infer that the author intended to convey the idea that the trees were suffering from some endemic malady, although it may have been due to long drouths, insect depredators, or other causes. A few years later Mr. Hough, in his "Elements of Forestry," refers to the subject again, and admits that "the cause of the malady is unknown." But as chestnuts continue to come to our markets in vast quantities from the Piedmont regions, there must be a goodly number of healthy trees remaining.

Uses.—The economic value of the chestnut, as food for mankind and the lower animals, has been, and is still, so well known, that no extended dissertation or compilation of historic instances of its usefulness are required here. For almost two thousand years it has been an important article of food throughout southern Europe, and in some of the mountainous districts it is almost the "staff of life" among the poorer people, who not only use these nuts in their raw state, but roasted, boiled, stewed, and even dried and ground into flour, from which a coarse but nutritious kind of cake or bread is made. These nuts are also used in the same way by the poorer classes of China and Japan, and probably in other oriental countries. In France, Italy, Spain and Portugal, the chestnut crop is of immense importance, not only for domestic use, but commercially, because all surplus is wanted by other nations, who are ever ready to take a share, and pay a good round price for the same.

In this country chestnuts are mainly used as a luxury or a kind of pocket lunch for the children, as they are rarely brought to the table, and it is very doubtful if the American housewife, or our cooks,—unless foreign born and bred,—know anything about preparing these delicious nuts for comestible purposes. Cereals, meats, fruits and vegetables have always been so abundant and cheap in this country, that the poorest of the poor could indulge in them without stint or limit; but all this will change sooner or later, and when our population has doubled or trebled, the edible nuts must become of much more importance than now, and a roast turkey stuffed with chestnuts may figure as the ideal of gastronomic art.

As our native chestnuts are now annually consumed by the thousands of bushels, and the imported varieties by millions of pounds, and all as a mere luxury,—not a necessity nor an article which we could not dispense with without any serious inconvenience,—we may well consider what the future demand must be, and make haste to meet it with an abundant supply.

CHAPTER VI.

FILBERT OR HAZELNUT.

Corylus, *Tournefort.* Name from *korys*, a hood, helmet or bonnet, in reference to the form of the calyx or husk enclosing the nut. Order, *Corylaceæ.* Deciduous trees or low shrubs. Male flowers appearing in the autumn in pendulous cylindrical catkins two inches or more in length, with a two-cleft calyx partly united with the bracts or scales. These catkins remain on the plants all winter, becoming fully developed, and shedding their pollen early the following spring. Female flowers minute, entirely hidden within the buds during the winter, but early in spring their bright red, thread-like stigmas push out from the tips of the lateral or terminal buds. Ovary two-celled, with one ovule in each. Nut globular, ovoid or oblong, often in clusters, but each enclosed in a leafy, two- or three-valved husk, fringed or deeply notched at the upper end. Leaves broadly heart-shaped, serrate, with sturdy, short leafstalks. The filbert and hazel always bloom before the leaves appear in spring, and the male catkins usually open and begin to scatter their pollen in this latitude during warm days in March, the females soon following, their bright-red stigmas pushing out from the ends of the buds, but as soon as fertilization has been consummated they shrivel and disappear. The trees may then remain leafless for weeks following, and yet produce a heavy crop of fruit.

The common English name, filbert, is from "fullbeard." All the varieties with husks extending beyond the nut, and with fringed edges, are filberts (Fig. 37);

while those with husks shorter than the nuts (Fig. 38)
are hazels, from the old Anglo-Saxon word, *hæsel*, a
hood or bonnet. The parentage, size, form or quality
of the nut, is not to be considered in this classification,
for when the nuts are ripe and fallen from the husks,

FIG. 37. LARGE FILBERT.

there is nothing left to distinguish the hazelnuts from
filberts, unless a person is sufficiently familiar with a
variety to know to which group it belongs. In France
these nuts are known under the general name of *Noysette;*
while in Germany it is *Haselnuss;* in Holland *Hazel-*

noot; and in Italy *Avellana,* from Avellana, a city of Naples, near which there is a valley where these nuts have been extensively cultivated for many centuries.

History of the Filbert.—It is claimed that the filbert was first known to the Romans as *Nux Pontica,* because introduced from Pontus; but it must have become naturalized throughout southern Europe in very early times. But the Italian name of *Avellana* appears to have been applied to the wild hazel of Britain, long before Linnæus adopted it as the specific name of the

FIG. 38. LARGE SEEDLING HAZELNUT.

indigenous species. John Evelyn, one of the most careful and learned of English arboriculturists of his time, in referring to these nuts, in his "Sylva," 1664, says: "I do not confound the filbert Pontic, distinguished by its beard, with our foresters or bald hazelnuts, which, doubtless, we had from abroad, bearing the names of *Avelan* or *Avelin,* as I find in some ancient records and deeds in my custody, where my ancestors' names were written Avelan, *alias* Evelin."

The filbert has been celebrated in prose and poetry from ancient times, as we may infer from a remark of Virgil, who says that it has been more honored "than the vine, the myrtle, or even the bay itself" (Eclogue vii).

The supposed occult power of a forked twig of the hazel as a divining-rod (*virgula divinatoria*) for finding hidden treasures, veins of metals, subterranean streams of water, and even pointing out criminals, is, of course, purely mythical, although so solemnly attested by many learned men in the past; and I would not consider this myth worthy of a notice here were it not for the fact that it was early imported into this country, and is still firmly believed by many persons among our rural population. It is true that the supposed attributes of the European hazel have been transferred to different plants in this country, mainly to the peach and our indigenous witch-hazel (*Hamamelis Virginiana*), but the myth still lives, a legitimate descendant of an Old World nut tree.

There is little to be said in regard to the history of the filbert and hazelnut in this country, but it is quite likely that both of the European species, and many varieties, were brought here and planted by the early settlers in the Eastern States, and bushes of the same could have been seen in many gardens a hundred years ago; but I have been unable to find any account of extensive plantings of these nuts, although nurserymen, all along, have been offering choice varieties to their customers. In the main, our pomologists have either remained silent in regard to these nuts, or, at most, referred to them very briefly in their published works.

William Prince, of Flushing, N. Y., in a "Short Treatise on Horticulture," published in 1828, refers to the filbert as follows: "This shrub or, in some cases, tree, accommodates itself to every exposition, and to every variety of soil, but prefers a moist loam on a sandy bottom, with a northern exposure. It is easily multiplied by seeds, layers or inoculation. In fact, these nuts, which are vended in large quantities in our markets, grow as well in our climate as the common hazelnut, and produce very abundantly. Such being the case, it is hoped, ere long, sufficient will be produced from our soil to supersede the necessity of importation, as plantations of this tree would amply remunerate the possessor; or if planted as a hedge, would be found to be very productive. A single bush of the Spanish filbert in my garden has produced a half-bushel annually."

Mr. Prince then names a few of the best varieties, which are about the same as those recommended at the present time, and he was, no doubt, honest in recommending filbert culture to his countrymen, for his own limited experience proved that the trees would grow here and fruit abundantly.

A. J. Downing, in the first edition of his "Fruits and Fruit Trees of America," 1845, says: "The Spanish filbert, common in many of our gardens, is a worthless, nearly barren variety; but we have found the better English sorts productive and excellent in this climate (Newburg, N. Y.), and at least a few plants of these should have a place in all our gardens." If a few plants will succeed in a garden, then we might reasonably suppose that the number might be safely increased, and this was the idea of Mr. Prince, and many other writers on the subject since his time, but I fail to find any record of extended experiments with these nuts in this country, and as there must be some good reason for this neglect, perhaps my own experience in the cultivation of the filbert and hazel, to be given in succeeding pages, may throw some light on this question.

Propagation.—Filberts are readily propagated by almost all the modes employed in the multiplication of ordinary fruit trees and shrubs. The nuts are not at all delicate, and may be planted in the fall, or stored in a cool place, mixed with sand or sphagnum, and then put out in spring, always selecting a rather light and rich soil for a seed bed, and in such beds plants from one to three feet high may be obtained the first season. The seedlings produce such a mass of fine roots that they are readily transplanted without danger of loss. Varieties are perpetuated and multiplied by budding, grafting, suckers, layers, and some grow quite readily from cuttings made of the young, vigorous shoots, cut up into proper lengths in the fall, and then buried in the ground until the following spring, then planted out in trenches, as usually practiced with currants, grapes and similar plants. The method of propagation most generally practiced in Europe and this country is by suckers, and as the cultivated varieties of the filbert usually produce these from the base of their stems in profusion, there is no lack of material; besides, they make as strong, healthy and productive plants as can be procured in any other way. To secure an extra number of roots on these suckers, they should be banked up with a few inches in depth of good rich soil, or old manure, about midsummer, and then late in the autumn dig down to the base and remove with knife or chisel, after which they may be headed down to about fifteen or eighteen inches, and heeled-in for the winter, to be planted out in nursery rows early in spring. If a greater number of sprouts are wanted than the plants naturally produce, the main stem may be cut down ; but this will seldom be necessary, because the young transplanted suckers will usually produce more or less new ones the first season, all of which can be utilized for multiplying the stock if they are wanted.

Soil, Location and Climate.—European varieties of the filbert thrive best in what may be termed a rich loam, with a dry subsoil. If the soil is too moist, the trees are inclined to run too much to wood, producing less fruit. In the famous nut orchards of Kent, England, the soil is loam upon a dry, sandy rock. The trees in these orchards are manured at least once in two years, especially after they reach the full bearing age. Almost any good soil that is rich enough to produce a good crop of corn, and is not submerged in winter, will answer for the filbert in this country.

In selecting a location for a filbert orchard, an open, airy one would probably be preferable to a spot so sheltered as to cause the flowers to appear so early as to be injured by frosts. Furthermore, I would warn cultivators to keep as far away as possible from any hedgerows or plantation of the wild native hazel bushes, for these are always loaded with disease germs that are fatal to the foreign species. We might reasonably suppose that filberts would succeed better in the Southern than in the Northern States, but if the experience of those who have tried them there count for anything, then these nuts are not adapted to the South, owing to the fact that the flowers almost invariably push out during warm days in winter, and these are destroyed later by frosts. In the more elevated regions of the northern border of the Southern, and in similar locations in the Middle States, these nuts will doubtless thrive, or at least the climate will prove congenial. The more equable the climate and free from extremes in temperature, the better; but the most important element in this country is moisture, especially in summer, when the nuts are filling out; and the best way to supply this, where irrigation cannot be practiced, is to keep the ground around the trees continually covered with a mulch of leaves or other coarse vegetable matter.

Planting and Pruning.—The space to be allowed between the plants, when set out for bearing, will, of course, depend very much upon the size they are expected to attain. Those varieties which assume and remain in the bush form may be planted very close together, or not more than six to eight feet between the plants; but those which become small trees must be given more room. The larger European sorts, which are at present the only ones worth cultivating for their nuts, should be set ten or twelve feet apart, and the rows fifteen to sixteen feet, then if properly pruned they will shade the ground and be in a convenient form for gathering the crop. The trees may be planted in the orchard when quite small, and some kind of vegetable crop grown among them for the first two or three years, but I would prefer keeping the plants in nursery rows until they were four or five feet high, and then transplant to the orchard, and set a short, stout stake by the side of each, to keep the main stem in an upright position until the tree is well established.

The first pruning,—except removing suckers from those in the nursery rows,—will be the heading back of the main or central stem to a hight of two or three feet, for the purpose of laying the foundation, as it were, of the head of the future tree. Three or four of the larger branches, which will push out from near the top of the severed main stem, are to be selected to form the top, and all others removed. Small lateral branches or twigs will spring out from the larger or main ones, and in this way the head of a bearing tree is formed. But before attempting to prune a mature or fruitful tree, we must consider the mode of fructification, for the filbert does not bear nuts on the young growth of the season, as in the chestnut, but on the small branchlets or spur-like twigs of the preceding season, or, as we may say, on the one-year-old twigs. The small fruiting twigs are seldom more than four to six inches long, and sometimes almost every well-developed bud on these contain pistillate flowers and embryo nuts, either singly or in clusters. In pruning the bearing trees, the main point to be observed is to head back the strong leading shoots, to prevent the trees growing too tall, as well as to force out the side or lateral twigs as fruiting wood for the ensuing year. If the heads of the trees become too much crowded to admit light and air to the center, some of the larger branches must be removed entire. The best time to prune is in early spring, when the trees are in bloom, for at this season we can readily determine the injured from the sound male catkins, and preserve enough of these to insure perfect fertilization. It is not necessary, however, that there should be healthy pollen-bearing catkins on every tree in an orchard, for if one in a dozen is well supplied, there will be sufficient to fertilize the flowers of all growing near by. It often happens, in our rather severe climate, that the catkins of some trees or varieties are winterkilled, while the pistillate flowers enclosed in the buds escape injury, and when this occurs it is well to have some hardy variety at hand, from which pollen can be obtained when needed. The inferior varieties are usually the most hardy, and the wild European hazel or our northern beaked hazel, will usually escape injury where all the large improved sorts fail, and it requires but a few minutes' labor to cut branches bearing sound catkins, and scatter these about through the heads of trees requiring such assistance to make them fruitful.

SPECIES OF AMERICAN HAZELS.

CORYLUS AMERICANA (Walters). Common hazel bush.—Leaves roundish, heart-shaped, pointed, coarsely serrate ; husk somewhat downy, with a wide, flattened, fringed border extending beyond the roundish nut. Shell rather thick and brittle ; kernel sweet and good, but the nut is too small to be considered of much value. A low shrub, with many stems springing from the roots.

Young shoots and twigs downy and glandular-hairy.
Common in woods and old fields from Canada to Florida.

CORYLUS ROSTRATA (Aiton). Beaked hazel.—Leaves
ovate or oblong, somewhat heart-shaped, pointed, doubly
serrate ; husk extending an inch or more beyond the
round or ovoid nut, forming before it opens a long tubu-
lar beak, hence the name. The husk is densely covered
with nettle-like bristles, which are quite irritating to
tender hands. The nuts are small, usually growing in
clusters at the ends of the twigs, only a few coming to
maturity. A low shrub or small tree, usually growing
in a dense clump, not spreading from subterranean
stems, as in the last species. Common on rather firm
and rich soil along the borders of streams, in the
northern border States, and southward on the Alleghanies, but most abundant in the north through Canada, and westward to the Pacific in Washington and
Oregon, where, in the mountains, it often assumes the
tree form, growing to a hight of twenty-five to thirty
feet, with a stem from four to six inches in diameter.
The wood is light, soft, and very white to the center.
It also extends southward to central California, but
here it is only a small bush, this form having been described under the name of *Corylus rostrata*, var. Californica, A. de C. This species probably reaches its high-
est development in the Cascade range, in northern Oregon. The same or a closely allied species of the hazel
extends far into northern Asia. There are no improved
varieties of either of our native species of the hazel in
cultivation.

EUROPEAN SPECIES OF CORYLUS.

CORYLUS AVELLANA (Linn.). Common hazelnut.—
Leaves roundish, heart-shaped, pointed, coarsely and unevenly serrate ; husk bell-shaped, spreading, with a
fringed or deeply cut margin. The original form of this

nut is supposed to have been ovate or oval, but with a plant indigenous to such a wide range of climate and country, and one that has been so long under cultivation, —running wild in many localities where it is not a native, —it would be very difficult at this time to determine its primary botanical characters.   A common shrub or small tree throughout the greater part of Europe and Asia.

CORYLUS COLURNA (Linn.).—Constantinople hazel.   Leaves roundish ovate, heart-shaped ; husk double, the inner one divided into three deeply cleft divisions, the outer with many long, slender, curved segments, giving to the calyx or husk a fringed appearance, but leaving the end of the nut fully exposed (Fig. 39).   Nuts small, and for this reason rarely cultivated.   Native of Asia Minor, where the tree attains a hight of from fifty to sixty feet.   It is, however, hardy in France and England, and was introduced into the latter country some three hundred years ago, probably by Clusius, who received either nuts or plants from Constantinople, hence its present name.

There are several other hazels and filberts, so distinct from the two common European types that botanists have, in a few instances, been inclined to elevate them to the rank of species, and among these I may name *Corylus heterophylla*, or various-leaved filbert, from eastern Asia, also the *Corylus ferox*, or spiny filbert, which has a long and deeply cut or fringed husk.   It is a native of the Sheopur mountain in Nepaul.   But from the two common European species, *C. Avellana* and *C. Colurna*, and their hybrids, many hundreds of varieties have been raised, and from among these we may readily select a dozen possessing all the distinct and estimable properties to be found in this genus of nut-bearing plants ; to multiply names without securing anything of intrinsic value, is but a waste of time and labor on the part of the cultivator.

As we have no popular varieties of American origin, I am compelled to consult European catalogues in making a selection of those most promising for cultivation here, and this is, perhaps, an advantage, inasmuch as our transatlantic cousins have had a long experience and

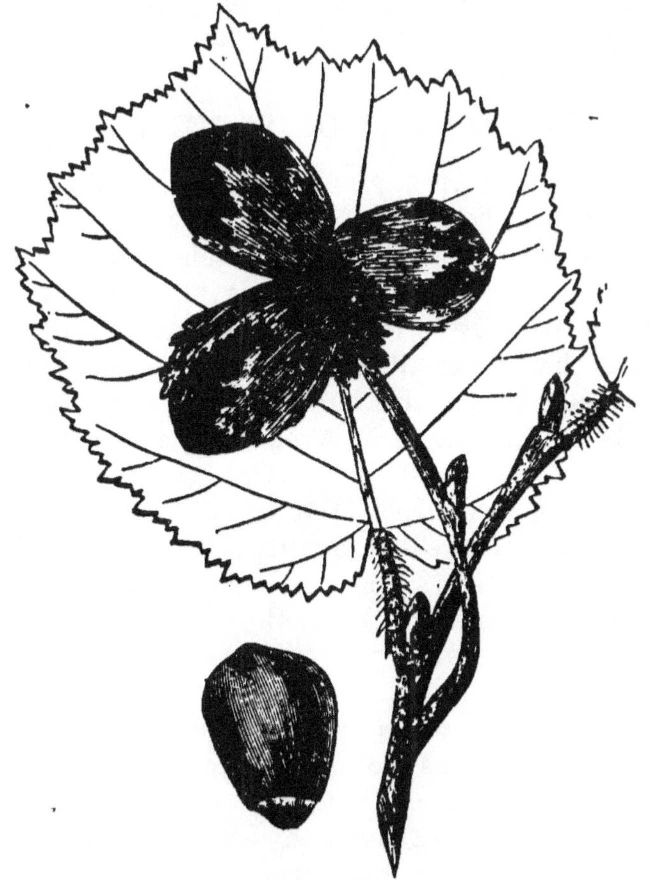

FIG. 39. CONSTANTINOPLE HAZEL.

abundant opportunities for determining the merits of the varieties they recommend. If hardiness and adaptation to our soil and climate are to be taken into account, in making a selection, then we may fail for the want of experienced guides, as it is undeniable that very

9

few persons in this country have ever attempted to conduct extended experiments in the cultivation of either the native or European species and varieties of the hazel.

Taking this view of the situation, I shall avail myself of the small but select list of varieties given in that standard work, "The Dictionary of Gardening," edited by Mr. George Nicholson, of the Royal Gardens, Kew, England.

SELECT LIST OF VARIETIES.

ALBA, OR WHITE FILBERT.—Considered in England one of the best varieties in cultivation. From the peculiar structure of the husk, which contracts rather than opens at the outer edge, this filbert can be kept longer in its cover than most others. As fashion demands that fresh filberts must be brought to the table in their husks, this variety deserves special attention. It is also known as Avelinier Blanche, Wrotham Park, etc.

COSFORD, OR MISS YOUNG'S THIN-SHELLED. — Nut oblong, of excellent quality; husk hairy, deeply cut, about as long as the nut. Highly valued on account of the thinness of the shell.

CRISPA, OR FRIZZLED FILBERT.—Shell thin, somewhat flattened; husk richly and curiously frizzled throughout, open wide at the mouth, and hanging about as long again as the nut. Ripens late, and one of the most productive.

DOWNTON LARGE SQUARE.—Nut very large; shell thick and well-filled; husk smooth, shorter than the nut. A peculiarly formed semi-square nut, of the best quality.

LAMBERT'S FILBERT (*Corylus tubulosa*). —Nut large, oblong; shell thick and strong, the kernel being covered with a red skin; husk long, rather smooth, serrated at the edges, longer than the nut. A fine, strong-growing, free-fruiting variety. It is quite popular in California, where it has been in cultivation for twenty years or more under the name of Red Aveline. Specimens I have received from there were not as large as those raised in England, but this can be accounted for by the difference in climate. This variety is cultivated in Europe under various local names, as, for instance, Great Cob, Kentish Cob, Filbert Cob, and Large Bond Cob.

GRANDIS, OR ROUND COBNUT.—Nut large, short, slightly compressed, very thick and hard; husk shorter than the fruit, much frizzled and hairy. This is supposed to be the true Barcelona nut of commerce, and is one of the finest grown. This is the large round hazel or filbert so largely imported for the trade in this country. It has many synonyms, and among them we may record Downton, Dwarf Prolific, Great Cob and Round Cob.

PURPLE-LEAVED FILBERT.—Usually cultivated as an ornamental shrub in this country, but under proper treatment it is one of the most valuable for its fruit. Leaves very large, and of a deep purple color. Nuts and husk of the same color, which they retain until cut by frosts. Nuts large, an inch in length; husks much longer than the nut, and slightly hairy. The catkins are tender and become winterkilled in our Northern States, but if the pistillate flowers are fertilized by pollen from some more hardy plant, this purple-leaved filbert is exceedingly prolific. I have gathered eighty nuts from a small bush in my garden, the flowers of which had been fertilized from another variety in early spring.

RED FILBERT. Red Hazel, Avelinier Rouge.—Nut medium ovate, not long as in the *tubulosa*, or Lambert's filbert; shell thick; husk long and hispid. A very productive variety of good quality.

Spanish filbert.—Nut very large, oblong; shell thick; husk smooth, longer than the nut. A very large variety, sometimes confounded with the Round cobnut and its synonyms.

PERSONAL EXPERIENCE WITH FILBERTS.

Believing that our failures are often of far more value, in the line of education, than our successes, I shall not hesitate to place my own on record as guide-posts to those who may be seeking the most direct road to success in nut culture. Having had a rather extended and expensive experience in the cultivation of filberts, I purpose giving a brief account of it here, with the hope that it may save some other enthusiast from losing time and money.

My attention was first specially drawn to these nuts in 1858,—while a resident of the city of Brooklyn, N. Y.,—by a neighbor who had a moderately large garden, on three sides of which he had planted a row of English filberts. These trees, at the time, had attained a hight of about fifteen feet, with broad, open heads, and they rarely failed to produce a heavy crop of nuts, which sold readily at very remunerative prices, for as they were always gathered in the husks and sold by the pound, the amount obtained from these few trees seemed to be enormous, considering the small space they occupied in this garden. The owner of these filbert trees, being an Englishman by birth, never tired of showing his English filberts to visitors, and of descanting upon their value, as well as upon the stupid indifference of the Yankees in neglecting the cultivation of these valuable nuts. I imbibed enough of my neighbor's enthusiasm to secure a good stock of his plants, a few years later, for cultivation in my grounds here. The third year after planting, quite a number of the bushes produced a fair crop of nuts, but I noticed that an occasional shoot was affected with blight, and these were immediately cut out and burned. The next season more of the branches were affected, and from these the blight extended downward on the main stems, and when these were cut away the sprouts from below made a very vigorous and apparently healthy growth, some reaching a hight of six feet the first season, but a year or two later these were also attacked and destroyed by blight.

Finding that the filberts in my grounds were doomed, I visited my old neighbor in Brooklyn, hoping to learn something of the origin or cause of the disease ; but the blight had invaded his garden, and not a tree remained. On my return from this visit I had every filbert and hazel plant on my place dug up and burned, thinking by such means to stamp out the disease. After waiting ten years, I thought it time to try filberts again, and to be certain of securing pure and healthy plants, I concluded to raise them from the nuts, and sent an order for a few pounds of the largest and best variety to be found in the celebrated filbert orchards of Kent, Eng. In due time the nuts arrived, and they were very large, and all of one variety, as ordered. They were mixed with sand and buried in the garden until the following spring, then sown thinly in shallow drills and covered with about two inches of rich soil.

At the close of the first season the plants were from one to two feet high and quite stocky, with a mass of small fibrous roots. The next spring they were transplanted into nursery rows, and set about one foot apart. The third spring I laid out about one acre for a specimen filbert orchard, and after the ground had been thoroughly prepared, the plants were set ten feet apart in the row, and twelve between the rows. No crop was planted among the trees, but the ground was kept clean and free from weeds during the summer, with cultivator and harrow. All suckers springing from the base of the

FIG. 40. ENGLISH FILBERT ORCHARD, FIVE YEARS FROM SEED.

stems were removed as soon as they appeared, and under
such treatment the plants made a vigorous growth.   Two
years later quite a number of the trees came into bearing, these showing that I was likely to have nearly as
many varieties in my orchard as there were trees.   Some
of the varieties might be better than the parent, but the
greater part were certain to be inferior in size.   The
fourth year after planting in the orchard the trees gave
me a heavy crop of nuts, and they made a fine appear-

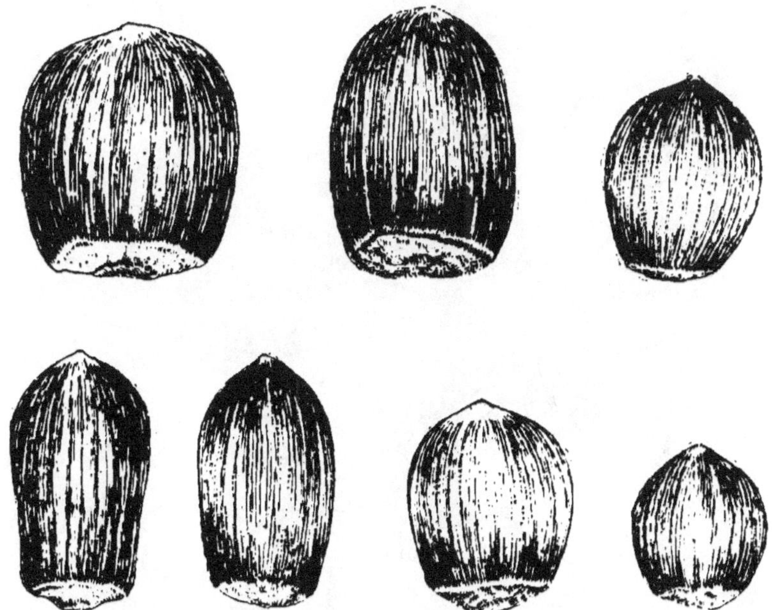

FIG. 41.   VARIETIES OF FILBERTS AND HAZEL SEEDLINGS.

ance as one looked down between the long rows, as
shown in Fig. 40.   But this season my old enemy, the
filbert blight, appeared again, and branches and main
stems began to blacken and the leaves to wither.   But I
had bushels of nuts and in great variety, and by sending specimen baskets of the long-husk varieties to dealers in New York, learned that there was an almost
unlimited demand for such nuts, at prices ranging from

FIG. 42. EXTRA LARGE HAZEL SEEDLING OR ROUND ENGLISH FILBERT.

FIG. 43. FILBERT ORCHARD STRUCK WITH BLIGHT, FIFTH YEAR FROM SEED.

thirty to seventy-five cents per pound, if sent to market
in their fresh, half-ripened husk; but later on, when
the nuts have fallen out and become thoroughly ripened,
as when imported, ten cents a pound may be considered
an average price for the larger varieties. Several of
these are shown in Fig. 41, of natural size and form.
Another extra-large hazel is shown in Fig. 42. The
fifth year after planting, my specimen filbert orchard
had suffered so much from blight that it appeared as
shown in Fig. 43; but a few dozen trees have been reserved, the rest being removed and reduced to ashes.

Name and Nature of the Filbert Blight.—The
reader must not suppose that one who has spent as much
time and money as the writer in experimenting with
these nuts, would make no effort to discover the origin
and name of such a virulent disease, and means of destroying it if these were known. For many years I had
been well aware of its presence in nearly all of the nurseries of the older States, as well as in the public parks
and private gardens. In the meantime I had diligently
examined the reports of the Division of Vegetable Pathology of the U. S. Department of Agriculture, as well
as the hundreds of bulletins of the various State experiment stations, treating of the fungous diseases of plants,
all without finding a hint or reference to this widely
distributed and destructive blight of the filbert. I also
sent many specimens of the diseased twigs and branches
to professional mycologists, with no better results.
With the nature of the disease, its mode of multiplication and distribution, I had become somewhat familiar, but the information sought was: Had it ever
been described and given a scientific name, and if so,
where, and by whom? This much of its history had
somehow escaped me, and, as it would appear from the
following correspondence, the chances were none too
good of finding it.

In reply to an inquiry directed to the U. S. Department of Agriculture, Division of Vegetable Pathology, I received the following:

WASHINGTON, D. C., Aug. 4. 1894.

DEAR SIR:

Your letter of Aug. 2, relating to the disease of the filbert, is at hand. In reply I have to say that we have not investigated this trouble, and are therefore unable to furnish you with any definite information upon it. Specimens of the disease, as you describe it, have never been, so far as I know, referred to the Division, nor am I able to find any record of any such disease in foreign or domestic literature. If you will send us specimens we shall be pleased to examine them and furnish you a report. We should also be pleased to have any information from you in regard to the manner in which the disease works. Very truly,

B. T. GALLOWAY, *Chief of Division.*

The specimens requested were forwarded promptly by mail, and in the absence of the Chief of Division, they fell into the hands of one of his assistants, who reported as follows:

WASHINGTON, D. C., Aug. 14, 1894.

DEAR SIR:

Your letter of Aug. 7 is received, together with the specimens. The stems of the *Corylus* are affected with one of the Pyrenomycetes. *Cryptospora anomala*, Pk. The fungus is described in "North American Pyrenomycetes," by Ellis and Everhart, p. 531. It attacks *Corylus Americana*, but appears to be worst on the European varieties, as you say. The pustules appear first on the young branches, and later on the older ones and on the trunk. The roots are not killed.

The only remedy known is to cut out and burn the diseased stems. Whether Bordeaux mixture or any other copper solution will protect the shrub from attack, is not known. So far as I know, it has not been tried. It is probable, however, that if the stems were thoroughly sprayed with the Bordeaux mixture they would be protected from attack. The mycelium of the fungus grows into the cambium and practically girdles the stems. The black pustules contain the spores. Very truly yours,

ALBERT F. WOODS, *Acting Chief.*

On the receipt of this note of Prof. Woods, I looked up Ellis and Everhart's work, a voluminous one of over 800 octavo pages, published by the authors at Newfield, N. J.   This filbert blight is briefly described under the scientific name of *Cryptospora anomala*, Pk., but Prof. Peck writes me that "the description was made from specimens discovered near Albany, N. Y., in May, 1874. In 1882 this description was republished by Saccardo, in his "Syllage Fungorum," Vol. I, p. 470, under the name of *Cryptosporella anomala*.   The original name in Report 28, p. 72, was *Diatrype anomala*.   In 1892 Ellis and Everhart, in "Pyrenomycetes of North America," p. 531, changed the name again, making it *Cryptospora anomala*."   So at present we have the names of this fungus in the following order :

Diatrypes anomal, Peck, 1876.

Cryptosporella anomala, Sacc., 1882.

Cryptospora anomala, E. and E., 1892.

Ellis and Everhart, after giving scientific description, add, "On living stems of *Corylus Americana*, Albany, N. Y. (Peck), Iowa (Holoway), on *Corylus Avellana*, Newfield, N. J.   The pustules appear first on the smaller branches, and are serrately arranged along one side of the branch ; afterwards they appear also on the larger branches and on the trunk itself, and in the course of two or three years the part of tree above ground is entirely killed.   The roots, however, still retain their vitality, and continue to send up each year a luxuriant growth of new shoots, destined to be destroyed the succeeding year by the inexorable pest.   The imported trees seem to be more injuriously affected than the native species."

The observations of Ellis and Everhart and Prof. Woods accord with my own, but I may say that the infested branches often show the presence of the mycelium in the bark and alburnum,—by a slight shrinking,—

weeks or months before the pustules appear, for these are merely indications of the last stage in the life of the fungus, and with the throwing off the spores from these pustules the old parasite perishes.

The pustules, when fully open, are from one-sixteenth to one-eighth of an inch in diameter, usually round, but sometimes slightly oval in form, and placed mainly in almost straight rows lengthways of the branch, as shown in Fig. 44. These pustules appear on wood of all ages, from two years upward, and in what may be termed patches, ranging from a few inches to a foot or more in length, and more frequently on the upper side than the underside of the branches.

This fungus is undoubtedly indigenous, and its host plant is the common American hazel (*C. Americana*). From a very careful search, I have not been able to find any clump of these bushes of any considerable size that was entirely free from pustulous stems. But on these wild plants it seems to do but little harm, for if a stem is killed, another soon springs up from the roots to take its place; but when·this fungus invades our orchards and gardens and attacks filbert trees, we recognize it as an implacable enemy. How far the spores of this fungus are likely to be carried by the wind, transported on the clothes of a person, or the hair of domestic animals, I do not know, but it certainly is not safe to plant the susceptible species and varieties within a mile of the wild hazel bushes, unless the planter is prepared to use fungicides freely on his trees. There are certain phases of this filbert blight that are rather

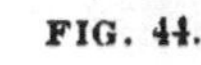

FIG. 44.

HAZEL FUNGUS.

obscure and scarcely explainable; as, for instance, its virulence among some species and varieties, and almost if not total absence among others. So far as my observation extends, I have never found it attacking the native beaked hazel (*Corylus rostrata*), and my correspondents in the Northwest and in the Pacific States assure me that no blight on the hazel has, as yet, been found there, and its absence is probably due to the fact that the common hazel (*C. Americana*) is not an inhabitant of these regions.

In a neighbor's garden just across the highway from my own, there are, at this time, four old European hazelnut trees, fully twenty feet high and as many years old. They are of two varieties: one a small round nut, the other a long, slender nut, but neither of much value, because of their small size. The trees, however, are perfectly healthy, never having suffered from the blight, although these four are all that remain of a long row of choice European varieties all planted at the same time. Blight destroyed the better varieties, while these inferior ones continue to thrive and are exceedingly productive.

This native fungus that causes blight in the hazels is but one of a large number of similar maladies which have appeared and often worsted the horticulturist, in his endeavor to introduce and cultivate foreign species and varieties of plants, and like the tropical fevers, they may pass unnoticed among the natives, but are terribly fatal to immigrants from cooler climates. The disease so well known as the black knot (*Otthia morbosa*, Schu.), and widely destructive to the European varieties of the plum, and Morello cherries, has existed for ages among our native plums and black cherries, doing comparatively little harm; but it seems to protest, by its virulence, against the introduction of some foreign species. The same is true with various blights and rusts which

attack the exotic pear, apple, quince, peach, and other
of the larger fruits, and we have only to ascend he
scale a few degrees from the microscopic fungi to the
microscopic insects, to meet on the very threshold of
this realm the minute but unconquerable grape louse
(*Phylloxera vastatrix*), which for more than two cen tu-
ries has prevented the successful cultivation of the European varieties of the grape in the open air everywhere
east of the Rocky mountains in North America; although
this minute insect has ever been present and a constant
parasite of the indigenous species of the grape, but
scarcely affecting the health of its host. The plum cur-
culio, chestnut and hickory weevils, bean weevil, and
many other similar species of insects appear to be ever
protesting against the introduction of exotic plants, as
well as the improvement of our indigenous kinds.

It is this blight, and nothing else, that has prevented the extensive cultivation of the improved varieties of the European filbert and hazelnut in this country, and not the uncongenial soil and climate, as has
been so often "officially" proclaimed by men whose theories are far greater than their practical knowledge of
such subjects. Men whose experience with these nuts
has been limited to a few isolated bushes or trees in gardens or nurseries, where they were protected, or beyond
the reach of the spores of the blight fungus, as has
already been noted in the experience of Prince, Downing,
Barry, and my neighbor Butler, of Brooklyn, could
scarcely understand why others should remain so indifferent to such a promising industry, or why the demand
for the trees remained so limited, with scarcely an
attempt to plant filbert orchards anywhere in this country. Nurserymen have continued to offer the choice
varieties at low prices per plant, and to advise their customers to cultivate filberts extensively, even to setting
them in hedgerows; and yet home-grown filberts remain

as rare in our markets as they were a hundred years ago, and all due to the simple reason that the insidious filbert blight still scatters its spores unrestrained.

With the present almost universal employment of various fungicides for the destruction of blights, mildews and rusts on cultivated fruits and vegetables, we may confidently assert that the diseases of the filbert may be readily controlled by the same means. The spraying of the trees with Bordeaux mixture and other copper solutions will certainly destroy the fungus spores, and with these out of the way filbert culture may become of as much importance and as popular here as it is in certain countries of Europe. In my own experience I have found no other nut tree (barring always the blight) that has been more satisfactory. The plants come forward rapidly, fruiting freely and abundantly when young, and if properly trained, the crop can be gathered with little labor, and as it is ready for use a month or more in advance of the arrival of fresh nuts from abroad, the home market during the time is at our command.

The number of applications of the fungicides that will be necessary during the season to rid the trees of blight, or the strength of the copper solution used, will depend somewhat upon circumstances and the condition of the subjects operated upon. If the trees are growing near hedges of wild hazels, where there is a constant or annual influx of the fungus spores, then greater care will be required to suppress them than if the trees are some distance from such sources of contagion; and it may be well for those contemplating planting filbert orchards, to examine their surroundings carefully in advance, in order to avoid local blight-breeding plants, and have these destroyed if any are found. I would also warn the cultivator against collecting branches of the wild hazel in the spring, carrying pollen-bearing catkins to be employed in fertilizing the pistillate flowers of the cultivated varieties, for by such means blight spores may be readily introduced into orchard and garden.

It will seldom be necessary to practice artificial fertilization, where any considerable number of trees are grown near together, because if ninety per cent. of the male catkins are winterkilled, the few remaining will be sufficient to supply pollen for the pistillate flowers. In my grounds filberts have never failed to produce annual crops after reaching a bearing age, although they have been subjected to great extremes of temperature in winter. One year the trees were in full bloom the last week in February, and although cold weather followed, the protected pistillate flowers were not injured. The winters of 1894 and 1895 were among the severest, in the way of continuous low temperature, I have ever experienced here, and while the filberts did not bloom until the first week in April, the crop proved to be abundant.

Insects Injurious to Filberts.—My personal observations lead me to believe that the filberts and hazels are, in this country, remarkably free from the depredations of noxious insects. Two species of nut weevils have been reported as breeding in the wild hazelnuts, viz., *Balaninus obtusus*, and *B. nasicus*, but among the many bushels of the European varieties of the filbert produced in my grounds I have never found one infested by a weevil or other insect. In Europe a nut weevil (*B. nucum*) is said to be very destructive to the wild hazel, often invading the filbert orchards, and this we can readily believe, because they are not at all uncommon in the imported nuts, but fortunately have not, as yet, become naturalized in this country.

The great hazel-leaf beetle, or as more generally known, elm-leaf beetle (*Monocesta coryli*), has been known in a few instances to attack and defoliate large

10

patches of the wild hazel bushes, but this insect seems to prefer the elm, hence is rarely found on the hazels. But should it ever invade our filbert orchards, it can be readily destroyed by dusting or spraying the trees with Paris green, London purple, or other well-known insecticides. There may be an occasional invasion of caterpillars, like the tent worms, spanworms, leaf rollers of various species, and what are called leaf miners, but as these infest almost all kinds of deciduous trees and shrubs, we cannot consider them specially injurious to the filberts and hazels.

CHAPTER VII.

HICKORY NUTS.

Hicoria, *Rafinesque.* Name probably derived from the aboriginal or Indian word hickery, or hickory, the common name for these nuts among the tribes formerly inhabiting the Middle and Southern Atlantic States.

Order, *Juglandaceæ* (Walnut family).—Native deciduous trees of large size, with compound serrate leaves with an odd number of leaflets, varying from five to fifteen in the different species, the three terminal ones usually much the largest, the lower ones on opposite sides of the rather stout leafstalk. Male catkins slender, cylindrical, pendulous, two to six inches long, three in a cluster, on a naked peduncle or stalk (Fig. 46) springing from the base of the terminal buds of the previous season's twigs, and just below the first set of new leaves in spring ; calyx unequally three-parted ; stamens three to eight. Female flowers two or more in a cluster, from the end of the new growth of the season, which becomes the common peduncle or fruit-stalk of a single nut or cluster of nuts. The flowers are destitute of petals ; stigma short, broad, and four-lobed ; husk fleshy or leathery, smooth, very thick in some species and thin in others, partly or wholly four-lobed, opening in some, allowing the nut to drop out at maturity, in others adhering, falling off entire when ripe. Nuts with hard, bone-like shell, round or oblong, smooth or deeply four to six angled, somewhat flattened or compressed in most of the species ; kernel two-lobed, oily, sweet and delicious, as in the common shellbark hickory, or extremely bitter, as in the bitter nut.

History.—The early white settlers of the Atlantic States found the hickory nut in common use among the Indians, who gathered and stored them in large quantities in the fall, for food during the winter months, and while our ancestors who sought to make homes in the western wilderness may have appreciated these luxuries, they needed land for cultivation, and to secure it the forests were destroyed, with no thought of preserving trees that would yield food for themselves or succeeding generations. Not only were the forests cleared away, as things to be banished from sight and mind, but as the hickories yielded superior timber for various agricultural and other implements, as well as for fuel, they were often sought for and utilized in advance of the general clearing of wood lands, and the first to feel the woodman's axe.

William Bartram, in the account of his travels through the Southern Atlantic States, from 1773 to 1778, and published in Philadelphia in 1791, says, in referring to these nuts, that they are held "in great estimation with the present generation of Indians, particularly *Juglans exaltata*, commonly called shellbarked hickory; the Creeks store up the latter in their towns. I have seen above an hundred bushels of these nuts belonging to one family. They pound them to pieces, and then cast them into boiling water, which, after passing through fine strainers, preserves the most oily part of the liquid; this they call by a name which signifies 'hickory milk;' it is as sweet and rich as fresh cream, and is an ingredient in most of their cookery, especially in hominy and corn cakes."

We can readily imagine what a delicious liquid hickory milk must be in which to cook hominy, rice, and similar kinds of grain; and there would be no danger from tuberculosis in this natural product of the vegetable kingdom. Perhaps at some future day, when

milch cows are as rare in this country as they have been
for ages in China and Japan, hickory milk will come
into vogue again and be more highly valued by our people than it ever was by the aborigines.

While we have no romantic tales to repeat in which
either hickory trees or the nuts have played an important
part, yet we can well imagine that such delicious food
must, in ages past, as well as in our own times, have
been a coveted luxury, enjoyed at many a social gathering
of friends and neighbors.   Many a country boy and girl
has welcomed the early autumn frosts, because they an-
nounced the opening of the nutting season, reminding
them of the long winter evenings near at hand, and that
the industrious and nimble squirrel was a sharp com-
petitor in the nutting field ; consequently, no time could
be wasted if a store of such luxuries was to be gathered
for home use, or to be sent to city or village market for
the benefit of less fortunate consumers.   It is to be
hoped that this source of pleasure and profit may continue long after the original forests of our country have
disappeared, and through the preservation and planting
of the noble food-bearing hickories by the roadsides, in
orchards, also for shelter, shade and ornament.   Valuable as hickory timber and hickory nuts have always been
to the inhabitants of this country, we might reasonably
suppose that there would be many thousands of these
trees planted every year, in order to keep up a supply
and make good the annual loss sustained in the destruction constantly going on in our forests.   But no such
plantings appear to have been undertaken in our Northern States, and only quite recently in the Southern,
where the pecan nut is attracting considerable attention,
on account of the increase in demand, and the advance in
price obtained for them in the markets.   Furthermore,
with the many millions of dollars expended by the general government to encourage the planting, preservation

and cultivation of forest trees, no special encouragement has been extended to the nut-bearing kinds, and the man who plants a cottonwood or worthless willow is given as much credit as though he planted and reared a tree a thousand times more valuable to himself and the country at large.

This may not be a very creditable phase of nut culture in the United States, but it is history, nevertheless, and to attempt to suppress it would merely be encouraging negligence, which has already become so general that the inferior varieties of hickory nuts command a much higher price in our markets than the very choicest did a few years ago.

The nomenclature of the walnut family has been subjected to various revisions by botanists, during the present century, and there are probably others yet to follow in the near or distant future. In all other standard botanical works published prior to 1817-1818, the hickories were classed with the butternut, black walnut and Persian walnut, and under the generic name of *Juglans.* But in the year 1818 Mr. Thomas Nuttall, an eminent English botanist, who had given years to wandering through our forests and studying American plants, separated the hickories from the older genus of *Juglans,* placing them in a new one, to which he gave the name of *Carya,* from an ancient Greek name of the walnut tree. This classification of Nuttall's was immediately adopted by the botanists of his time, and has been observed, scarcely without question, by the authors of all the numerous botanical works published in America and Europe during the past seventy-five years. But now we are informed by some of our noted botanists that, in deference to the law of priority dominant in matters scientific, Nuttall's name for this genus must be abandoned, inasmuch as Mr. C. S. Rafinesque, an erratic Frenchman possessing considerable ability for botanical research, and who came to this country several years before Nuttall,—as some recent investigations appear to prove,—defined the distinct characteristics of the hickories, and not only proposed, but published the name *Hicoria* for this genus in 1817, while Nuttall's *Carya* did not appear until one year later, viz.: 1818. For these dates I am mainly indebted to Dr. N. L. Britton, who appears to have been delving among "first editions" of the works of the authors named (Bulletin, Torrey Botanical Club, 1888).

It seems strange, however, at this late date, that such eminent botanists as the late Dr. John Torrey and Dr. Asa Gray, who were both intimately acquainted with, in fact associates of, Rafinesque, should have ignored his rights in regard to the name of *Hicoria*, if he was really entitled to the honor of founding this genus and separating the hickories from the *Juglans*. But for some good reason they left the matter in abeyance, for their successors to settle. Dr. Torrey does, in a way, recognize Rafinesque, in his "Catalogue of Plants Within Thirty Miles of the City of New York," published in 1819, but in a manner which shows that he had no confidence in Rafinesque's claim, but did approve of Nuttall's classifications and name of *Carya*, for on page 74 he refers to the hickories as follows: "*Carya*, Nuttall; *Hickoria*, Rafinesque."

From this it appears that Dr. Torrey did not adopt *Hicoria* as the proper mode of spelling this word, but retained the letter k in giving it a Latin form. This is not strange, inasmuch as Rafinesque had no settled form of his own, and varied the spelling at different times; as, for instance, *Scoria*, *Hicoria*, *Hickorius* and *Hicorius*. It is but reasonable to suppose that Dr. Torrey was familiar with Rafinesque's earlier writings, and also whether his proposed generic name of *Scoria*, in 1808, was legitimate, or a misspelling of *Hicoria*, as suggested by Dr. Britton.   But of one thing we may rest assured, and that is, Dr. Torrey would not knowingly detract from, nor fail to give every man full credit for his labors in any branch of natural history or elsewhere, and he certainly must have known Rafinesque in all his eccentricities and moods, for when in New York city he was usually the guest of Dr. Torrey, and these relations continued for many years.

A few of our leading botanists, having recently decided that Rafinesque's name of *Hicoria* must be restored, in deference to the laws of priority, and Nuttall's *Carya* be relegated to the position of a synonym, I have concluded to adopt it in this work, although 1 am well aware that a large majority of our botanists have protested against this change, probably because of the confusion it is likely to cause in the botanical literature of our times.   My own reason for adopting *Hicoria* is not so much from any special reverence to the laws of priority, but because it is derived from an old American Indian name, and for all such I have a profound regard, and would retain and adopt them whenever and wherever they are at all appropriate to products indigenous to this country.   The hickories being purely American, and unknown to Greece or Greeks, a semi-native name is all the more acceptable.   It is not to be expected that botanical quibbles are of any special interest to the practical nut culturist, for a pecan or a shellbark hickory will taste just as sweet and command as high a price in market under one scientific name as another; but the cultivator may have occasion to look up the botanical name of his trees in some school botany, or other botanical work, and fail to find it, in the absence of some guide to the various changes that have been made in the name of the genus, as well as in the name of the synonyms of the different species.   Then, again, propagators and dealers in trees are prone to employ unfamiliar names, whether they are old or new, this adding to the confusion, without benefit to either purchaser or cultivator.

To assist those who may have occasion to consult these pages for either the common or botanical names of the different species of the hickory, I shall endeavor to give the greater part of those compiled by Prof. C. S. Sargent (Tenth Census), Dr. Britton, and other eminent authorities whose works I have had occasion to consult in writing this treatise. It is not certain, however, that these revisions and readjustments of the scientific names of this genus of trees will remain undisturbed for any considerable number of years, for we have "many men of many minds" at work in the line of botanical research, and it can scarcely be expected that all will reach the same conclusion, either in fact or fancy; besides, it is often difficult, if not wholly impossible, to determine a species from the description given by the earlier botanists, for they are generally very brief and vague, and will often apply equally well to two or more species of the same genus. In some instances not a word is given in the way of description, merely a name, as in "Bartram's Travels" (1791), where he speaks of *Juglans exaltata*, a tall-growing hickory found in the region through which he was traveling, and we now know that it may have been any one of two or three species indigenous to the Southern States.

Under such confusing circumstances I shall make no claim of infallibility in applying names to species, but attempt no more than my predecessors have in the same direction, and my contemporaries are now attempting, *i. e.*, make as close a guess as possible as to the species or variety of hickory which the earlier authors intended to name and briefly describe. The date of publication of some of the earlier works consulted are given, as an earnest of my desire to assent to the law of priority in such matters.

FIG. 45. FOURTEEN YEARS OLD PECAN TREE IN MISSISSIPPI.

Pecan nut, Illinois nut (*Hicoria Pecan.* Marshall).—Leaves with thirteen to fifteen leaflets, oblong-lanceolate, serrate, pointed; nuts mostly oblong, smooth; husk thin, somewhat four-angled and four-valved, these at maturity shrinking, and falling apart when dropping to the ground. Shell of nut generally thin, smooth or slightly corrugated, varying widely in both form and size from less than one inch in length to nearly or quite two inches, abruptly blunt, or long and sharp pointed; the two-lobed cotyledon or kernel oily, sweet and delicious. A large, tall, but usually slender tree, with smooth or slightly furrowed bark, as seen in Fig. 45. Mainly indigenous to river bottoms in the Southern and Southwestern States, extending northward to Indiana, Illinois, Missouri and Southern Iowa.

Synonyms and their authors:

Juglans Pecan, Marshall, Arboretum Americanum, 1785.

Juglans Pecan, Walter, 1787.

Juglans olivæformis, Willdenow, 1809.

Carya olivæformis, Nuttall, 1818.

Juglans Illinoiensis, Wangenheim, 1787.

Juglans angustifolia, Aiton, Hortus Kewensis.

Juglans rubra, Gærtner.

Juglans cylindrica, Lamarck.

Shellbark or shagbark hickory (*Hicoria alba.* Clayton).—Leaflets mostly five, occasionally seven, the three upper ones obovate-lanceolate, the lower pair much smaller and oblong-lanceolate, as shown in Fig. 46, all taper-pointed, finely serrate, and slightly downy underneath. Terminal buds large and scaly. Fruit globose, somewhat depressed; husk smooth, very thick, firm, scarcely shrinking at maturity, but opening and falling with the nuts when ripe. Nuts variable in size, mainly thin-shelled, white, compressed or flattened, four-angled, with deep corrugations, blunt, rarely sharp-pointed;

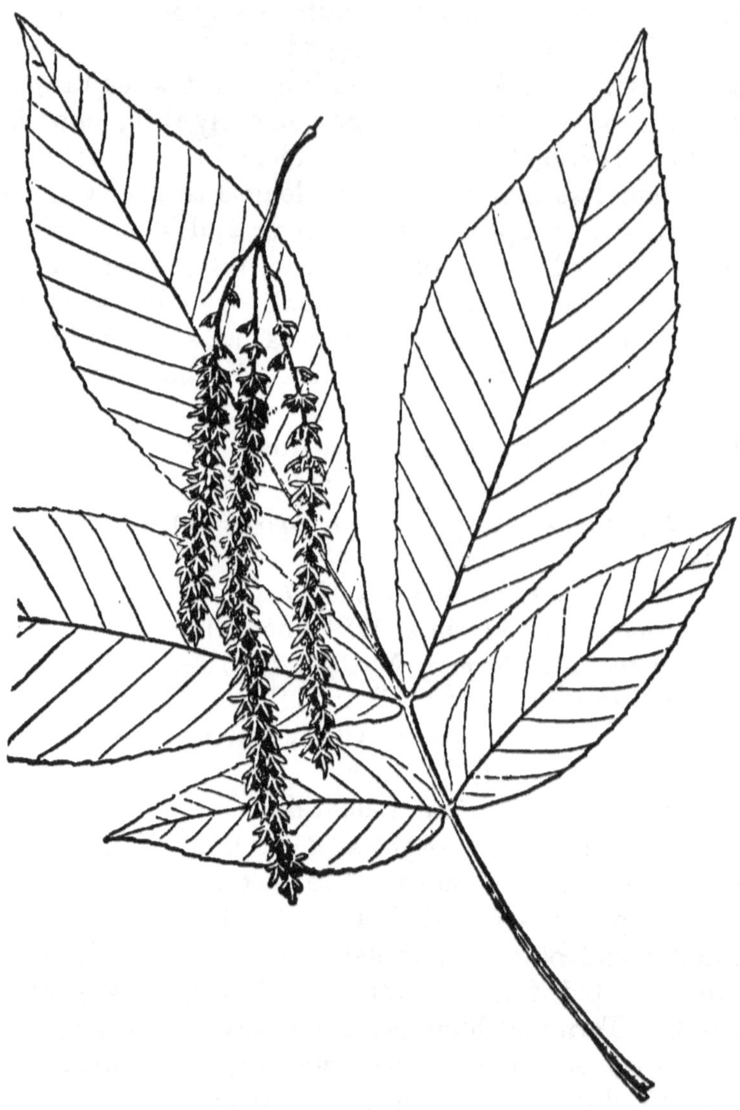

FIG. 46. LEAF AND STERILE CATKINS OF SHELLBARK HICKORY.

kernel large, sweet and excellent. One of the most common and popular of the indigenous edible nuts, collected in large quantities as they ripen in autumn, for home use and for sale, as the demand for this excellent nut is almost unlimited. A large tree, fifty to eighty feet high, and stem one to three feet in diameter, with a shaggy or scaly bark, which on old trees may be readily pulled off in long, shell-like plates. Timber well known as valuable for many purposes. This species has a very wide range, or from Maine to Florida in the Eastern States, and westward to Minnesota, thence southward through eastern Kansas, Missouri, Indian Territory and eastern Texas.

Synonyms :

Juglans alba, Clayton, Flora Virginica, 1739.
Juglans alba ovata, Miller, Gard. Dict., 1754.
Juglans alba, Linn., Spec. pl., 1754.
Juglans alba ovata, Marshall, 1785.
Juglans compressa (?), Willdenow, 1809.
Juglans exaltata (?), Bartram, 1791.
Juglans alba, Nuttall, 1818.
Juglans var. *microcarpa*, Nuttall.
Juglans squamosa (?), Lamarck.
Juglans ovalis (?), Wangenheim.

Although Clayton, as with most of the earlier botanists, fails to give any description of the foliage of the hickories he mentions, and all have the affix *alba* (white), yet his reference to the form of the nut and the scaly bark of the tree is sufficient to enable us to identify the species as that of our common shellbark hickory of the Atlantic States, which extends through the regions where he gathered his botanical specimens.

BIG SHELLBARK, THICK OR WESTERN SHELLBARK, ETC. (*Hicoria laciniosa*. Michaux).—Leaflets seven to nine, obovate-oblong, finely serrate, roughish-downy or pubescent beneath. Buds large, composed of rather

loose grayish scales ; the young twigs stout, with a gray
bark, most noticeable in winter. Fruit large, oval to
oblong, usually four-ribbed above the middle, with de-

FIG. 47.   WESTERN SHELLBARK.

pressions between ; husk
thick, somewhat spongy,
shrinking at maturity, and
splitting open from top downward. Nut large, with prominent ridges, and strongly
pointed, but slightly compressed at the sides, as seen
in Fig. 47 ; shell thick and of
a dull yellowish color ; kernel
moderately large, as shown
across section of nut in Fig.
48, but much smaller in proportion to the size of the nut
than in the two preceding
species, but it is sweet, well flavored, and easily removed
from the shell when cracked. The very large size of
these nuts makes them a favorite, especially where the
pecan and the true shellbarks are
not plentiful.   These nuts were
formerly known as the Springfield
or Gloucester nut.   A very large
tree, sixty to eignty feet high, and
two to four feet in diameter, with
thick, scaly bark, the scales somewhat thicker than in tne common
shellbark hickory of the Atlantic
States.   A rare tree, except in the
valleys west of the Alleghanies,
although it is reported to have

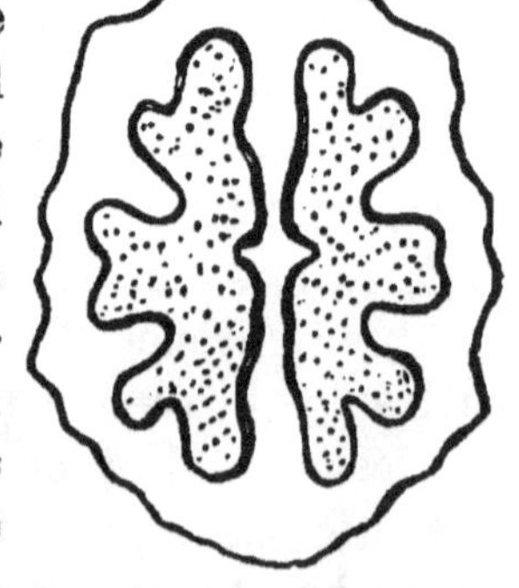

FIG. 48.   SECTION WEST-
ERN SHELLBARK.

been found in Chester county, Pennsylvania, and thence
west to southern Indiana, Illinois, Missouri, eastern
Kansas, and the Indian Territory.   Plentiful in the

bottom lands along the Ohio, Mississippi and lower Missouri. Elliott, in "Botany of South Carolina and Georgia" (1824), says it is rare in the low country of Carolina, but he does not say that it is found plentiful anywhere in the South. That he was sometimes in doubt in regard to the identification of this and other species may be inferred from his remark, namely: "The greater part of our hickories resemble each other so closely in their leaves and vary so much in their fruit that it is very difficult to discriminate the species."

It is this difficulty of identification which has led to so much confusion in the application of the specific names, for the earlier botanists rarely had an opportunity of a close and careful examination of the trees or other plants which they attempted to describe. In relation to the species under consideration, we find that the specific name of *sulcata*, so long in use, was adopted by Nuttall, from some earlier or contemporaneous author, —a system he followed with all the different species of the hickory, but without, in some instances, any discrimination or regard to their adaptation or validity. If there was anything to show that Willdenow (1796) had this Western shellbark in mind, or that he or his correspondents in this country had ever seen or collected it, then we might adopt the name of *sulcata* as the original and true one; but in the absence of such information, with a full and accurate description of the species and its habitats by Michaux, under the name of *laciniosa*, I think, in common justice to one of the most eminent dendrologists who ever visited this country, the name given should stand as the true one for this species. See Michaux, "North American Sylva," Vol. I, p. 128.

Synonyms:

Juglans sulcata (?), Willdenow, 1796.

Juglans laciniosa, Michaux, 1810.

Carya sulcata, Nuttall, 1818.

Carya cordiformis, Koch, Dendrologie.

The three preceding species are probably the only ones worthy of propagation for their fruit, or that have and are likely to yield varieties of any considerable economic value; but as it is important that the nut culturist should know the materials he is using, and whether they be of the best or otherwise, I shall admit all the species, without regard to their merits or value for cultivation.

MOCKER NUT, BULL NUT, BIG-BUD HICKORY, KING NUT, WHITE-HEART HICKORY, ETC. (*Hicoria tomentosa.* Michaux).—Leaflets mostly seven, occasionally nine, large, oblong-obovate, rather long pointed, slightly serrate, smooth on both sides while young, becoming roughish downy underneath when fully developed in summer; leafstalks and catkins also somewhat downy. Fruit medium to very large, round or ovoid, with a very thick woody husk, which splits nearly or quite down to the base, but usually falling with the enclosed nut entire, or bursting open as they strike the ground. Nut very thick shelled, smooth, or strongly four to six angled, white at first, but becoming a dull brown when exposed to the light. The kernel is sweet, but so small and firmly imbedded in the thick shell that it is only to be removed in minute sections, but this is successfully accomplished by the squirrels, who often throw down the entire crop from large trees before the shells harden, and then pack them away in the ground, in old logs, and under the leaves, where they will not dry for some weeks or months later. An exceedingly variable species, especially in the size and form of the nuts; on some trees they are scarcely an inch in diameter, while on others they are nearly or quite two inches, but always with such a thick, hard shell as to be nearly worthless for their meats. The largest of these nuts I have ever seen grow in central and western New York, where they are called "King" or "Bull" nuts.

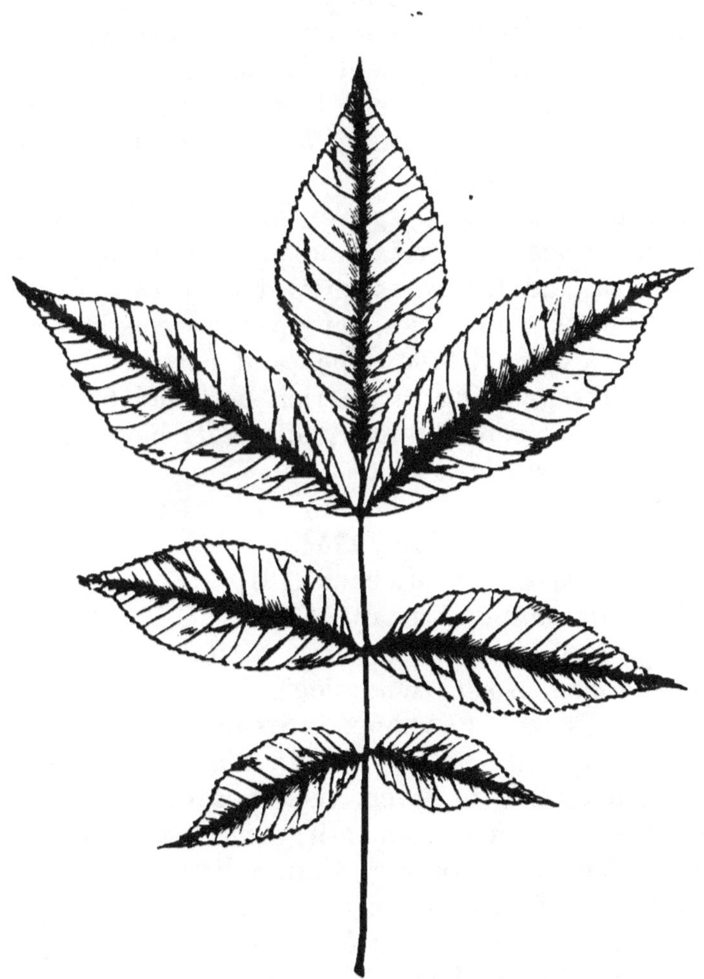

FIG. 49. LEAF OF PIGNUT.

The trees grow to a very large size, or from sixty to eighty feet high, and two to three feet in diameter, with a thick, deeply furrowed bark, not scaly. The wood is white, heavy, tough, and nearly as valuable as the common shellbark hickory. The terminal buds, and especially those on the young seedlings and suckers springing up in clearings, are very large, round, short, and covered with brownish scales, hence one of the local names of big-bud hickory.

A widely distributed species, or from the valley of the St. Lawrence to Florida, and along the great lakes to Nebraska, and thence southward to Texas. Unlike most of the other hickories, this species seems to prefer thin soils, rocky sandstone ridges, and here in New Jersey almost disappearing in the rich bottom lands along our creeks and rivers; at least, this is its habit here in the northern part of the State.

Synonyms :
Juglans alba (?), Linn., 1754.
Juglans tomentosa, Michaux, 1810.
Carya tomentosa, Nuttall, 1818.
Carya tomentosa var. *maxima*, Nuttall.
Carya alba, Koch, Dendrologie.

PIGNUT, HOGNUT, BROWN HICKORY, BLACK HICKORY, SWITCH-BUD HICKORY (*Hicoria glabra*. Miller).—Leaflets five to seven, mostly seven (Fig. 49), ovate-lanceolate, serrate, smooth; fruit pear-shaped or roundish-obovate; husk very thin, splitting about half way down into four sections or valves, these usually remaining attached to the nut for some time after falling, in fact, may often be found within the husk all through the winter; shell of nut moderately thin but tough, with a small, bitterish-sweet kernel. A large, rather slender tree in similar and same localities as the last, with a close bark but not so deeply furrowed as in the mocker nut (*H. tomentosa*). Of no special value except

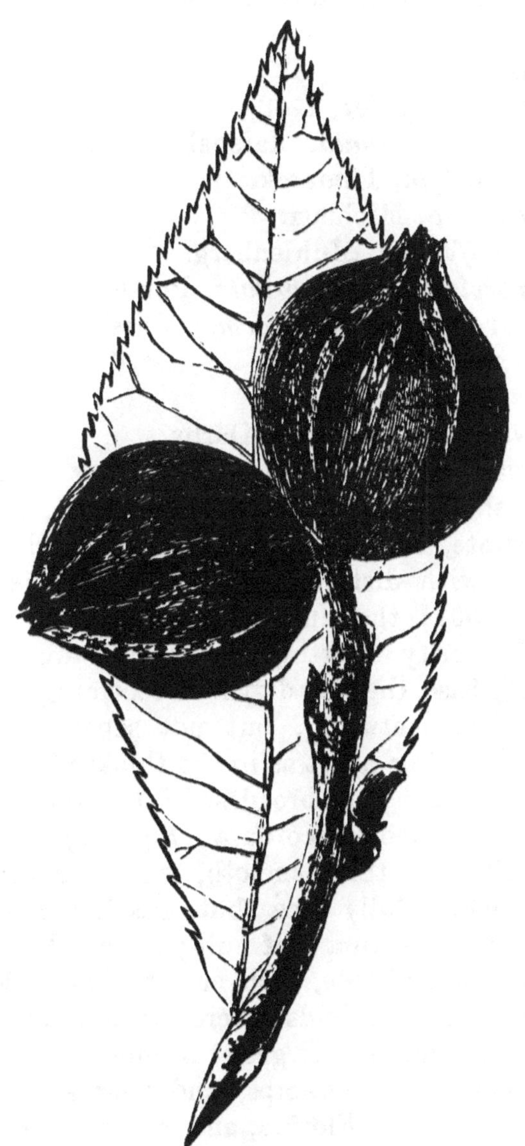

FIG. 50.   BITTERNUT.

as a timber tree, and its slow growth makes it less deserving of attention than those species that bear large and edible nuts.

Synonyms :

Juglans glabra, Miller, 1768.
Juglans alba acuminata, Marshall, 1785.
Juglans obcordata, Lamarck.
Juglans porcina, Michaux.
Juglans pyriformis, Muhlenberg.
Juglans porcina, var. *obcordata,* Pursh.
Juglans porcina, var. *pyriformis,* Pursh.
Carya porcina, Nuttall.
Carya glabra, Torrey.
Carya amara, var. *porcina,* Darby.

BITTERNUT, SWAMP HICKORY, PIGNUT (*Hicoria minima.* Marshall).—Leaflets seven to eleven, oblong-lanceolate, serrate, smooth and thin; fruit globular, with distinct ridges at the seams (Fig. 50); the husk very thin, and at maturity splitting about halfway to the base, the four divisions becoming reflexed in maturing, but not separating and falling apart as in the thicker-husk species. Nut broadest at the top, sharp-pointed, obcordata (Fig. 51), slightly

FIG. 51. BITTERNUT.

depressed; shell very thin, smooth, white; kernel intensely bitter when fully ripe, but greedily eaten by squirrels when fresh or in a half milky state. Usually a medium-sized, graceful tree, with smooth bark, slender twigs, and small, oblong buds covered with a dense yellow pubescence in winter. It grows in moist soils, along streams and borders of swamps, and near springs on hillsides, from Maine to Florida, and westward to Minnesota, Nebraska and Kansas. Humphrey Marshall described this species so accurately in his "American Grove," under the name of *Juglans minima,* p. 68, that there is no good reason to doubt its identity, nor question the validity of this name, which should remain as the true and original one, and all others of later date be placed among the synonyms.

Synonyms:

Juglans (*alba*) *minima*, Marshall, 1785.

Juglans cordiformis, Wangenheim, 1787.

Juglans angustifolia, Lamarck, 1791.

Juglans amara, Michaux, 1810.

Hickorius amarus, Rafinesque, 1817.

Carya amara, Nuttall, 1818.

NUTMEG HICKORY (*Hicoria myristicæformis*. Michaux).—Leaflets five to seven, ovate-lanceolate, pointed, quite smooth on both sides, the terminal leaflet sessile, not stalked; fruit oval; husk wrinkled and rough, thick; nut small, oval, short-pointed; the shell furrowed and very hard, and of a brownish color marked with white lines. Michaux says: "The shell is so thick that it constitutes two-thirds of the volume of the nut, which, consequently, is extremely hard, and has a minute kernel. It is inferior to the pignut."

A medium-size tree with slender branches, found in a few localities in South Carolina, near swamps and borders of streams, and westward to Arkansas, where it reaches its greatest development. This hickory has been so rarely seen by botanists that Michaux's specific name, given it more than eighty years ago, has fared a better fate than those of our more common and abundant species; consequently, I have only one synonym to record, viz.: *Carya amara*, var. *myristicæformis*, Cooper, in Smithsonian Report, 1858.

WATER HICKORY, SWAMP HICKORY, BITTER PECAN (*Hicoria aquatica*. Michaux).—Leaflets nine to thirteen, generally eleven, narrow and obliquely lanceolate-pointed, slightly serrate, thin and smooth; fruit globular or somewhat egg-shaped, four-ribbed; husk thin, dividing at maturity down to the base; nut thin-shelled, four-angled; kernel much wrinkled and very bitter. This is closely allied to if not a more Southern form of our common bitternut. A small tree in swamps and river bottoms from North Carolina south to Florida, and west to Texas.

Synonyms:

Juglans aquatica, Michaux.
Hicorius integrifolia, Rafinesque.
Carya aquatica, Nuttall.
Carya integrifolia, Sprengel.

Varieties of the Hickories.—Every one who has ever had occasion to gather or examine hickory nuts in the forest, or has seen them in market, must be aware of the fact that there is an almost endless variety of each and all the different species. But as it is only the varieties of the pecan and thick- and thin-shelled shagbark hickories that are likely to be of any economic value to the nut cultur-ist, all others will be omitted. Of the first or pecan nut the natural varieties are not only exceedingly numerous, but vary wide-ly in size, form, thickness of shell, and productive-ness of the individual trees. In some the nuts

FIG. 52. LARGE, LONG PECAN NUT.

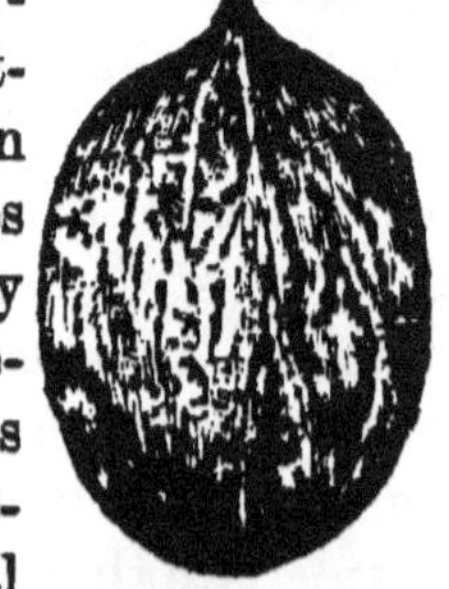

FIG. 53. OVAL PECAN NUT.

are produced singly or in pairs, and from this number up to clusters of seven or eight; these large-clustered and extra-prolific varieties are most worthy of special attention, especially when the nuts are of good size and thin-shelled, as in the large, long pecan (Fig. 52). From this size they vary, as shown in Figs. 53, 54, 55. Some of the wild varieties have received local names, and a very few propagated by grafting, which is probably the most practical means known of multiplying them, and at the same time preserving their varietal characteristics. Choice and extra fine ones are constantly being discovered and brought to notice, and doubtless many more will follow as the old fields and forests of the South and West are explored; besides, there are many thousands of seedling ·trees now under cultivation, and from these we may expect some marked variations from the original or wild forms. In Bulletin 105, of the

FIG. 54. SMALL OVAL.

FIG. 55. LITTLE MOBILE

North Carolina Agricultural Experiment Station for 1894, and in Report of Assistant Pomologist of U. S. Department of Agriculture for same year, we find the following-named varieties of pecans:

ALBA.—Size below medium, cylindrical, with pointed apex; cracking qualities good; shell of medium thickness; corky shell lining thick, adhering to the kernel; kernel plump, light colored; quality good.

BILOXI (W. R. Stuart, Ocean Springs, Miss.).—Medium size, cylindrical, pointed at each end; surface quite regular, light brown; shell thin; cracking qualities medium; kernel plump, with yellowish-brown surface; free from astringency, of good quality, and keeps well without becoming rancid. Introduced several years ago by W. R. Stuart as Mexican Paper Shell, but the name has since been changed to Biloxi.

COLUMBIAN (W. R. Stuart, Ocean Springs, Miss.). —Large, cylindrical, somewhat compressed at the middle, rounding at the base; pointed and somewhat four-sided at the crown; shell rather heavy; cracking qualities medium; quality good. In size and form this nut closely resembles Mammoth, which was introduced in 1890 by Richard Frotscher, of New Orleans, La.

EARLY TEXAN (Louis Biediger, Idlewild, Tex.).—
Size above medium, short, cylindrical, with rounded
base and blunt conical crown; shell quite thick, shell
lining thick, astringent; cracking qualities medium;
kernel not very plump, of mild, nutty flavor; quality
good.

GEORGIA MELON.—Size above medium, short,
rather blunt at apex; cracking quality medium; shell
rather thick; kernel plump, brown; meat yellow, moderately tender, pleasant, good.

GONZALES (T. V. Munson, Denison, Tex.).—Above
medium size, with firm, clear shell; quality excellent.
Originated in Gonzales county, Tex.

HARCOURT.—Size medium, short, slightly acorn-
shaped; cracking qualities medium; shell rather thick,
but very smooth inside; kernel short, very plump; meat
yellow, very tender, rich, very good.

LONGFELLOW.—Size medium, oblong, cylindrical,
somewhat irregular, enlarging from base to near crown,
then sharply conical to the apex; cracking qualities not
first-class; shell of medium thickness; kernel plump
but rather thin, light-colored; meat white, sweetish,
rich, good.

PRIMATE (W. R. Stuart, Ocean Springs, Miss.)—Of
medium size, slender, rather long; shell thin; quality
good; ripens in September, thirty days before other
nuts.

RIBERA.—Size above medium, oblong ovate; cracking qualities good; shell thin; kernel plump, light
brown, free from the bitter, red, corky growth which
adheres to the shell; meat yellow, tender, with rich,
delicate, pleasant flavor.

FAUST.—A South Carolina variety of medium to
large size, medium shell and good quality.

FROTSCHER.—A Louisiana variety of large size, very
thin shell, and plump kernel of good quality.

JEWETT.—From Mississippi; a large, long nut, rather irregular; shell medium; quality very good.

STUART.—A large, roundish, oblong nut from Mississippi (Fig. 56).

FIG. 56. STUART.

TURKEY EGG. — A variety from Florida; large and thin-shelled.

VAN DEMAN. — A large variety from Mississippi, of oblong form and thin shell (Fig. 57).

From other sources we collect other names, namely:

IDLEWILD.—An oval shaped nut from Idlewild, Texas. Report of U. S. Department of Agriculture, 1890.

FIG. 57.
VAN DEMAN.

RISIEN.—A very broad, thick variety, about one inch in diameter, very blunt at both ends. From San Saba, Texas (Fig. 58).

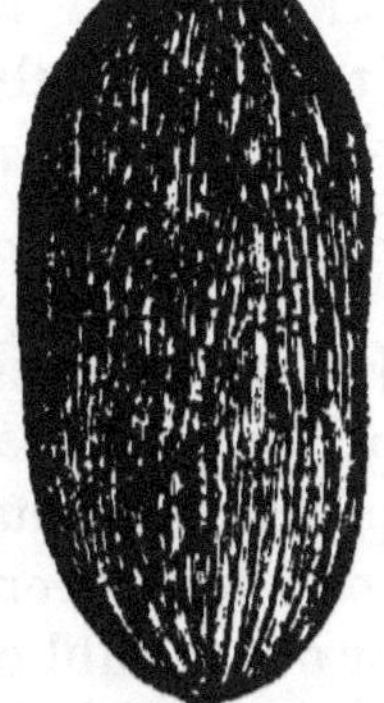

FIG. 59.
LADY FINGER.

A peculiar s h a p e d pecan nut is shown in Fig. 59, from Louisiana, sent under the name of Lady Finger.

From the report of the Georgia State Horticultural Society, 1893, we obtain certain local names without description, as, for instance, Turkey Egg, Mexican, Colorado, Pride of the Coast, etc. Col. W. R. Stuart, of Ocean Springs, Miss., who has been called the "father of pecan culture"

FIG. 58. RISIEN.

in that State, and is the author of "The Pecan and How to Grow it," adds two more varieties to the above list, viz. :   Beauty and Columbia ; the latter, as figured in the book named, is a very large variety, tapering from a broad base to a sharp point.   Judge Samuel Miller, of Bluffton, Mo., found some very large and fine varieties of the pecan in his neighborhood several years ago, on the farm of a man named Meyers, and he purchased the nuts from the tree bearing the largest in the grove and planted them, and the seedlings have since been distributed under the name of "Meyers' Pecan."

Judge Miller kindly sent me a quantity of these nuts, from which I raised some fifty or more trees, and all have thus far been uninjured by the cold of our severest winters.   From my own experience in raising pecan trees, and I may add, that of some of my neighbors, those grown from nuts gathered in the more Southern States are almost invariably tender here in the North ; but those raised from thoroughly acclimated trees, along the northern limits of this species, will give us a hardy race, and probably allow of extending their cultivation far north of their natural range.   Those who intend to try pecan culture in the Northern States should bear this in mind, and secure nuts and cions from hardy acclimated trees.

Varieties of the Shellbark.—Of this species (*H. alba*) there are as many distinct natural varieties as of the pecan, and while local or neighborhood names are plentiful enough, they have not, except in a very few instances, been placed on record in agricultural reports or other publications.   Three small thin-shelled varieties are named in the Report of the Pomologist of the U. S. Department of Agriculture for 1891, viz. :   Milford, Shimar and Leaming, but neither has been propagated, and they are probably not worthy of it, because there

FIG. 60. THE ORIGINAL HALES' PAPER-SHELL HICKORY TREE.

are plenty of larger ones with thin shells which would
be far more valuable for cultivation.

A careful research extending over a period of a
quarter of a century yields only a solitary instance of
the propagation and dissemination of a variety of the
shellbark hickory, and this one is Hales' Paper-shell,
which I named, described and figured in the *Rural New-
Yorker*, Nov. 19, 1870, p. 382, Vol. XXII. I am thus
particular in regard to time and place, because years
hence these facts may be of more importance than at
the present day.

The original tree of this remarkable variety is growing upon the farm of Mr. Henry Hales, near Ridgewood,
N. J., and on bottom land within a few rods of the
Saddle river. The tree is probably more than a hundred years old, and is about seventy-five feet high, and
nearly two feet in diameter at the base, and of the shape
shown in Fig. 60, taken from a sketch made in the fall
of 1894. There
are a large num-
ber of the shellbark
hickories growing
near by, and while
there are several
excellent and very
large varieties
among them, the
one I have named
is by far the largest and most distinct in form, and with
the thinnest shell; in fact, the shell is much thinner
than in many of the pecan nuts that reach our Northern
markets from the South. The size and form of these
nuts is clearly shown in Fig. 61, while the thin shell and
thick, plump kernel is seen in the cross-section, Fig. 62.
It will be noticed that these nuts differ from the ordinary varieties of this species in the absence of the sharp

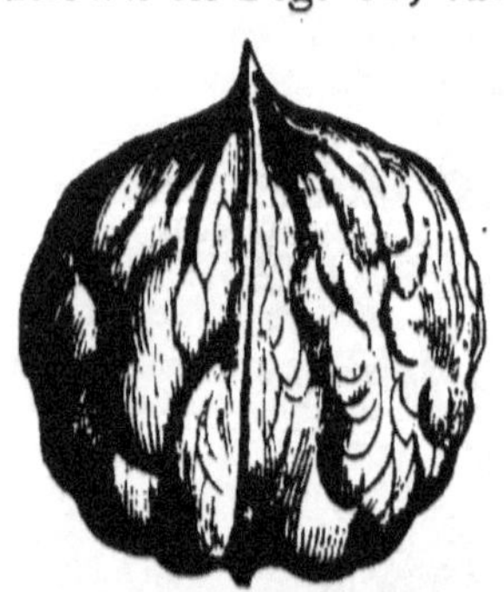

FIG. 61. HALES' HICKORY.　　FIG. 62. SECTION OF HALES' HICKORY.

ridges and depressions running from base to point, the surface of the shell being broken up into irregular, wavy lines, somewhat resembling the shell of the more common varieties of the Persian walnuts. I have occasionally seen very similar varieties,—but of smaller size,—among the mixed lots of hickory nuts on sale in our city markets, also oblong nuts, as shown in Fig. 63, but of course there is no way of tracing these to the trees producing them.

Another merit, in addition to the large size and thin shell of the Hales' Paper-shell, is its keeping qualities, the kernels rarely becoming rancid, even when two or more years old, and from a long acquaintance with this nut and hundreds of other varieties gathered from all parts of the United States, I am inclined to place it at the head of the list, and as the most valuable sort as yet

FIG. 63. LONG SHELLBARK HICKORY.

discovered. It is true, however, that I have found in the forests, and also received, many very large and superior nuts of this species, that are well worthy of propagation and cultivation, but they have been, in the main, of the typical form, and not of so distinct a type as this Paper-shell. Judge Miller sent me a few nuts of a shellbark found in Missouri, that were even larger, and with fully as thin shell

FIG. 64. SHELLBARK MISSOURI.

as that of the Hales' (Fig. 64), but upon making further inquiries in regard to the tree that produced them, I learned that an incoming railroad line had destroyed it, and thus one more tree of inestimable value had been sacrificed in the march of this progressive age.

Varieties of the Western Shellbark.—The typical form of the thick or Western shellbark (*H. laciniosa*) has already been shown on a preceding page, but some remarkable and valuable varieties have been found in the Western States, and no doubt others will be, when more attention is paid than at present to the natural food products of our forests. The tendency of this species, in its variations, is usually in the direction of an elongation of the nuts, even when there is no decrease in the thickness of the shell, as shown in Fig. 65, taken from one of a number of long varieties collected in the Western States ; and while they do not possess any special merit, they attract attention, owing to their unusual form.

FIG. 65. LONG WESTERN SHELLBARK.

NUSSBAUMER'S HYBRID. —Several years ago I received a specimen of a very remarkable nut from Judge Samuel Miller, of Bluffton, Mo., under the name of "Nussbaumer's Hybrid Pecan." Judge Miller informed me that he had received it from Mr. J. J. Nussbaumer, Mascoutah, St. Clair Co., Ill., who claimed that it was a hybrid between the pecan and the large western shellbark hickory (*H. laciniosa*). I had an illustration made of this specimen, and it appeared, with a brief description, in the *American Agriculturist* for Dec., 1884, p. 546. Soon after receiving the specimen nut from Judge Miller I opened correspondence with Mr. Nussbaumer, and learned from him that only one tree bearing such nuts

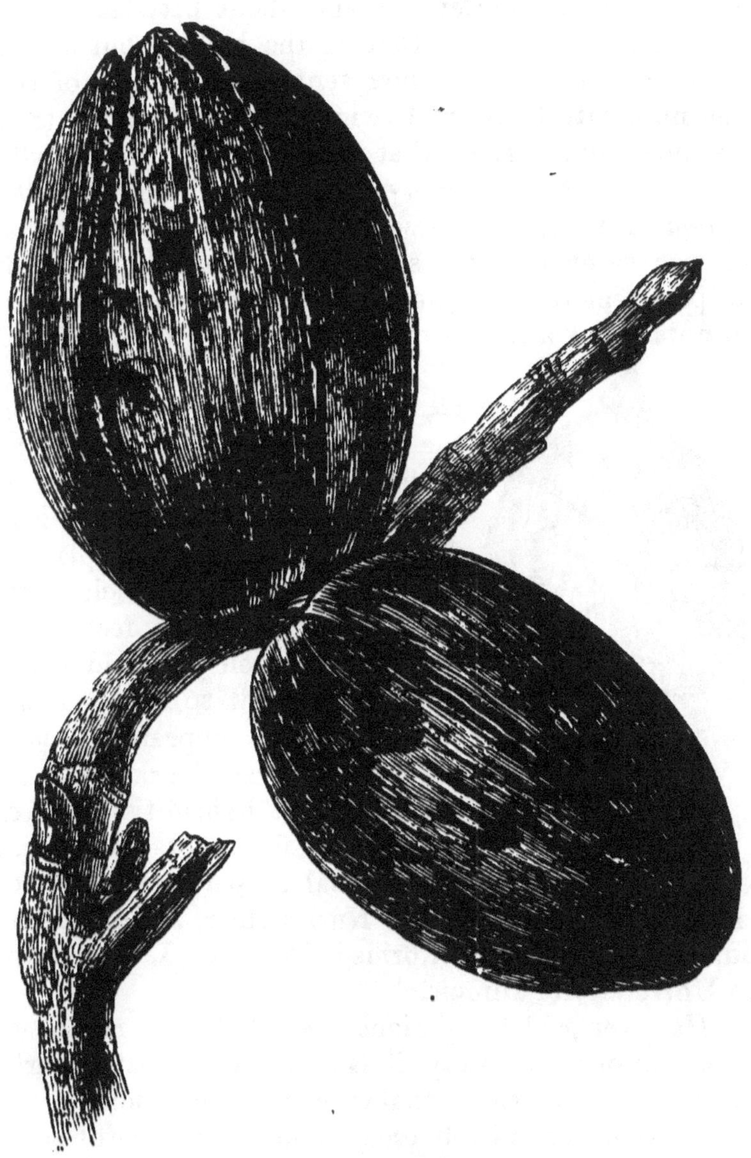

FIG. 66. FRESH NUSSBAUMER HYBRID.

had ever been found, and this was of large size, six and a half feet in circumference, and about fifty feet high, the bark somewhat like that of the hickory but nearer the pecan. Mr. Nussbaumer sent me specimens of the green nuts with leaves and twigs, from the original tree. The nuts, however, of that season (1884), were badly infested with the "hickory-shuck worm" (*Grapholitha caryana*, Fitch), and these had so ruined the shucks, and even eaten into the shells of the nuts, that few of the specimens received were fully developed. But from two nuts I had a sketch made while they were fresh and of natural size, as shown in Fig. 66, the dark, irregular marks on the husks showing where the shuck worm had attacked them. One of these nuts is shown in Fig. 67, also natural size. I planted one of the nuts, from which I now have a tree about ten feet high, but although ten years old it has not fruited, and, so far as I can judge from its appearance, is a pure Western shellbark, with no indication of hybridity; but of course this does not prove that the original or parent tree is not

FIG. 67.
NUSSBAUMER'S HYBRID.

a hybrid, as claimed by Mr. Nussbaumer, Judge Miller, and, if I am rightly informed, Prof. T. J. Burrill, of the University of Illinois.

However widely opinions may differ in regard to the origin of this variety, it is certainly a most remarkable nut, and I regret that the exact location of the original tree has entirely escaped my most careful seeking; and of late years I have been unable to learn anything of Mr. Nussbaumer, further than that he had moved from Mascoutah to Okawville, Ill., the last letter received from him being dated Dec. 13, 1887. In one of his letters he said that he had raised a large number of seedlings from this supposed hybrid, and if these are still alive they would be of much scientific interest, especially if any of them showed the distinct characteristics of either of the supposed parents.

It would certainly be a pity to have such a remarkable nut lost to the world, because if propagated by grafting or by any other mode to insure perpetuating its varietal characteristics, its value could scarcely be estimated. The nuts are as thin-shelled as the common pecan, the kernel sweet and good, and in addition, the tree is a native of a northern State, and would, no doubt, prove as hardy as our common shellbark hickories.

THE FLOYD PECAN.—This is another supposed-to-be hybrid, and of the same species of hickory as the last; but the one nut which I received differed from the Nussbaumer by being somewhat larger, and the shell with more prominent ridges and a little thicker. It was said to have been found somewhere in southern Indiana by a Mr. Floyd, who, believing it to be of great value, refused to give any information likely to aid any one else to locate the original tree, neither would he part with any of the nuts except the one specimen which eventually came into my hands. Of course all horticulturists know that seedlings raised from such freaks among nut trees are far too uncertain to be of much value, but ignorance in such matters often leads the possessor of an article slightly differing from the ordinary to permit his imagination to warp his good sense.

Cultivation of the Hickories.—The hickories have been so seldom planted in our Northern States for any purpose, that anything like a systematic cultivation of these trees is a thing almost unknown. Of course there is no good reason why the hickories should not be multiplied and cultivated as well as other kinds of trees,

12

but in some unknown way the idea became prevalent that these trees could not be transplanted with any assurance of success, and this has been kept alive, either through ignorance or by those whose interest led them to encourage the planting of the rapid-growing and easily propagated kinds, instead of those which, though less profitable to the producer, would be of far greater value to the purchaser. It must be admitted, however, that the hickories are not so tenacious of life as the willows, poplars, elms and similar kinds of trees, requiring more care in their cultivation if they are to be transplanted when of a proper size for setting along roadsides or elsewhere, for shade and ornament, but they are certainly no more difficult to make live than the beech, oak, tulip and various species of the magnolia.

The slow growth of the hickories while young is another objection often urged as a fault of these trees, but there is nothing lost but time in waiting, and this passes just as swiftly whether we plant trees that may in ten years yield a golden harvest, or nothing but leaves; besides, the hickories respond as readily to stimulants and good care generally as the common fruit trees of our orchards. While the farmers of our Northern States are generally quite indifferent as to what becomes of their old hickory trees, and seldom attempt to preserve the wild seedlings that spring up in the fields and on the borders of forests, their fellow countrymen of the Southern States have, within the past two or three decades, discovered that they possess an inexhaustible source of wealth in their common pecan nut. Formerly these trees were sacrificed whenever a choice piece of tough timber was wanted, and often merely to secure the entire crop of nuts without waiting for nature to drop them within reach; but the advent of many lines of railroads, steamboats, and other means of communication with the great cities and their markets, has changed this inclination to destroy into one of preservation. The old pecan trees are not only appreciated as a source of income, but thousands and tens of thousands of seedlings are now annually raised and planted, to insure larger returns in the near or distant future. In fact, pecan culture has already become an important industry in several of the Southern States, although in point of age it is little more than a fledgling. We have no statistics to show what the annual crop averages in pounds or bushels, but it must be something enormous if we make our estimate from the quantities received and distributed in the Northern States. But with all the efforts put forth to secure a supply of these nuts, and the high prices they command at both wholesale and retail, the demand seems to keep well in advance of the supply, and this will, in all probability, continue as our population increases. In the way of demand, the same is true with our northern species of the shellbark hickories, which were formerly very abundant, but of late years have become rather scarce, for reasons too obvious to call for any explanation at this time.

In selecting a location for planting and cultivating the hickories, including the pecan, a moist, deep soil is certainly preferable to any other, especially for the three species and their varieties most promising for this purpose, because we find them growing wild in such situations and soils. But while these naturally deep, rich and moist soils are to be preferred, no one need hesitate to plant hickories on light, dry, and even poor soils, if they are properly enriched, or a few shovelfuls of fine old stable manure is thoroughly mixed with the earth in which the roots are set, and then a mulch applied to the surface to keep the soil moist. Almost any old waste fibrous material, such as leaves, straw, hay, weeds or coarse manure, will answer for mulching newly planted trees, and it should be applied to a depth of three or four inches, and renewed annually, or as often as necessary to prevent the growth of grass or weeds growing within three or four feet of the stem of the tree.   In all dry climates and soils mulching should be considered an important operation, not to be omitted until the trees are from six to ten years old, and it may usually be continued a longer time with benefit.

Propagation.—All the species of the hickory are very readily grown from nuts gathered when ripe and planted within a few weeks; or they may be mixed with or stratified between layers of sand and light soil and buried in the open ground for the winter, and the planting deferred until the following spring. They are not at all delicate and will withstand considerable drying and neglect, and will grow, if stored in a cool cellar, without being packed in either soil, sand or other material.   But as I have had no occasion to determine how much neglect these nuts will withstand, nor to what extremes of adverse conditions it is safe to subject them, I shall leave investigation in this direction to others, because in general practice no valuable seed or plant grows any too readily and freely to satisfy the cultivator, and for this reason I recommend either planting hickory nuts in the fall, or burying them between layers of light soil or sand, sifting out and planting early the following spring. If any considerable quantity is to be planted they should be dropped three or four inches apart in shallow trenches and covered about two inches deep. The distance between the rows may be from two to three feet, depending upon the implements to be used in their cultivation.

The soil for a seedbed should, of course, be made rich and deep, or the same as recommended for chestnuts, and all the means usually employed to assist the growth of cultivated plants are applicable to nut trees. I may also add that cutworms, white grubs and other

noxious insects are enemies of nut-tree seedlings as well
as garden vegetables. The seedling hickories should
be treated as advised for chestnuts; that is, dug up
when one or, at the latest, two years old, and their
central or taproot shortened to at least one-half their
original length, and then reset in nursery rows, and at
a distance of twelve to fifteen inches apart in the row.
If grown in ordinary upland, the transplanted seedlings
will make a better growth if heavily mulched than under the usual system of clean cultivation, and it is usually less expensive; besides, by keeping the surface of
the soil cool and moist, we encourage and assist the production of fibrous lateral roots, which, as a rule, are
none too abundant on seedling hickories, no matter
under what conditions or system of cultivation they
are raised.

When the seedlings have grown in the nursery rows
two or three years, they will probably be large enough
for planting where they are to remain permanently; but
if, for any reason, they are not disposed of, then they
should be again transplanted,—the larger roots shortened,—and re-set in good rich soil. The object of transplanting is to insure the production of small fibrous
roots, and a frequent renewal of the same, close to the
main stem or stock, as long as the trees remain in the
nursery, whether this be two or twenty years. This
is somewhat of an expensive operation, but the value of
stock thus handled is enhanced far more than the cost
of such transplanting, and purchasers are, or at least
should be, willing to pay a fair price for such trees.

It is the natural habit of the hickories, as well as
many other kinds of deciduous trees, to produce in their
earlier stages of growth rather large, deeply penetrating,
naked roots, with few small fibers, and in this condition
they are not so readily and successfully transplanted as
the kinds possessing a more ramified root system. This,

perhaps, has misled many persons to believe that certain kinds of trees, like the hickories, could not be moved at all, or at least not with any assurance of being made to live. This idea has become so prevalent among inexperienced cultivators, and, I regret to add, often reiterated by theorists, that it has discouraged many who otherwise would have raised and planted nut trees in preference to other kinds.

Admitting that it is the general habit of most kinds of forest trees to produce deeply penetrating taproots, when grown from seed, it proves nothing more than that these parts may be of some importance to the plants while they are young, and under natural conditions, yet they are not absolutely necessary, and, at most, are only temporary organs, like the tails of tadpoles, always disappearing with maturity.

Any one at all observing, and having had an opportunity of examining limited or extended areas of forest trees thrown over by hurricanes, must have noticed that no tree of any considerable size and age possessed a taproot, but had been for years kept in its upright position by lateral brace-roots, and through these it had also obtained nutriment from the surface soil. Some of my correspondents in the South have expressed their surprise at not finding any trace of the original central roots on old pecan trees, when blown over by severe wind storms. But it is the same everywhere with forest trees and where the soil is naturally loose and moist: the principal or supporting roots spread out widely and remain near the surface, and the central roots·or taproots disappear much earlier than in dry soils.

In multiplying trees under artificial conditions, we remove the taproots, not only for convenience in transplanting, but also to hasten and increase the production of surface lateral roots, and more than this, we lessen the years of luxuriant sterility, securing earlier fruiting by such operations as root pruning and frequent transplanting.

Budding and Grafting.—I have never known of an instance of successful budding of the hickory, at least in the ordinary way during the summer months. What is called "annular budding" in early spring with buds of the previous season, is said to have been successfully practiced with the pecan at the South, but this mode of propagation is more of the nature of grafting than of what is usually understood as budding. But I have been unable to obtain any statistics in regard to the proportion of buds that any propagator or experimenter has made live by this or other modes of propagation. Col. Stuart says, in "The Pecan," p. 45, "There is a method known as 'annular budding,' which proves quite successful." He then proceeds to describe the operation, as given in all works on the propagation of trees and plants during the past hundred years or more, but not a word to indicate what he considers a "success,"—whether it be once or fifty times in a hundred, or if he ever succeeded in making an annular bud unite to the stock; I am more inclined to think that he never did, than otherwise.

In Bulletin No. 105, "Nut Culture for North Carolina," issued from the N. C. State Experiment Station, 1894, Mr. W. A. Taylor, Assistant Pomologist U. S. Department of Agriculture, in referring to budding and grafting of these trees, says: "These latter operations are less successful with the pecan than most fruit trees, though they are by no means impossible to accomplish. On seedlings one or two years old annular budding in early summer succeeds best." But here again we are left in doubt in regard to what the writer considers "a success." Then, again, the line between the "possible" and "impossible," in horticultural matters, is a rather difficult one to determine, and Mr. Taylor fails to cite a single instance in which either annular or any other form of either budding or grafting had been successfully practiced. The Bulletins issued from the Division of Pomology of the Department of Agriculture, give us no information whatever on this subject of propagation of the hickories, further than to repeat the old formulas of annular, splice and cleft grafting ; but as to results they have always been provokingly silent.

Having been repeatedly assured, by men who presumed to know, that the pecan tree was successfully propagated in the South by grafting, and many thousands annually raised in this way, it seems strange that such plants are so rarely offered by nurserymen. Seedlings of choice varieties are, of course, abundant enough, but a man might, with as much propriety, offer seedling Bartlett pears or Baldwin apples, as pecan trees, expecting to perpetuate varieties. In corresponding with Mr. P. J. Berckmans, of the Fruitland Nurseries of Augusta, Ga., whose experience and acquaintance with the fruits of the South are, without doubt, in advance of any other horticulturist of the past or even the present generation, in reply to my request for information on grafting pecans, he writes : "For the past five or six years we have grafted various varieties of the pecan nuts. I do not know of any other nurseryman South who offers grafted trees. I presume the reason of this is, the great difficulty in having the grafts take, as we seldom have more than fifteen to twenty-five per cent grow. We usually crown graft in February, using one-year-old seedlings grown in nursery rows. Owing to the small percentage of grafts which grow, grafted trees must, necessarily, be quite expensive, and for this reason there are so few attempts made in this method of propagation."

Mr. Berckmans makes no reference to annular budding of the pecan, so strongly and frequently recommended by the several writers already quoted, although

I am certain that he is as familiar with this mode of propagation as any one else, and would have practiced it had he found it in any way superior to crown grafting. From all that I have been able to learn through a rather extended correspondence, in regard to the propagation of the pecan nut tree in the South, I conclude that they are occasionally and sparingly grafted, but with such indifferent results that they are not at all numerous in either orchards or nurseries.

From certain remarks of Col. Stuart, in his essay on "Pecan Culture," I infer that he has sold grafted trees, for he says: "It costs no more to care for the grove of choice trees than of poor ones; then, again, the grafted or budded ones come into profitable bearing three years earlier than seedlings. Here is a case in point: Last November (1892) we paid, in cash, two hundred and forty-eight dollars for the nuts which grew upon one tree, the crop of one year. The tree is twenty inches through at its base, and forty-five feet high; such a size tree would grow in twenty or twenty-five years. Now small nuts from the same size tree will sell for not more than fifteen to twenty dollars. Another tree only ten years old bore thirteen and a half dollars worth. These choice nuts are such as we grow seedlings from; we sell a great many more seedlings than we do grafted or budded trees, simply because they are so much cheaper, and people in general do not realize that such a vast difference exists between the profits of seedling and grafted or budded trees; but such is the case, and such it will always remain for aught we can see." Soon after I published the description of the Hales' Paper-shell hickory in 1870, requests for cions were received from nurserymen and many amateur horticulturists, who were anxious to try their skill in grafting this excellent variety. Mr. Hales generously responded, and sent cions to a large number of correspondents in various parts of the

country, because he was desirous of having the variety
preserved and propagated.   During the following ten
years the old original tree was kept pretty well pruned,
in filling orders for cions; those sent to nurserymen
were to be raised on shares, one-half of all the successfully grafted trees to be returned to Mr. Hales.   Being
a near neighbor, my opportunities for keeping informed
as to the result of this arrangement was all that I could
desire.   To one nursery firm in central New York Mr.
Hales sent about one thousand cions per annum for four
successive years, and in return received just four feeble
grafted plants as his share of the total product of the
four thousand cions.   But as the four plants received
soon died, he closed that account as one of total loss.
Previously, however, he had sent a quantity of cions to
Mr. J. R. Trumpy, of the Kissena Nurseries, Flushing,
N. Y., whose skill as a propagator of ligneous plants is
probably second to that of no man in·this country; the
result proved that our faith in the man was not mis-
placed, for Mr. Hales received for his share of the experiment something over two dozen grafted trees, and
most of these are now handsome specimens ten to twenty
feet high.   Just what percentage of the cions set were
made to unite and grow I have not been informed, but
the experiment was, doubtless, rather unsatisfactory as a
commercial transaction.

In addition to the plants sent to Mr. Hales, there
have been quite a number distributed among the customers of the nurseries named; consequently, we are
pretty well assured of the perpetuation of this remark-
·ably fine variety, even when the original tree succumbs
to old age, or should it be accidentally destroyed.   I am
inclined to give Mr. Trumpy credit for being the first
man to graft the shellbark hickory in this or any other
country, and make the cions unite and grow, for I
have failed to find any instance of success in this mode

of propagating these trees, prior to his with the Hales' Paper-shell.

In reply to a note sent him a few months since, asking: "How did or do you graft the hickories?" he replied as follows: "I put the hickory stocks in pots in the spring, and graft them the following spring, say in April, and in the house. The cions are cut during the winter, so as to keep them in good order until wanted for use. I find it is better to operate in April than earlier in the winter. I also graft them out of doors about the beginning of May, when the stocks are growing. They will succeed very well out of doors, provided the stocks are large enough for the cions. Any kind of grafting will do, but crown grafting is the best. I have not done much of late in the way of grafting hickories in the nursery, not having suitable stocks; besides, when the weather becomes warm enough for outside work, vegetation pushes far too rapidly to give a man a chance to do much of this kind of grafting."

Since the above was written and while these pages were being put in type, Mr. Jackson Dawson, of the Arnold Arboretum, Jamaica Plain, Mass., has given his method of grafting the hickories, in *Garden and Forest*, Feb. 19, 1896, as follows:

"My method," writes Mr. Dawson, "has been to side-graft, using a cion with part of the second year's wood attached, binding it firmly and covering it with damp sphagnum until the union has been made. The best time I have found for the operation under glass has been during February, and the plants have been kept under glass until midsummer, and wintered the first year in a cold frame. In all the genera I find certain species which may be called free stocks,—that is, stocks which take grafts more readily than others. Thus, nearly all the oaks will graft readily on *Quercus Robur;* the birches will graft more easily on *Betula alba* than on others ; so of the hickories, observation has led me to believe that the best stock is the bitternut, *Hicoria minima.* This species grows almost twice as rapidly as the common shagbark hickory, and while young the cambium is quite soft. I should advise anyone who wishes to propagate hickories on a large scale to grow stocks of this species in boxes not more than four inches deep. In this way all the roots can be saved and there will be no extreme taproot, and when shaken out of the boxes the plants are easily established in pots and ready for grafting. If taken up in the ordinary way from the woods, it requires almost two years to get them well rooted, and often the stocks die for want of roots after the grafts have really taken. If grown in rich soil, the stocks will be large enough to use in one or two years. I should then pot them early in the fall, keeping them from heavy frosts, and bringing them into the house about the first of January, and as soon as they begin to make roots. I should side-graft them close to the collar and plunge them in sphagnum moss, leaving the top bud of the graft out to the air. The graft ought to be well united about the last of March, when the plants should be taken from the sphagnum and set in the body of the house to finish their growth."

All who have had any experience in the propagation of trees by grafting in spring, are well aware of the flight of time, in the hurry of work that must be done in a few days or not at all. It is true that the season for grafting may be prolonged or extended a little by cutting the cions in winter and storing them in a cool, moist place, where they remain dormant after vegetation has started in the open air ; but this does not affect the stocks, and these may come on slowly or rapidly, varying with the seasons, and the grafter must not only watch for opportune moments, but take his chances of striking the right time and conditions, in order to be successful.

With such hard wood trees as the hickories it is better to be a little ahead of time than a few days too late, for frosts, and even quite a severe freeze, will not injure a dormant cion, and under the most favorable conditions the union between stock and cion is a rather slow process. For this reason I advise giving as much time as possible, and while I do not claim to having had any personal experience as a grafter, in the South, still I am inclined to think that grafting in the fall, and not later than December, would be preferable to later in winter or spring. By giving the cion and stock two or three

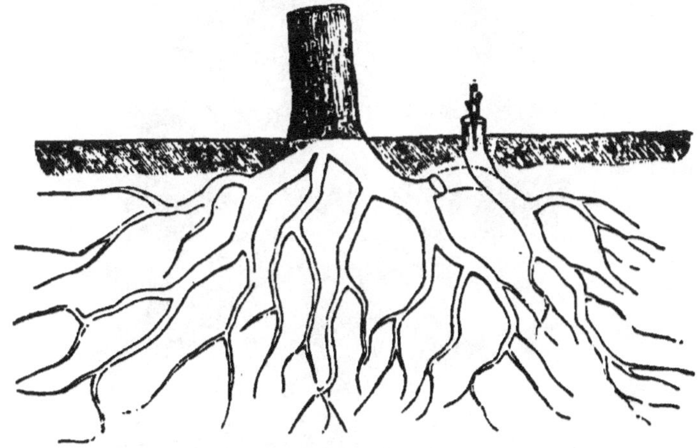

FIG. 68. CROWN GRAFTING ON ROOTS OF THE HICKORY.

months in which to form granulations and cohesion, there would be more certainty of success. Of course, I now refer to what is called crown grafting on the root below the surface of the ground, and when the cion is fixed in place with the usual ligatures of waxed paper or cloth, the soil is drawn back into place and the cion entirely covered with it, but very lightly over the terminal bud.

Where small stocks are not at hand, the roots of large trees may be severed and the end partly lifted towards the surface, as shown in Fig. 68, and when

grafted, allowed to remain in position until the following season, and then taken up entire or with roots
enough to insure future growth. The same or a similar process may be practiced to propagate a choice variety of the hickory, and a mere severing of the roots will
insure the production of suckers from near the severed
end, as shown in Fig. 69.

In grafting isolated stocks in this way, a small or
large stake should be placed by the side of each, to indi-

FIG. 69. SPROUTS FROM SEVERED HICKORY ROOTS.

cate their position, and also protect them from being
trampled upon. I make this suggestion because, in my
own experience, it has often proved successful with various kinds of hard-wooded trees and shrubs that failed
when grafted in the spring. Here in the North it is
rather difficult, as well as expensive, to protect cions set
in the open ground in the fall; but in the South it is

different, and a handful of almost any coarse litter would be sufficient to prevent severe freezing.

But grafting in the fall in the open ground is unnecessary, where small seedling stocks are used in the propagation of any kind of tree; in fact, nurserymen do very little grafting of this kind in spring, for they learned, by long experience, that the most economical and certain method of multiplying such trees is to take up the stocks in the fall, and then graft them indoors during the winter, having stocks and cions stored in cool cellars or pits, where they will be readily accessible when wanted. Apples, pears, quinces, grapes, and many other kinds of hardy trees, shrubs and vines are now extensively propagated by grafting during the winter months, and I do not know of any good reason why the hickories and other closely allied nut trees should not be multiplied in this way. I have tried it, on a limited scale, with the shellbark hickories, and with fair success, and in my opinion it is the only way by which the hickories, including the pecan, can be multiplied cheaply enough to become of commercial importance.

The small stocks of one or two years old should be taken up in the fall, and then crown grafted any time from December to March in the Northern States, but the earlier the better; then pack away the grafted stocks in moss or soil, in a cool cellar, or heel-in elsewhere, as, for instance, in pits or frames, where they will not be frozen, and yet cool enough to prevent active growth.

In the spring the grafted stocks should be planted out in nursery rows, and deep enough to have the top of the cion just level with the surface after the soil has been settled about it by a shower or heavy rains. The plants must be handled with care, so as not to disturb the cions. Mulching will, of course, be beneficial in dry seasons, and especially if the stocks are set in ordinary well-drained soils. In selecting wood for cions, twigs of the previous season's growth are usually preferred, but it is not necessary, nor is it advisable to discard all except the extreme end of the shoot or that containing a terminal bud, as some writers have advised, to prevent rapid loss of moisture by evaporation, for a drop of wax will seal the end of a cion as thoroughly and effectually as a natural bud ; besides, the lower part of the annual twigs is often more firm and really better for grafting than the upper and less sturdy wood, and the lateral buds on it will push just as readily as the terminal one. The cion may be three or four inches long, and contain two or more buds. The sealing of the upper end of a cion that is not protected by a terminal bud is certainly important with all of the hickories, for in this genus of trees the pith is large and continuous, not intersected or cut off by a thin partition of wood at the joints, as seen in many trees, shrubs and vines. This large and continuous pith in the hickories is another reason why the cions succeed best if set below the crown and in or on the fleshy roots having no pith. They may be set on one side, as in splice grafting, or in the center, or in a cleft made for their reception with a sharp knife, then bound with waxed paper, or wrapped with bass, raffia, or other similar material, and afterwards covered with melted wax to exclude air and water from the joints and wounds.

In this mode of grafting hickories it is not necessary to employ the entire root or stock, if it is of large size, for a single cion ; for pieces of from six to twelve inches long, containing a few lateral fibers, will answer the purpose, and it will be found, in practice, that these sections of the large fleshy roots contain so much vitality that, if the cions set in them fail to grow, they will throw up sprouts from adventitious buds during the ensuing summer. Almost any fair-sized piece of root left in the ground, when digging up hickory trees large or small, is pretty certain to throw up sprouts, this not only showing their great vitality, but that propagation by root cuttings is perfectly practicable and may be utilized whenever and wherever it may be desirable. The man who attempts to raise hickories from root cuttings must have patience, for very frequently the cuttings will remain apparently dormant in the ground one entire season before the sprouts appear above the surface. I will also add that this slow or retarded germination frequently occurs with the nuts, especially if they have become somewhat dry before planting.

For commercial purposes root-grafting small stock, as described, during the fall and winter, gives promise of being the best and most practicable system of multiplying varieties; but there is much yet to be learned in regard to details, and hundreds of carefully conducted experiments may be necessary to determine the exact time, condition and mode of operation. It may be that very early grafting is better than late, or that we have not, as yet, found the best species for stocks, and that a half-ripened one will be preferable to one fully matured. Neither has it, as yet, been determined what kind of material is best in which to store the grafted roots: sand, soil or sphagnum (moss) from the swamps; or whether they should be kept very moist, or comparatively dry; very cold, or moderately warm. Here is a wide field for experiments, and a most interesting one; for the successful propagation of the hickories by any mode that will insure the perpetuation and rapid multiplication of varieties, means millions of dollars added to the wealth of the country.

Age of Fruiting.—We hear much of the precociousness of pecan trees in the South, and many are reported as coming into bearing at the age of six to ten years from the time of planting the nut; but these are probably exceptional instances of early fruiting and not

13

the rule, although in a favorable soil and climate it is to be expected that such trees will push forward more rapidly than under less favorable conditions. Grafted trees will, of course, produce fruit in less time than seedlings, and as this mode of propagation becomes more general, and repeated in a direct ancestral line, the cions for each successive generation of trees being taken from mature or bearing specimens, the precocious and productive habit will eventually become intensified, as it has been in all of our long-cultivated fruit trees propagated by artificial methods. We have so intensified the productiveness of many kinds of cultivated fruits by selection, that it has become more of a fault, than a merit to be encouraged.

The nut trees are amenable to the same physiological laws as other kinds, and in their propagation by grafting with cions from bearing specimens we hasten maturity in the offspring. This has been fully demonstrated in many varieties of the Persian walnuts and European chestnuts. Here in the Northern States we have had so little experience with grafted hickories of any species, that really nothing is yet known as to how they will respond to this mode of propagation, further than that they grow rapidly and give promise of being fruitful. Seedling trees are, as a rule, of slow growth, rarely attaining a bearing age and size under twenty years, and with the shellbarks thirty or forty years usually pass before anything like a crop of nuts is gathered. Something may be gained, in the way of time, by frequent transplantings and pruning, but more by grafting seedlings from old and mature trees. Two grafts of the Hales' hickory commenced bearing at the age of sixteen years.

Planting for Profit.—There are, doubtless, many thousands of acres of half-denuded woodlands in almost every State in the Union, both North and South, that could be readily utilized for growing hickory timber, and much of such lands is almost useless for other purposes; but timber culture and forestry is a subject which I have discussed elsewhere,* while the object of this work is to aid my readers in producing something that may be utilized as food. When the hundreds and thousands of miles of our public highways are shaded with hickory and other nut-bearing trees of the best species and varieties, it will be time enough to begin planting such kinds elsewhere. As roadside trees they cannot fail to be profitable, largely enhancing the value of adjoining land; for in addition to being equally as ornamental as other kinds, they yield fruit always in demand at remunerative prices. The three species of the hickory and their varieties recommended for cultivation all thrive best in moist soils, but by occasional watering or thorough mulching they will succeed almost anywhere, especially in naturally dry locations.

Insect Enemies.—The hickories, as with all other nut-bearing trees, have numerous insect enemies, but these are neither so numerous nor destructive as to seriously interfere with their growth in general, or with their productiveness. Insects may occasionally become exceedingly numerous in certain localities for a few years, then suddenly or slowly disappear; but this we must expect, as one of the coexisting phases of all agricultural pursuits.

Collectively the hickories have no considerable number of destructive insect enemies, but if we count all the species of the various orders that have been found occasionally, or otherwise, feeding on the leaves, buds, fruit, twigs, bark, or boring in the solid wood, they make a very formidable list of names, or about one hundred and seventy-five in all; but fully ninety per cent of these

---

*Practical Forestry.

depredators are scarcely known, except to a few professional entomologists, and unless they become more destructive in the future than they are at present, or have been in years past, nut culturists have little to fear from their depredations. Among the most common species of insects injurious to the hickory, the following may prove most annoying to the cultivator.

THE HICKORY-TWIG GIRDLER (*Oncideres cingulatus*. Say).—A small yellowish-gray beetle, a little less than an inch long, usually appearing in this latitude during August, the females depositing their eggs in the twigs of from a quarter to a half-inch in diameter.

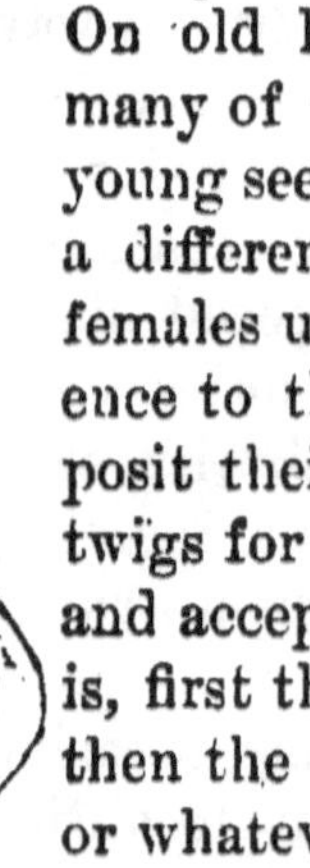

FIG. 70.

On old large trees the loss of a few or many of these is scarcely noticed; but on young seedlings or grafted stock it is quite a different affair, for on such plants the females usually select the leader in preference to the lateral twigs in which to deposit their eggs. The female girdles the twigs for the purpose of providing proper and acceptable food for her progeny; that is, first the green, then the slowly drying, then the perfectly hard, seasoned hickory or whatever kind she may have attacked. Selecting a suitable twig, she rests upon it, usually with head downward (Fig. 70), and with her mandibles cuts out a ring of bark about one-twelfth of an inch wide, and deep enough to reach the firm wood underneath. The place selected for this annular incision may be only a few inches from the terminal bud, or a foot below it, and in some instances she will cut two incisions on the same twig some distance apart, but usually there is only one on a twig. While cutting this incision she will sometimes rest long enough from her labors to deposit an egg in the bark above. The number of eggs she deposits in the twig is probably variable, but three full-grown grubs is the most I have ever found, and the larger proportion examined had only one. This girdling of the twig prevents the flow of sap, and the leaves soon wither and drop off, and the bark and wood shrivel and become hard and dry; but in the meantime the eggs have hatched and the minute grubs have bored their way through the soft bark and reached the pith, feeding in this while acquiring size and strength of jaws that will enable them to consume more solid food later and during the succeeding winter, spring and summer. Some do not reach maturity until the second summer; at least, in this latitude, as I have found after very careful observation and while collecting many hundreds of specimens. I will say, however, that this insect is usually referred to by entomologists as rather rare, and in general it is, but some years ago, in an old clearing near by where there was a great number of young hickory seedlings and sprouts, it was for a season or two very abundant; then it suddenly disappeared, and I have not taken a half-dozen specimens since. The grubs bore out the wood in the infested twig, and in most instances so completely as to leave only a thin shell of the wood or bark, by the time they have reached maturity and are ready to pass into their imago or perfect-winged stage.

This species of twig girdler also attacks the apple, pear, persimmon, elm, and other kinds of trees, and with those like the apple, with a soft and brittle wood, the girdled twigs are frequently broken off by the winds; but this rarely occurs with the hickories, and we can usually find the stumps remaining on the trees years after the beetles have emerged. The only way to keep this pest in check is to cut off and burn the girdled twigs any time before the larvæ have reached maturity, and as the girdled dead twigs are readily seen, the gathering is not difficult, from medium-sized trees.

THE PAINTED HICKORY BORER (*Cyllene pictus.* Drury).—This is, perhaps, one of the most common and widely distributed of all the hickory borers, but, so far as my observations have extended, it rarely attacks young or healthy trees of any age; in fact, I have never found it in or about growing trees, but I have seen it, by the thousands, breeding in decaying specimens and in hickory cordwood cut during the winter months and ranked up in shady places. A hickory tree cut down in fall or winter, and left on the ground or cut up into cordwood, is pretty sure to attract this borer early in spring, the females swarming over the bark, depositing their eggs upon it, and by the ensuing autumn the wood will be fairly honeycombed if this insect is at all abun-

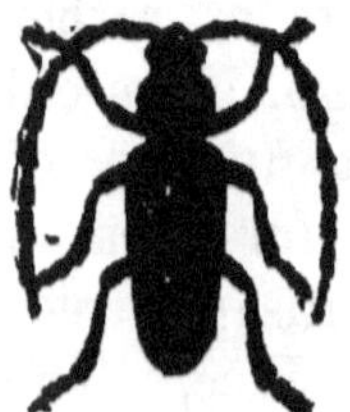

FIG. 71.
HICKORY BORER.

dant. The general color of the beetle is black, and the size as shown in Fig. 71. There are three narrow, whitish bands across the top of the thorax, and one slightly broader band at the extreme point of the wing-covers; but the next band is in the form of an inverted $\vee$; the point of the $\wedge$ does not quite touch the broad lateral band, as in the closely allied species known as the locust borer (*C. robiniæ*), with which it is often confounded; besides, in the latter the markings are of a deep yellow, and not white or of a faint yellowish tinge. The hickory borer always appears in spring, and the locust borer in the fall, not later than September in this part of the country. Below or behind the $\vee$-shaped band there are three others, but all broken up into mere dots, and not continuous.

In the South, and especially in Texas, there is a somewhat smaller but closely allied species (*Cyllene crinicornis*) that attacks the pecan tree and its wood in the same way as our common hickory borer, but in the Southern or Southwestern species the bands on the wing-covers are all interrupted or broken up into small white spots or dots. I have no remedy to suggest, further than to cut down old, infested trees, and to haul the wood out into the sun and spread it out where it will quickly dry and become seasoned. If the felled tree and wood is stripped of its bark as soon as cut, the female beetles will not deposit their eggs upon it.

There are other long-horned beetles (*Cerambycidæ*) that are occasionally found breeding in the hickories, and among these may be named the Belted Chion (*Chion cinctus*), Tiger Goes (*Goes tigrinus*), Beautiful Goes (*Goes pulchra*), and the Orange Sawyer (*Elaphidion inerme*), but they are usually quite too rare to be considered as very destructive insects.

Hickory-bark borer (*Scolytus 4-spinosus.* Say). —Only once within my memory has this minute but destructive beetle appeared in any considerable numbers in my neighborhood, although I have occasionally received a few specimens from correspondents in various parts of the country, even as far west as the Pacific coast in Washington. This borer is a very small, cylindrical, dark brown beetle, about one-fifth of an inch or less in length, and one-sixteenth in diameter. The hind part of the body is quite blunt (truncate), the males having four short but distinct blunt spines, two on each side, projecting from the hind part of the abdomen, hence the name "4-spinosus." In the females these spines are absent, otherwise they closely resemble the males. These bark borers usually appear here in the Northern States the last of June or early in July, and both sexes attack hickory trees of all species, but appear to prefer the old and nearly mature trees to the young and small with thinner bark. After boring through the bark and reaching the soft cambium layer underneath, upon which these insects feed, the female cuts a vertical channel in this substance, of little over an inch in length.

This burrow is a little larger than the diameter of her body, and along on both sides she deposits her eggs, to the number of ten to thirty, placing about an equal number on each side. When these eggs hatch, the young larvæ begin to feed on the soft material by which they are surrounded, making minute burrows at first, and at nearly right angles with the parent one; but as they increase in size they are forced to diverge, those above the center working upward, and those below downward, as shown in Fig. 72. These burrows enlarge as the grubs increase in size, as shown, most of them reaching their full development by the time cold weather sets in, but some do not cease feeding until spring, then pass to the pupal stage, and later to the perfect or beetle form, and from the extreme end of these burrows they bore a hole straight out to the surface, and are then ready to begin the cycle of life again, either on the tree from which they have

FIG. 72. BURROWS OF HICKORY SCOLYTUS.

emerged, or others near by. Some fifteen years ago I noticed that the leaves of some of the old hickory trees on my place were turning yellow prematurely, and upon examination I found the bark perforated with minute holes not larger than small bird shot, indicating the presence of the bark borer under consideration. Seven of the very largest and, presumably, the oldest, appeared to be affected, and these were immediately cut down and stripped of their bark, exposing the little grubs to the air and attacks of insect-eating birds. These trees appeared to have been infested for several years, as there was scarcely a spot on the surface of the wood that had not been scarified with this pest. Since the destruction of these trees I have not been troubled with bark borers, although there are still a number of very old and large hickories thriving in the same grove. The only remedy I can suggest is to cut down infested trees as soon as they are discovered, and also encourage the insect-eating birds to remain in and near the nut groves.

There are several other species of bark borers that occasionally attack hickories, one of these, the *Chramesus icoriæ*, Leconte, infests the small twigs, while another, the *Sinoxylon basilare*, Say, after boring through the bark, continues its course far into the heart-wood, showing a preference for this kind of food instead of the living tissues. These pests, however, are rarely constant, but very erratic, in their attacks, and while they may be rather abundant on a few or many trees a season or two, they then disappear, and not one may be seen for several decades.

THE HICKORY-SHUCK WORM (*Grapholitha caryana.* Fitch).—The parent of this pest is a minute moth of the family *Tortricidæ*, the small caterpillars mining and boring the green husks, and sometimes into the immature shell, causing the nuts to wither and drop off prematurely, although an occasional one may reach maturity, even in its scarified condition. This insect appears to be somewhat rare in the East, but very abundant some years in the West, where it is frequently destructive to the thick shellbark hickory and pecan. The first fresh specimens of the Nussbaumer Hybrid pecan nut (referred to on a preceding page) were so badly bored and scarified by this worm when received, that they would have been nearly or quite worthless for either planting or other purposes. As this insect attacks the nuts on the very largest trees in the forest and elsewhere, I cannot suggest any other remedy than to gather the immature and infested nuts as they fall, and burn them, with their contents.

Among the larger Lepidoptera (butterflies and moths) there are many species, the caterpillars of which occasionally feed on the leaves of the hickories, but not exclusively; consequently, they cannot be considered as the special enemies of this genus of trees. When they do attack them, it is as much due to accident as design. This is certainly true with the great Luna moth (*Attacus luna*) and the American silk worm (*Telea polyphemus*), and various species of the *Catocala*, as well as the Tent caterpillar (*Clisiocampa sylvatica*).

There is also a hickory-nut weevil, closely allied to the species infesting the chestnut; and while not quite as large, its habits are similar, and its ravages may be checked by the same or similar means. The grubs bore into the green nuts, causing some to fall before half-grown; others may remain in the nuts until they are ripe and gathered in the autumn; consequently, per-forated hickory nuts are not at all rare, even on the stands of venders in our cities.

Bud worms, leaf miners, leaf rollers and plant lice, —and among the latter several gall-making species,—are to be found on the hickories; but with all these natural enemies to contend with, the hickories thrive, grow, and yield their fruits in greater or less abundance. To enu-merate, describe and illustrate all the insects known to be enemies of the hickory would require a large volume, but fortunately there are many special works published on the insects injurious to vegetation, and these are readily obtainable by all who may have occasion to con-sult their pages.

CHAPTER VIII.

THE WALNUT.

Juglans. The ancient Latin name, first used by Pliny, contracted from *Jovis glans*, the nut of Jove or Jupiter. A genus of about eight species, three or four of these indigenous to the United States.

Order, *Juglandaceæ* (Walnut family).—Medium to large deciduous trees with odd-pinnate leaves; leaflets from fifteen to twenty-one, serrate, mainly oblong and pointed. The sexes of flowers separate (monœcious) on the same tree, the males in pendulous green cylindrical catkins two to three inches long, solitary or in pairs, sessile,—not stalked, as in the hickories,—issuing from the one-year-old twigs, and at the upper edge of the scar left by the falling leaf of the previous season (Fig. 73), showing that the male organs emanate from an aggregation of bud-cells in the axils of the leaves during the preceding summer and autumn. Female flowers terminal on the new growth in spring, also single, in clusters, and occasionally in long pendulous racemes with a four-cleft calyx, four minute petals and two thick curved stigmas. Fruit round or oblong (Fig. 74); husk thin, drying up without opening by seams, as in the hickories. Shell of nut either rough and deeply corrugated, with sharp-pointed ridges, or quite smooth, with an undulating, wavy surface, very thick in some species and thin in others; kernel two- or indistinctly four-lobed, united at the apex, fleshy, rich and oily.

History.—The common walnut, so long and widely known in commerce under various names, such

as Persian, English, French, Italian and European walnuts, also as Madeira nut, and recently Chile walnut,
are now all believed to have descended from trees native
of Persia, most plentiful in the province of Ghilan on
the Caspian sea, between latitude 35° and 40°, hence the

FIG. 73. PERSIAN WALNUT, SHOWING POSITION OF SEXUAL ORGANS.

old Grecian name of the fruit, viz.: Persicon and Basil-
icon, or Persian Royal nut, probably because either
introduced by the Greek monarchs, or sent to them by
the Persian kings. Later,—according to Pliny,—the
Greeks called the trees *Caryon*, on account of the strong

FIG. 74. BEARING BRANCH OF ENGLISH WALNUT.

scent óf the foliage, and from this name Nuttall coined his word, *Carya*, for our indigenous hickories, as explained in the preceding chapter. It should also be noted here that the elder Michaux, in 1782–4, was the first modern botanist to visit the province of Ghilan, and he determined, by personal investigation, that this species of the walnut was really indigenous to that region of country, along with the peach and apricot.

Earlier European authors claim that the walnut was first introduced into Italy by Vitellius (emperor) early in the first century of the Christian Era,—but this is uncertain,—the Romans giving it the name of *Juglandes*, or the nut of Jove or Jupiter, both being the same mythical personage. The nuts, at this early day, were highly prized, and also the wood of the tree, the latter being even more valuable than that of the citron (orange and lemon). Ovid wrote a poem about these nuts, entitled *De Nuce*, from which we learn that boys were employed to, or did of their own accord, knock off these nuts; and that at marriages walnuts were thrown by the bride and bridegroom among the children, a ceremony which was supposed to indicate that the bridegroom had left off his boyish amusements, and' that the bride was no longer a votary of Diana, and it is quite probable that the French word for nuptials, *des nóces*, was derived from this ancient custom. The ancients also believed that walnuts possessed powerful medicinal properties, even to the curing of hydrophobia; but in these latter days they have lost most of their curative virtues, in the opinion of the medical fraternity.

As with the chestnut, the planting of the walnut extended northward into Gaul (France), hence the earlier name of Gaul nuts, which became corrupted into walnuts by the English-speaking people. The Italian name is *Noci;* in France, *Noyer;* and the Germans, with their usual habit of compounding names, call it *walnuss-baum* or walnut tree.

Joannis De Loureiro, in his work on the plants of China, "Flora Cochinchinensis," published in 1790, claims that this Persian walnut is also a native of the northern provinces of China, with two other species which he describes (p. 573), adding, however, that one of these is cultivated in Cochin China, and the other is found wild in the mountains.

The wild form of this world-wide-famous nut is, doubtless, quite different from the varieties with which we are familiar, for two thousand years or more of continuous cultivation and selections have greatly changed the character of these nuts, as well as the habit of the trees. The nuts from the wild trees are said to have a rather thick shell, and to be much smaller than the best of the improved cultivated varieties, or very like those we now obtain in China and Japan. The Persian walnut, in its many varieties, has been planted almost everywhere in Europe as far north as Warsaw, but does not appear to have run wild and become naturalized, as with many other kinds of fruit and forest trees. In Great Britain it has probably been cultivated ever since the invasion of the country by the Romans, although a much later date is named by some of our modern horticultural authorities. Dodoens (1552), Gerarde (1597), Parkinson (1629), and other of our early authors of works on cultivated plants, speak of the Persian walnut as common in various countries of Europe, Great Britain included. John Evelyn, in his "Sylva" (1664), says: "In Burgundy, walnut trees abound where they stand, in the meadows of goodly lands, at sixty and a hundred feet distance, and so far as hurting the crop, they are looked upon as great preservers, keeping the ground warm, nor do the roots hinder the plow." Evelyn, no doubt, had read what Pliny had said on this point, viz.:

"Even the oak will not thrive near the walnut tree; which, if it be true, may be owing to the interference of their roots in the subsoil; but it is certain that neither grass nor field nor garden crops thrive well under the walnut."　Evelyn was far too good a gardener and close observer to fall into the error of attributing noxious properties to the walnut tree, although Pliny's assertion, which has no foundation beyond his imagination, has been many times repeated in these days of supposed general intelligence.　Small plants may fail, under the shade of large trees, or when deprived of moisture by the roots of such trees, but the walnut is no exception to the rule; in fact, such deep-rooted kinds are less injurious than those with roots nearer the surface. Evelyn, in continuing his account of the walnut in Germany, says:　"Whenever they fell a tree, which is only the old, decayed, they always plant a young one near him, and, in several places betwixt Hanau and Frankfort, no young farmer whatsoever is permitted to marry a wife till he bring proof that he is a father of such a stated number of walnut trees; and the law is inviolably observed to this day, for the extraordinary benefit which this tree affords the inhabitants."　What a pity that some such custom could not have prevailed during the past century in the United States.　The author from whom I have just quoted adds that the Bergstrasse, which extends from Heidelberg to Darmstadt, is all planted with walnuts.

Cold winters, however, have occasionally played havoc with the walnut trees in Europe, and one of these occurred in 1709, when the greater part of the trees were seriously injured, especially in Switzerland, Germany and France.　Many trees were cut down for their timber, which is always in great demand for gun-stocks and furniture.　Certain Dutch capitalists, foreseeing the scarcity of walnut timber, bought up all they could procure, and years afterwards sold it at a greatly advanced price. In the year 1720 an act was passed in France to prevent the exportation of walnut timber, and this led to the planting of these trees more extensively than at any previous date ; this practice has continued to the present time, hence the immense revenue secured from the exportation of these nuts. The people of the United States are good customers for the surplus stock of Europe, and will probably so continue, until we wake up to a sense of our folly of perpetually buying articles that could be readily produced at home, and at a very large profit.

Persian Walnut in America.—The date of the first experiment in planting this nut in this country is now probably unknown, but the oldest tree that I have been able to find with anything like a satisfactory history, is still growing vigorously at Washington Heights, on Manhattan Island, near 160th street and St. Nicholas avenue. I gave a brief history of this noble monarch of its race in the *American Garden* for September, 1888, from which the following account is condensed : "In 1758 Roger Morris, an English gentleman, built a spacious mansion on his estate, at what, in later years, became known as Washington Heights. His grounds were well laid out for that time, and many rare foreign trees and shrubs planted, among them several, as then called, English walnuts. Whether these trees were raised from the nuts, or plants of some size imported, is not now known. Mr. Morris may have procured the seedlings from the Prince Nursery, Flushing, L. I., for this famous garden was established in 1713, or forty-five years previous to the building of the Morris mansion and the planting of the grounds about it.

"At that period no one doubted the hardiness of the so-called English walnut in America, and as most of the nuts and trees procured for planting came from accli-

14

mated stock in Great Britain or the cooler region of Europe, success usually attended such experiments. Our pioneers and horticulturists fully expected that the trees would thrive and bear nuts in abundance, and time has shown that they were not mistaken, although we frequently see it stated at this late day, that the Persian walnut is not hardy north of the latitude of Washington, Philadelphia, or other cities south of New York.

"One hundred and thirty-eight years have rolled by since walnut trees were planted at Washington Heights, and at least one of the originals has escaped destruction and holds its head aloft, defying the tempests which frequently sweep over that elevated and exposed spot on Manhattan Island. This veritable patriarch of its race in America is a monster in size, its stem between four and five feet in diameter at the base and more than seventy-five feet high, with wide-spreading branches.

"In the summer of 1776 the Battle of Long Island was fought, and the American forces were compelled to retreat in confusion to New York, thence northward up the island; but when they reached Fort Washington, not far from the eleventh milestone on the old Albany post road, they made a stand and proceeded to entrench themselves at that place. This was in September, 1776, and General Washington took possession of the Morris mansion near by, making it his headquarters, and, as this was at the season when the walnuts had reached an edible stage, we may safely presume, from his well-known predilection for such delicacies, that he tested the quality of the Morris walnuts. One hundred and twenty years later I am writing this, with some fresh specimens of nuts before me from that same old tree.

"This old patriarch has cast its shade over many a noted person in its time, for in 1810 the Morris estate passed into the hands of Madame Jumel, a lady long famous for her hospitality and the good cheer she extended to the surviving patriots of the Revolution. From 1810 to the time of her death, 1865, Madame Jumel's household always had an abundance of walnuts from the old tree, and one of the workmen on the place informed me that about two cartloads was considered a fair annual crop."

It cannot be many years before this old tree will meet the same fate that has overtaken many of its younger contemporaries which were once growing in the neighborhood, for with the rush for building lots and the opening of new streets and avenues, trees are usually in the way, and in such cases even patriarchs are not sacred, nor do they command much respect from our urban population.*

A half-century ago there was quite a large number of walnut trees scattered about on the northern half of Manhattan Island, many of these probably descendants of the old Morris trees, but of this nothing definite is now known. A number of persons whose ages permitted them to scan the early days of the present century, have assured me that in their childhood they had often collected walnuts from goodly sized trees on farms, from Harlem northward on the island. The largest number of Persian walnut trees planted in any one place was on the Tieman farm at Manhattanville, these being set out as roadside trees, some of which are still standing, although in the march of improvements they must soon disappear. These trees have always been noted for their productiveness, bearing a full crop every alternate year, and a lighter one in what is termed the "off season."

While the old Morris walnut tree, and the large number growing on the Tieman estate, and scores of others scattered about New York city and its suburbs,

---

*Since writing the above, and while these pages are being put in type, accidentally I learn with regret that the old Morris walnut tree has been destroyed.

have been, and many still are, living witnesses of the fact that varieties of the Persian walnut will thrive in this latitude, certain horticultural authors and essayists have continually asserted the contrary.

Mr. F. J. Scott, in his superb and voluminous work, "Suburban Home Grounds," in speaking of this species of the walnut, says, p. 351: "Though greatly valued in England and on the continent for its beauty, as well as for its nuts, its want of hardiness in the Northern States, and lack of any peculiar beauty in the South, has prevented its culture to any great extent in this country. South of Philadelphia it may be grown with safety." This seems strange language to have come from such an eminent authority as the late Mr. Scott, inasmuch as he must have passed a hundred times within sight, if not in the very shadow of the rows of old walnut trees growing at Manhattanville, when going from New York city to Newburgh, where he studied landscape gardening under the lamented A. J. Downing, and to whom the work from which I have quoted is dedicated. It is quite evident, however, that our author, like many others, failed to see things that should have interested him.

As an offset to Mr. Scott's idea of the northern limit for the successful cultivation of this nut, I may refer to the work of Mr. George Jacques, "Practical Treatise on Fruit Trees, Adapted to the Interior of New England," published at Worcester, Mass., 1849. In referring to the European walnut, p. 238, he says: "It is perfectly hardy on Long Island, and to the south of New York, and as far north as the city of Charlestown in this State (Mass.), where there may be seen, in the enclosure of a residence on Harvard street, two fine trees of this kind, either of them much taller and larger than our large-sized apple trees. We have eaten nuts from these trees well ripened and fully equal to any of those imported. The trees often bear a crop of some bushels." It is unnecessary to search for further proof to show that certain excellent varieties of the Persian walnut do thrive and bear abundantly in our Northern States; not, perhaps, in the extreme boreal borders of New England, nor in those of the northwest, but the acclimated sorts are pretty safe as far north as 42° of latitude, and in protected locations may crowd up a half degree more. I have found very productive trees of this nut in northern New Jersey, several in Bergen county, others in Passaic, and thence southward, and while they are few in number, they are sufficient to prove that this tree is adapted to the soil and climate of the entire State. We seldom find more than one or two trees in any garden, and these are probably more the result of accident than design, their owners seeming to be satisfied in possessing something in the way of a tree not common in the neighborhood, never thinking that it might be well to plant enough of such trees to have them become a source of revenue. The parentage of quite a number of these bearing trees is readily traced to the Morris and Tieman stock, showing that these old trees are of a hardy and prolific race, which are well worthy of perpetuation for cold climates. Very old and large walnut trees are reported as growing in Pennsylvania and other of the Middle States, but they are far from being numerous. It has long been claimed that this species of nut succeeded best in the Southern States, and it is probably true, especially with the tender varieties; but for some reason, unknown to me, they have not been planted there in sufficient numbers to have, as yet, become of any commercial importance.

During the past twenty-five years these nuts have been more extensively planted in California than elsewhere in the United States, and we may expect soon to know something definite in regard to results. Nearly all of the favorite French varieties have been introduced, and are now being tested in different parts of the State, and it is quite likely that the greater part will succeed, although some of the early-blooming sorts may fail in localities subject to late spring frosts. Previous to the introduction of grafted trees of the named varieties, the only trees of this kind planted in California were seedlings raised from the common imported nuts; but I have no statistics at hand to determine the date of the first plantings of this kind.

Of late years there has been received, at some of our seaports, and especially at New York, some quite large consignments of walnuts from South America, under the name of "Chile walnuts," but they are only varieties of the Persian raised in Chile. They are generally of good size, moderately thin shelled, with plump kernels of excellent flavor. They are in great demand for confectionery, and are really better for such purposes than the larger and fancy bleached walnuts imported under the somewhat general name of Grenobles, or French walnuts. Owing to the difference of climate, these Chile walnuts arrive here late in winter, or about the time those coming from European countries the previous autumn begin to become somewhat stale.

Of our native species of this genus (*Juglans*), the almost everywhere common butternut ranks first in flavor and general estimation, but owing to its hard, rough shell, and the difficulty in extracting the kernel, it has never become of any considerable importance, although usually found in our markets in limited quantities. Of course, it is a general favorite in the country, and wherever found in sufficient quantities the boys and girls lay up a goodly supply for winter use; and cracking butternuts during the long winter evenings is a pastime and pleasure not to be ignored nor forgotten. The flavor of the butternut is far more delicate, and better, than any of the Persian species, but the difficulty in extracting the rather small kernel is a serious objection.

The black walnut has a larger kernel, in proportion to its size, than the butternut, and it is not so difficult to extract when the nuts are dry, but the flavor is too rank for most palates, although it has often been referred to as excellent by the earlier botanists who visited this country; but it has never been considered of much value until quite recently, or since the manufacturers of confectionery discovered that heat somewhat subdued the rank flavor, and now many tons of the meats are annually consumed in candies and walnut cakes. I am credibly informed that cracking black walnuts and shipping the meats to our larger cities has become quite an extensive industry in several of the Middle and Western States. We have two other but smaller native species of the walnut that will be described further on, under the head Species and Varieties.

Propagation of Walnuts.—The propagation of the walnut in the natural way, or by seed, is exceedingly simple, for the nuts grow readily and freely if planted soon after they are ripe, or any time before they become old and the kernels shriveled. It is, of course, best to plant them while fresh, but they are not at all delicate, and may be transported a long distance in a dry condition without seriously affecting their vitality. If walnuts are given the same care as recommended in the preceding pages for other kinds of nuts, so much the better.

The seedlings of walnuts, like those of other species, usually produce long taproots, and if grown in a compact soil, these will have few small lateral fibers the first season, as shown in Fig. 75; but when taken up and the vertical main root shortened at *a*, and then replanted, they produce fibrous roots in abundance. The trees of almost any age from one to twenty years old, are not at all difficult to make live when transplanted, provided the branches or tops of the trees are reduced, to correspond with loss of roots in digging up at the time of removal. It may be well to give a word of caution to the novice in nut culture about pruning nut trees in spring, after the sap begins to flow; for if done at this time they will bleed freely and leave unhealthy wounds and black, unsightly spots on the bark. Prune walnuts in summer or early in winter, to give time for the wounds to season before the buds swell in spring. If young trees are to be dug up, prune after they are taken from the ground, then the sap will not flow from the wounds. This is true of all deciduous trees, vines and shrubs. If the trees have few small roots when taken up, prune severely; but if roots are abundant, little pruning will be required. It is seldom, however, in transplanting walnuts, that the pruning need be as severe as recommended for the chestnut; in fact, having transplanted walnuts of various species, and of all ages from one to twenty years, without the loss of a plant, I have

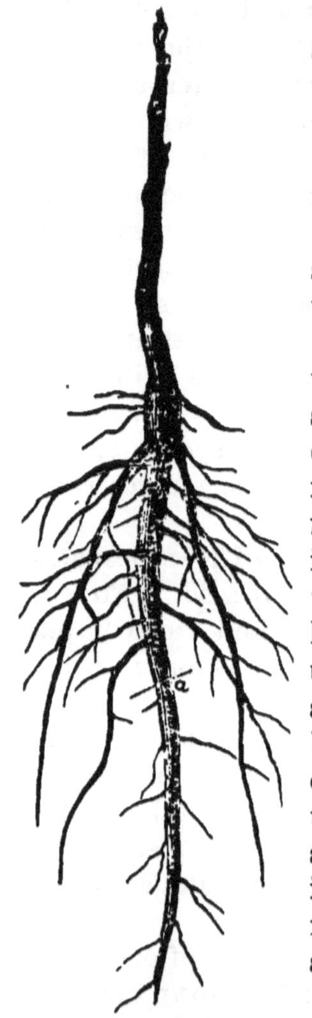

FIG. 75. SEEDLING WALNUT. come to the conclusion that they are pretty safe trees to handle, in this climate, at least, if not elsewhere.

In seeking walnuts from a distance, for planting anywhere in the Middle or Northern States, it will be well to learn something in advance about the climate in which the nuts are raised; for it would be folly to send for either trees or nuts to a warm or semi-tropical region, like that of southern France or Spain, for a stock to cultivate in a climate as cold as that of New York, New Jersey, and States on the same line westward. We might, perchance, from such importation, secure one hardy plant in a hundred or thousand, but there would be no certainty of even this small number.

This idea of acclimation and adaptation of trees to conditions and climate should not be overlooked by the nut culturist, no matter from what source he procures his stock, whether from abroad, or some distant region of his own country. If it can be obtained from a region where it has been growing under conditions similar to those to which it is to be transferred for cultivation, then the chances of success will certainly be largely augmented. Acclimation is a slow process; in fact, too slow for us to expect to secure any appreciable advantages from it in a lifetime, but in nature we seek final results, leaving time out of the question.

In raising seedling trees we cannot expect much more than a reproduction of the species, and not that of the parent tree. Plants that have been subjected to unnatural conditions and surroundings, as usual under cultivation, are far more likely to show a wider range of variation in the seedlings than those growing wild in their native habitats; but even the latter cannot be depended upon to reproduce exact types from seed. In other words, there is nothing certain about seedling nut trees; the large nuts may produce trees bearing very small ones, the early-ripening give late ones, the tall dwarf trees and the precocious fruiting some of the most tardy varieties; and yet, with all this uncertainty, we still think it best to select for planting the best nuts obtainable, *i. e.*, best and most promising for the conditions under which the seedlings are to be grown.

For the multiplication and perpetuation of choice varieties we must resort to artificial modes of propagation, mainly by budding and grafting. These modes, however, while the best at present known, are so difficult and uncertain in cool climates,—even in the hands of the most skilful propagators,—that grafted walnut trees have never been very plentiful in the nurseries of this or other countries with which we have commercial relations. In the south of France nurserymen appear to have been more successful in the propagation of walnuts by budding and grafting, than elsewhere; but in the northern provinces, as well as in Great Britain, we hear little of this mode of propagation. So difficult has this mode of propagating the walnut been considered in England, that Thomas Andrew Knight, president of the London Horticultural Society, early in the present century discouraged all attempts to propagate this tree by such means; but later, in a paper read before the Society April 7, 1818, he admits to having changed his mind, especially in regard to budding the walnut, and says :

"The buds of trees of almost every species succeed with most certainty when inserted on the shoots of the same year's growth; but the walnut tree appears to afford an exception; possibly, in some measure, because its buds contain within themselves, in the spring, all the leaves which the tree bears in the following summer, whence its annual shoots cease to elongate soon after its buds unfold; all its buds of each season are also, consequently, very nearly of the same age, and long before any have acquired the proper degree of maturity for being removed, the annual branches have ceased to grow longer or to produce new foliage. . . . To obviate the disadvantage arising from the preceding circumstances, I adopted means of retarding the period of the vegetation of the stocks comparatively with that of the bearing tree : and by these means I became partially successful. There are, at the base of the annual shoots of the walnut and other trees, where these join the year-old wood, many minute buds which are almost concealed in the bark, and which rarely or never vegetate but in the event of the destruction of the large prominent buds which occupy the middle and opposite end of the annual wood. By inserting in each stock one of these minute buds and one of the large prominent kind, I had the pleasure to find that the minute buds took freely, while the large all failed without a single exception."

From the above and other remarks of Mr. Knight, in the paper read by him, I infer that he kept the stocks in pots stored in a cool place in spring, until he could obtain shoots of the season from bearing trees, and from these minute undeveloped axillary buds for inserting in the stocks. These buds, as he informs us, are inserted in the wood of the preceding season, and near the summit or top. He does not give any directions for holding the buds in place, whether by waxed or plain bass ligatures ; the former, however, would probably be preferable, for the purpose of excluding the air and water.

Some twenty years later (1838) J. C. Loudon, in "Arboretum Britannicum," etc., refers to the propagation af the walnut as follows : "Much has been written on the subject by French authors, from which it appears that in the north of France, and in cold countries generally, the walnut does not bud or graft easily by any mode ; but that in the south of France and north of Italy it may be budded or grafted by different modes, with success. At Metz, the Baron de Tschoudy found the flute method (Fig. 76) almost the only one which he could practice with success. By this mode an entire ring of bark, containing one or more buds, is removed from a twig on a tree to be multiplied, and transferred to the stock, and made to fit as shown. If the ring is too large, a slice may be cut off; and if too small, a piece of the bark of the stock may be left to fill the space." Both stock and parent tree must be in about the same condition or stage of growth when this ring budding is done, in order that the bark containing the bud may peel off freely from the wood, and this is always

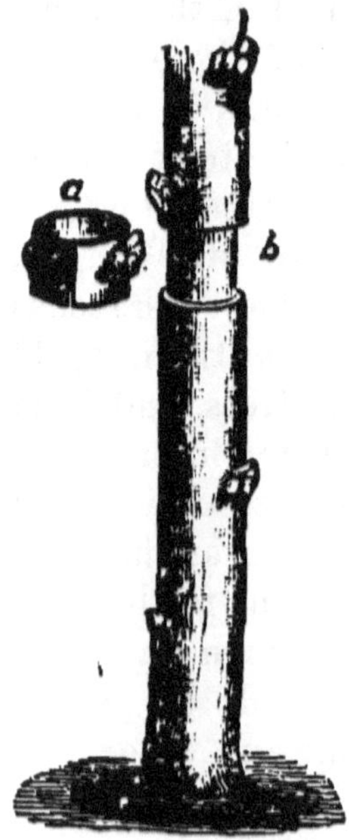

FIG. 76.
FLUTE BUDDING.

in the spring, soon after the buds begin to unfold and the sap is in motion. Loudon says that in Dauphine, France, young plants in the nurseries are budded chiefly by this mode, which succeeds best the closer the operation is performed to the collar of the plant; and the same is true in grafting, the nearer the root the better, as has been found by experience with hickories.

Charles Baltet, in his "L'Art de Greffer," recommends grafting in the usual mode of crown grafting, also flute or ring grafting, in April or May, and ordinary cleft grafting close to the root and at the forks of the branches, etc. He says that the cion should be cut, as much as possible, obliquely across the pith, so that it may be exposed on one side only. He also advises using cions whose base consists of wood of two years' growth, and these furnished with a terminal bud. He cautions propagators against grafting early-growing kinds upon those of later vegetation. If walnuts of any of the native or foreign species have been successfully propagated by budding or grafting, at any of the nurseries in our Eastern States, it has not been made known in the nurserymen's catalogues.

Michael Floy, who early in the present century had quite extensive grounds devoted to fruit and ornamental trees, near what is now the center of New York city, as we learn from his "Guide to the Orchard," published in 1833, claims, in this work, that the Persian walnuts thrive well in this country, but admits that he had never succeeded in grafting the trees, and with the hickories had no better success, although he had tried them many times; but he adds: "Still I do not say it is impossible either to bud or graft them; but there is something peculiar about it, for both the bud and graft turn black when cut, almost instantaneously. Others may succeed better, but let them try it before they affirm it upon hearsay; they may succeed very well by inarching."

Coming down to the present day, in our search for facts and information in regard to the propagation of varieties of the walnut, we may find it interesting to visit California, which, of all the States of the Union, is perhaps the best adapted to nut culture in general; besides, a larger number of nut trees of various kinds have been planted there than elsewhere in this country. It is in California that we find such men as Felix Gillet, of Nevada City, an enthusiastic propagator and cultivator of fruit and nut trees, and especially of the latter, if we may judge by his works and writings on this branch of horticulture,—and so far as I have been able to learn, he is the only nurseryman in the United States who has grafted walnut trees of many different varieties for sale.

In regard to modes of propagation, Mr. Gillet says that the common mode of shield budding, as employed on fruit trees, fails entirely with small walnuts from one to three years from the seed, and it does but seldom succeed even on larger stocks. When tried on large, old stocks, he advises removing all the wood from the inner side of the strip of bark on which the bud is situated, and at the same time have this strip not less than two inches long and as broad as possible. He describes his mode of grafting walnuts, which does not differ materially from those already given. That he has never attained any very remarkable results may be inferred from the following:

"We will add that the 'grafted walnuts' that we offer were grafted expressly for us, regardless of cost, by the most reliable firm to be found in the walnut district in France, through a process discovered several years ago, and which we will briefly describe for the benefit of people who may be inclined to try this new method of grafting very young walnuts.

"One-year-old seedlings of the size of the little finger, or about one-half inch in diameter at the butt, are selected, the root cut back short enough to permit the planting of the trees in pots of three inches in depth; the trees, previously to being potted, are grafted with cions exactly of the same size, whip or cleft grafting being used; the pots are then taken to a hot, or propagating house, and a glass bell set over them to prevent the outside air getting to the grafts, the temperature of the house being kept day and night, at least for fifteen days, or till the grafting has taken, to 70° F. When the grafts are well taken and growing, the glass bells are removed, and the grafts allowed to grow three or four inches, before the little grafted trees are set out in nursery rows; it may be preferable, especially in certain parts of the country, to keep the trees in the pots till the ensuing spring. Forty to fifty per cent of the grafts will succeed, and it is the best that can be done.

"This mode of grafting the walnut, besides requiring a hothouse, needs the care of a skillful person to make it succeed. So are grafted the little trees that we import from France, and that we plant in nursery rows and offer to the public."

For other modes of root grafting, I refer the reader to those recommended for the hickories, in the preceding chapter. Propagating walnuts by layers is practicable, where the small trees have been cut down to force out new shoots near the surface of the ground, then bent down and covered with soil in the usual method of layering woody plants.

Planting and Pruning.—The plants will produce a greater number of fibrous roots if the nuts are planted in light, loose, but rich soil, than in a heavy, tenacious one; but with all kinds it is best to transplant when one or two years old, and cut off a portion of the tap-roots, as recommended for the hickories. When removed from the nursery rows for final planting, prune away nearly or quite all side branches, leaving only the terminal bud if the trees are not more than six to eight feet high. After final planting where the trees are to remain permanently, very little pruning will ever be required, further than to cut away branches that may cross each other, or to shorten some to give proper form to the head. No tree in cultivation requires less pruning than walnuts.

As a genus of trees the walnuts flourish best in deep, rich loam, rather light than heavy, and in this country require considerable moisture at the roots, and some, like the butternut, succeed best in bottomlands, near creeks and larger streams. If the soil is naturally too dry for such trees, the fault can be readily remedied by the use of some form of mulch applied to the surface of the soil around the stem after planting, renewing this annually, or oftener if necessary, until the trees are large enough to shade the ground.

Walnut trees, as well as the closely allied hickories, are well adapted for roadside planting, and when set in such positions are far less likely to be injured by insects than when planted in orchards or large groups, besides serving a double purpose, being ornamental as well as useful. They may also be planted around buildings, and where other and less valuable trees are generally grown. There are also millions of acres of rocky hillsides and old fields which might be utilized for nut orchards, and if rather widely scattered over such land they would prove beneficial in shading the pasture grasses. First of all, however, let us have rows of these trees along all our country roads, after which it will be time enough to begin planting them elsewere.

SPECIES AND VARIETIES OF WALNUTS.

Native of the United States (*Juglans cinerea.* Linn.). Butternut. White Walnut.—Leaflets fifteen to nineteen, oblong-lanceolate and sharp-pointed, rounded at the base, downy, especially on the underside, petioles covered with viscid hairs; fruit oblong, two or more inches in length, with a clammy husk, not opening when ripe, but closely adhering to the deeply corrugated and rough, thick shell. Trees with widespreading branches, and of medium hight, or from forty to fifty feet, but in deep forests sometimes sixty to seventy, with stems two to three feet in diameter. A common tree in moist soils almost everywhere, from the Canadas southward to the highlands of northern Georgia, Alabama, and sparingly in Mississippi and Arkansas, and all the States bordering the Mississippi river northward to Minnesota. A valuable timber tree, with soft, light wood, much used of late for furniture and inside house finishing. In early times the inner bark was employed for making a yellow dye, also as a medicine, the extract being a mild cathartic, hence one of the specific names, *Cathartica.*

Synonyms.
Juglans oblonga alba, Marshall.
Juglans cathartica, Michaux.
Carya cathartica, Barton, 1818.
Wallia cinerea, Alefeld, 1861.

Varieties of the Butternut.—There are to be found many varieties of the butternut, varying mainly in the size of the nuts, and only slightly in the thickness of the shell; but I am not aware that any of these have ever been propagated, all the trees in cultivation or elsewhere having been grown from the nuts. This nut is, no doubt, susceptible of great improvement, as well as others of the genus, and it is worthy of being experimented with for that purpose, especially in cold, northern climates, where there are few or no other kinds of edible nuts. Probably the most direct and surest way to secure improved varieties is by hybridizing, taking the butternut for the female parent, and the Persian walnut for the male. Hybrids between these two species are already known, and they will, no doubt, become more plentiful as soon as skillful horticulturists are encouraged to produce them. Several hybrid walnuts of other species are figured and described by European horticulturists, but, so far as known, they are mainly accidental productions, and not the result of any direct effort of man; nature, in this instance, merely giving a hint of the possible, leaving us to avail ourselves of the lesson if we feel so inclined.

J. Le Conte, in a list of four hundred and fifty plants, collected by him on the island of New York (Manhattan), and published in the "Medical and Philosophical Register," Vol. II, 1812, mentions a hybrid walnut among the number. Dr. John Torrey, in "Catalogue of Plants," etc., 1819, refers to this tree under the name of *Juglans hybrida*, and says that it is growing near where Eighth avenue intersects the road called

15

Lake Tours, about three miles from the city, and is a large tree. This specimen probably disappeared long ago, and we have no means now of determining its origin or between what two species it was a hybrid.

Recently Prof. C. S. Sargent has discovered other hybrid walnuts in the neighborhood of Boston, and figured and described one in *Garden and Forest* for Oct. 31, 1894. He says: "My attention was first called to the fact by observing that a tree which I had supposed was a so-called English walnut (*Juglans regia*), in the grounds connected with the Episcopal school of Harvard college, at Cambridge, was not injured by the cold of the severest winters, although *Juglans regia* generally suffers from cold here, and rarely grows to a large size. This individual is really a noble tree ; the trunk forks, about five feet above the surface of the ground, into two limbs, and girths, at the point where its diameter is smallest, fifteen feet and two inches. The divisions of the trunk spread slightly and form a wide, round-topped head of pendulous branches of unusual symmetry and beauty, and probably sixty to seventy feet high. A closer examination of this tree showed that it was hardly to be distinguished from *Juglans regia* in habit, in the character of the bark, or in the form and coloring of the leaves, and that the oblong nut, with its thick shell deeply sculptured into narrow ridges, was the slightly modified nut of our native butternut, *Juglans regia*. Two other trees with the same peculiarities were afterwards found. One is a large, widespreading specimen, with a trunk diameter of four feet three inches about two feet above the surface of the ground, and just below the point where it divides into three large limbs. This is on the grounds of Mr. Eben Bacon of Jamaica Plain, and is supposed to have been planted between fifty and sixty years ago. The other has a tall, straight trunk, with a diameter of three feet one inch at three feet above the surface of the ground, and is growing on a farm near Houghton's Pond, in Milton, at the base of the southeastern slope of the Blue Hills."

That there should be hybrid walnuts is nothing strange or wonderful, and we often marvel that there should be so few of them in regions where two or more species are growing in close proximity in the same forest or elsewhere, but from whence came these specimens in Massachusetts is somewhat of a mystery. We may safely conclude, however, that the hybridizing did not occur there, but somewhere else, and either the nuts or small seedling trees were introduced and planted where these hybrid specimens are now growing. It is possible that they are descendants of the old hybrid walnut tree of New York city, mentioned by Le Conte and Dr. Torrey, some one having sent nuts or seedlings to friends in Massachusetts, and the three trees described by Prof. Sargent are merely those which have survived until the present day, these retaining the hybrid characteristics of their parent. These hybrids may or may not possess any special economic value, but they are of considerable scientific interest, and for this reason alone are well worthy of careful preservation and extensive propagation.

Butternut Sugar.—It has often been claimed that sugar can be made from the native butternut tree, and while it is true that the sweetish sap flows readily from wounds made in this tree in early spring, the amount and quality of sugar to be obtained from it is scarcely worthy of serious attention. In my boyhood days butternut syrup and sugar were considered as "sticky jokes" of the sugar camp.

Hybrids in California.—Mrs. Ninetta Eames, writing, in the *American Agriculturist,* of new varieties of walnuts in California, refers to certain species and varieties growing in that State, as follows:

FIG. 77. FLOWERING BRANCH OF HYBRID WALNUT.
J. regia × *J. Californica.*

"On one of the avenues in Santa Rosa there are some dozen or so ornamental shade trees, which invariably attract the passers. It is not only that they are uncommonly beautiful, but that there is something unfamiliar about them. One unhesitatingly pronounces them 'walnuts,' from their unmistakable likeness to both the English walnut and the native species found growing along the streams of middle and southern California. They are, in fact, a cross between the *Juglans regia* and *J. Californica*, the wild black walnut of this State. In its appearance, this magnificent hybrid is nicely balanced between both parents, but it is superior to either of them in beauty and luxuriance of foliage, and in its phenomenal growth. There is, indeed, but one tree, the eucalyptus, that grows more rapidly. In speaking of this quality in the new walnut, Mr. Luther Burbank says: 'It often excels the combined growth of both parents, adding twelve to sixteen feet to its hight in one year. Given like conditions, a budded six-year-old hybrid is twice as large as a black walnut at twenty years of age.'

"The clean cut, bright green leaves make a remarkable showing, being all the way from two feet to a yard in length, and of graceful, drooping habit (Fig. 77). They are sweet-scented, too,—a delightful fragrance, resembling that of June apples. Another admirable feature of this hybrid walnut is its smooth, grayish bark, with white marblings not unlike the Eastern sugar maple. The wood is compact, with lustrous, satiny grain, and takes an elegant polish, which gives it unmistakable commercial value. Like the majority of hybrids, though blossoming freely it yields a scant crop of nuts, one or two annually on a single tree, and this only after twelve years of persistent barrenness. The seed, when planted, goes back to its parent distinctiveness,—one-half turning out to be English walnuts and the other

FIG. 78. HYBRID WALNUT. *J. nigra* × *J. Californica*.

FIG. 79. HYBRID WALNUT, SHELL REMOVED. *J. nigra* × *J. Californica*.

half black walnuts,—the true hybrid being only reproduced by grafting on a thrifty young *Juglans Californica.*

"Another handsome novelty in shade trees, is a hybrid from the *Juglans nigra,* or well-known Eastern black walnut, and *J. Californica* (Figs. 78 and 79). It makes a charming ornamental tree, and bears, in its season, a prolific crop of unusually large nuts, which have little value except in the eyes of school children. Several of these hybrids are growing in Santa Rosa, and present an interesting study to the pomologist.

"A still more unique species of the walnut genus is the *Juglans Sieboldiana,* a Japanese walnut which grows abundantly in the mountainous districts of the island of Yesso, and also in the more southern divisions of the empire. Several of these remarkable trees are to be found in the Kew gardens, but only one specimen is said to be grow-

FIG. 80. JUGLANS SIEBOLDIANA RACEME.

ing in America, and this has recently come into profuse bearing on the Burbank experimental farm, eight miles from Santa Rosa, California. According to good authority, this Japanese walnut not only attains its greatest perfection in this favored climate, but it thrives equally well in countries too cold for the common walnut, *J. regia.* In its wild state in Japan, the *Juglans Sieboldiana* (whose curious raceme of nuts is shown in Fig. 80) makes a wide-spreading tree about fifty feet in hight, with pale, furrowed bark; nuts an inch and a half long, with a diameter one-third less, and a kernel having much the flavor of the common walnut. The tree bearing so thriftily on California soil, suggests its possible value as a marketable nut, while it already furnishes a remarkable addition to horticultural interests."

FIG. 81. BLACK WALNUT IN HUSK.

JUGLANS NIGRA, Linn. Black Walnut.—Leaflets eleven to seventeen, rarely more; ovate-lanceolate, smooth above, moderately pubescent beneath, pointed, somewhat heart-shaped at the base; leafstalks slightly downy, usually of a pale purplish color early in the season, especially on young trees; fruit large, mostly globose (Fig. 81); husk thin, roughly dotted; shell thick, hard, deeply and unevenly corrugated with rough, sharp ridges and points (Fig. 82); kernel large, sweet, but usually with a strong, rather rank taste, but less oily than the butternut.

Trees grow to an immense size, with deeply furrowed
bark; wood dark colored, valuable for cabinet work,
inside finishing, gun stocks, etc. Common in deep, rich
soils, from western Massachusetts west to southern Minnesota, and southward to Florida. Most abundant west
of the Alleghany mountains, and especially in the rich
valleys of the Western States distant from railroads and
water communication; elsewhere the trees have long
since been cut for their
timber. I have only one
synonym to record, and
this is scarcely worthy of
notice, viz. : *Wallia nigra.*
(Alefeld in "Bonplandia,"
1861.)

Varieties of the
Black Walnut.—As with
the butternut, there are no
varieties of the black walnut
in cultivation; at least,
none propagated by means

FIG. 82. JUGLANS NIGRA, HUSK
REMOVED.

which will insure the perpetuation of their varietal characteristics. It is true that there are plenty of wild varieties to be found, these varying widely in size and form,
and somewhat in thickness of their shell, as well as the
ease with which the kernels may be extracted, but none
of these have been perpetuated by artificial means.
Among the earliest varieties recognized by botanists,
one was called Oblong Black Walnut, *Juglans nigra
oblonga,* by Miller, 1754, and perhaps in earlier editions
of the "Gardener's Dictionary." He says this is from
Virginia, and only a variety of the common black walnut. Marshall, in 1785, describes this "black oblong
fruited walnut," and adds: "There are, perhaps, some
other varieties." These oblong, or, more correctly
speaking, oval nuts, often sharp-pointed at both ends,

are rather plentiful at this time.   There are rarely any considerable number of bushels reaching market from Virginia and adjacent States, among which these oval or oblong nuts cannot be found.   I have a number before me measuring from one inch to one and a quarter in diameter, and from one and a half to nearly two inches in length.   Other varieties found, perhaps, in the same lot, are broader than long, or one and seven-eighths inches broad, by one and one-half in vertical diameter. These measurements are of the cleaned shell, after the husks have been removed.

For several years a "thin-shelled black walnut" has been offered by at least two nurserymen, in whose catalogues they are described as "with unusually thin shells, the kernels coming out whole." I have endeavored to ascertain the origin of this variety, but failed, for both of the nursery firms who advertised the trees for sale admit that they do not know from whom they obtained the nuts planted, or where the original tree is growing. As the trees offered are only seedlings, there is no certainty that they will produce nuts with "thin shells." We can safely drop this supposed variety from the list until something definite is known about it.

JUGLANS CALIFORNICA, Watson.   California Walnut.—Leaflets in from five to eight pairs, more or less downy, but sometimes smooth, oblong-lanceolate, sharp-pointed, narrowing upward from near the base, two to two and a half inches long.   Male catkins much larger than in our Eastern species, or from four to eight inches, often in pairs.   Fruit round, slightly compressed, three-fourths to one inch and a quarter in diameter; husk thin, slightly dotted or roughened; shell dark brown, very faintly sculptured (Fig. 83), almost smooth, thick, the kernel filling two broad cavities upon each side; edible and fairly good.   A tree or large shrub in the vicinity of San Francisco and along the Sacramento (where it is sometimes cultivated), growing to the hight of forty to sixty feet, and two to four feet in diameter; ranging southward to Santa Barbara, and eastward through southern Arizona to New Mexico and Sonora (Thurber, "Botany of California"). This species has been considered by some botanists as only a variety of the next, or *Juglans rupestris,* var. *Major,* Torrey. Scarcely hardy in the latitude of New York city, except an occasional seedling from nuts gathered along the northern limits of the species, or from the cooler elevated regions of the Pacific slope. It is of no special value, only adding one more edible nut tree to the list.

FIG. 83.
JUGLANS CALIFORNICA.

JUGLANS RUPESTRIS, Engelmann. Texas Walnut. New Mexico Walnut.—Leaflets thirteen to twenty-five, smooth, bright green, small, narrow, and long-pointed; male catkins short, or about two inches long, and quite slender; fruit round or oblate; husk thin, nearly smooth; nut small, one-half to three-fourths of an inch in diameter; shell very thick, rather deeply furrowed, the narrow grooves on the greater part continuous from base to apex, the broad edges of the ridges smooth, not jagged as in the butternut and black walnut. Kernel sweet and good, but so small (Fig. 84) as not to

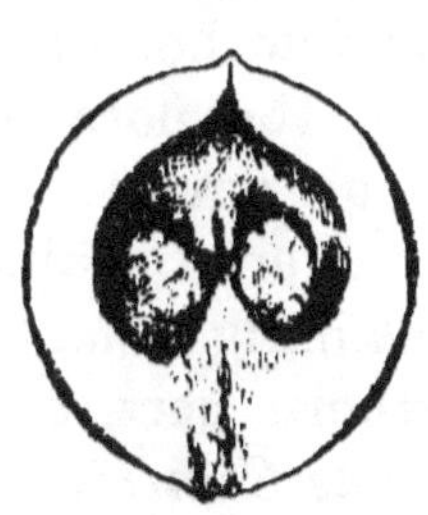

FIG. 84. JUGLANS RUPESTRIS, SHOWING SMALL KERNEL.

be worth the trouble of extracting. A small and neat tree twenty to forty feet high, native of the bottom lands of the Colorado in Texas, and throughout the western part of the State, extending through southern and central New Mexico to Arizona. In New Mexico it reaches an elevation of seven or eight thousand feet, though the climate is often severe, the temperature dropping to zero and below during the winter. Seedlings raised from nuts obtained near the northern limits of this species in Texas and New Mexico would probably be hardy in most of the Northern States, but they are scarcely worth cultivating for their nuts, owing to the small size and thick shell; but as the trees are neat and graceful they are worthy of a place among other useful and ornamental kinds. An occasional bearing tree of this Texas walnut may be seen in the gardens and parks of the Eastern States, and probably in some of the Western, but I have no direct information in regard to their locations or age.

Synonyms:

Juglans rupestris, Torrey.

Juglans Californica, Watson, Bot. California.

Oriental Walnuts.—How few or many species of the walnut are indigenous to China, Korea, Japan and other Oriental countries it would be very difficult to determine, with our present limited knowledge of the forests of that part of the world. The few botanists who have had opportunities of studying the flora of those regions do not agree as to names or number of species of the genus. Loureiro, in his "Flora Cochinchinensis" (1788), names three species as indigenous to China, viz.: *Juglans regia* in the northern part, but this is now considered very doubtful; *Juglans Camirium*, Rhumphius, a medium-sized, heart-shaped nut, the trees found in the forests, and also under cultivation; *Juglans Catappa*, a large forest tree in the Cochin China mountains, with oblong, edible nuts, with husk and shell of nuts of a reddish color. Many years later Siebold describes a Japan walnut under the name of *Juglans Japonica*, and still later the Russian botanist, Maxiomowicz, renames this, in honor of Siebold, *Juglans Sieboldiana*, and describes another native of Japan as *Juglans cordiformis*. But prior to any of the authors

named, Thunberg had described a Japan walnut under
the name of *Juglans nigra*, probably the same as Loureiro's species, with reddish husk, but as this name had
already been given to an American species it had to be
dropped. Maxiomowicz also describes what he supposed
to be a distinct species, found in the forests of Mand-
shuria under the name of *J. Mandshurica* (1872), but
it is doubtful if it is anything more than one of the
many wild forms of the species found widely distributed
over eastern Asia. The red or black fruited walnut of
Loureiro (*J. Catappa*), and Siebold's black walnut (*J.
nigra*), are probably the same as the Ailantus-leaved
(*J. ailantifolia*), recently described in Nicholson's
"Dictionary of Gardening," London, Eng., 1884, the
origin of which is said to be uncertain. It is *Juglans
Mandshurica*, Maxim, in Alphonse Lavallée's "Catalogue of Arboretum Segrezianum." As described in
this work, the young fruit is violet-red, and produced in
long pendulous clusters, the latter being one of the
marked characteristics of these Oriental walnuts. But
whether we admit that there is but one or a dozen species of these Eastern walnuts, it cannot be of any special
interest to the practical nut culturist, for to him their
economic and commercial value is of more importance
than scientific nomenclature.

Up to the present time we have only succeeded in
obtaining two species of these walnuts, or perhaps only
one species and one variety; but we certainly have two
distinct forms, both coming from Japan, and distributed under the names given them by Maxiomowicz, viz.:

JUGLANS SIEBOLDIANA (Siebold Walnut).—Leaflets
sessile, usually fifteen, five to seven inches long, oblong-
pointed, thin, soft, downy, serratures very shallow, pale
green above and somewhat lighter beneath; footstalks
densely clothed with clammy hairs; fruit in long pendulous clusters of a half dozen to a dozen, one and a

half inches or more long by a little more than one inch broad in the middle; husk thin, downy or clammy; nut somewhat compressed, the point usually bending to one side; shell smooth, with two shallow grooves from base upward on the sides opposite to the sharp, prominent ridges at the seams of the two lobes, the shell ending in a strong, sharp point (Fig. 85). The shell is very hard and thick; the kernel small, sweet, oily, resembling in taste our common butternut; tree a rapid and stocky grower, the coarse shoots and large leaves resembling those of the Ailantus tree at first, but soon spreading branches appear, forming an open, roundish head. The seedlings, as raised here, are abundantly supplied with small fibrous roots, which insures transplanting with safety. Apparently perfectly hardy in our Northern States, as I have heard

FIG. 85. JUGLANS SIEBOLDIANA no complaints of winterkilling of the young trees, although they are now widely distributed and in considerable numbers, but none, so far as I have been able to learn, have reached a bearing age here in the North.

Mr. P. C. Berckmans, of Augusta, Ga., in writing me under date of Dec. 3, 1894, says: "Last year we fruited *Juglans Sieboldiana* trees four years from the seed. Fruit was produced in long clusters, and trees exceedingly ornamental, but this year these same trees were killed to the ground on the 26th of March, after they had set a crop of fruit and made a young growth of more than twelve inches. This untimely frost may not happen again in years, but it goes to show that many varieties of trees which are considered hardy further north, are sometimes destroyed here by spring frosts."

As these Japanese and Chinese walnuts are natives of cold climates they may be better adapted to the Northern than Southern States, but there is no locality entirely exempt from late spring frosts, as most farmers and fruit growers learned to their cost the past season. There can be little doubt of this species of walnut being the one described by Rhumphius under the name of *J. Camirium*, and more fully later by Loureiro, as already noted; but having come to us from Japan as Siebold's walnut, this name will answer as well as any other, even if it is not the proper one.

JUGLANS CORDIFORMIS, Maxim.—In foliage and growth of tree this is almost, if not absolutely, identical with the last; the difference observed is in the nuts, which are also produced in pendulous clusters. The form of the nut is almost round (Fig. 86), rather blunt-pointed, but the shell is deeply and unevenly furrowed, and indented somewhat like our black walnut; the ridges, however, are not as sharp. The specimens I have received from various sources are not as large as the Sie-

FIG. 86. JUGLANS CORDIFORMIS.

bold, and the shell not quite as thick, but the kernel is small. I may note here that there appears to be some confusion in regard to this variety or species, for in several nurserymen's catalogues this form of nut is figured as Siebold's, and the one that I have described under that name is called *Cordiformis*. The specimens received from California, Japan, and also from Mr. Berckmans, correspond with the names here given, but further investigations may show that they should be reversed. The one I have received as *Cordiformis* is, doubtless, the nut described by Loureiro as *J. Catappa*, as an ovate-oblong nut, with a fibrous, leathery, reddish husk.

While I do not suppose that these Oriental walnuts will ever become of any considerable commercial value, they are worth planting for shade and ornamental trees. They are rather precocious, coming into bearing at an early age, and the nuts are not only edible, but will always be an acceptable addition to the unimportant although agreeable household supplies.

Persian Walnuts. *Juglans regia*, Linn. Royal Walnut, Madeira Nut, English Walnut, French Walnut, Chile Walnut, etc.—Leaflets five to nine, oval, smooth, pointed, slightly serrate; fruit round or slightly oval; husk thin, green, of a leathery texture, becoming brittle and cleaving from the nut when ripe and dry; nut roundish-oval, smallest at the top; shell smooth, with slight indentations, thin, two-valved, readily parting at the seams; kernel large, wrinkled and corrugated, the two lobes separated below with a thin, papery partition, but united at the top; sweet, oily, and generally esteemed.

This species has been in cultivation many centuries, and in different countries and climates, and under such variable conditions that many of the varieties have departed widely from the normal type. There are now an almost innumerable number of varieties, varying greatly in size and form. Some are not larger than a good-sized pea, as seen in the "Small Fruited Walnut" (Fig. 87), while others are nearly as large as a man's fist, as in the thick-shelled or "Gibbous Walnut" (Fig. 92), while in others the nut is greatly elongated, as in the "Barthere Walnut" (Fig. 88), and hundreds of other intermediate forms. There are also varieties that bloom early in spring, others late. Some are very hardy, others quite tender in cold climates. There are also dwarf and tall-growing, as well as the precocious and tardy fruiting varieties. But very few

FIG. 87. SMALL FRUITED WALNUT.

of these have ever been cultivated in our Eastern States, consequently little is known of their value here; but more may be in the near future, when our horticulturists and farmers begin to plant nut trees as freely as they have other kinds, or are awakened to the fact that such trees can be made a source of pleasure and profit.

Here in the Northern States our main dependence for hardy and productive trees of this species will be upon seedlings or cions from those acclimated specimens which have already been thoroughly tested and found to be both hardy and prolific. There are plenty of these, as I have stated elsewhere, and they are well worthy of attention and multiplication until something better is produced or discovered. In the meantime, the most promising European varieties could be imported and tested, although it is not probable that those originating in southern France and Italy would be of much value for planting in the latitude of New York city or north of it, but south of this line the chances of success would be somewhat greater; and to escape injury from late spring frosts, the more elevated regions are preferable to the lower and warmer anywhere in the Southern States. In anticipation of the question being asked, I will say that, at present, I do not know of any nursery-man in the Eastern States who propagates or imports named varieties of walnuts for sale. Of course, seedlings of these are offered, but it is well known that there is but a remote chance of these coming true from seed. Even the little dwarf French walnut *Præparturiens*, or Early Prolific, cannot be depended upon to produce dwarf or early bearing trees beyond the first generation from the nut, and these must be the product of grafted trees, to insure this much. The following list contains the names of only a few of the most noted varieties, the greater part having originated in Europe.

16

AILANTUS-LEAVED WALNUT.   See Oriental walnuts.

BARTHERE WALNUTS.   See Fig. 88.—A very long nut, pointed at both ends.   Shell thin; kernel large and of excellent fla-vor.   N a m e d after M. Bar-there, a horti-culturist of T o u l o u s e, France, who discovered i t growing among a n u m b e r of other trees; consequently, its origin is a mystery.   M. Barthere says that it is very productive, and even the

FIG. 89.   CHABERTE.

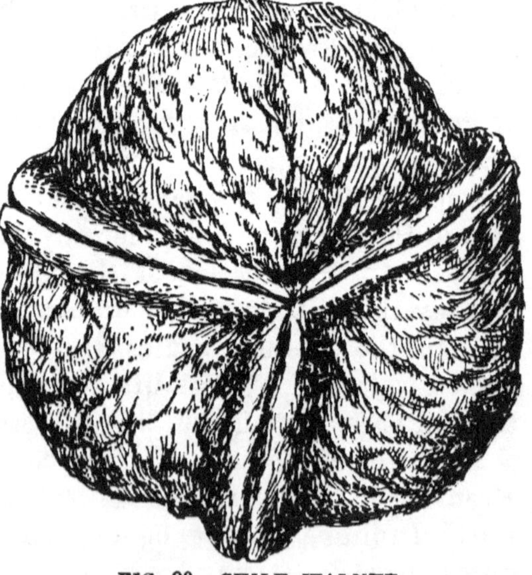

FIG. 88.
BARTHERE WALNUT.

seedlings of this va-riety begin to bear very early.

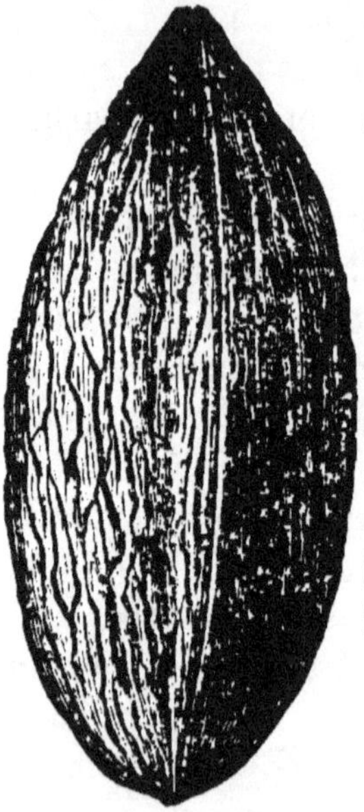

CHABERTE.—An old standard French variety, of an oval shape; me-dium size, with very full and rich flavored k e r n e l (Fig. 89).   The

FIG. 90.   CHILE WALNUT.

tree buds and blooms late, therefore especially valuable in localities where late spring frosts are likely to occur.

CHILE WALNUT.—This name is given, in a general way, to all the walnuts received in our markets from

South America. The nuts are usually of good size, with a dark grayish shell; thin but firm, with plump kernels of excellent flavor. These nuts arrive in February and March. Many of the Chile walnuts have three valves (Fig. 90), instead of the normal two. Such freaks are occasionally found among the European varieties, also in the native hickories, but these tri-valved nuts appear to be very abundant among the Chile walnuts.

CLUSTER WALNUT. RACEMOSA OR SPICATA.—Described by Mr. Gillet as a variety of the Persian walnut, producing medium, thin-shelled nuts in long clusters of from eight to twenty-eight. He also says that he introduced it into this country, but from whence we are not informed. Lavellée (1877) records it as a variety of *J. regia*, under the name of *racemosa*, giving its synonym as *Juglans Californica* of the horticulturists. I have not found it mentioned elsewhere.

CUT-LEAVED WALNUT.—A variety with deeply cut leaves; very ornamental, as seen in

FIG. 91. CUT-LEAVED WALNUT.

Fig. 91. Nuts quite small, but of good quality.

FRANQUETTE.—Another old standard French variety, with large, elongated-oval nuts with a distinct point. Shell thin; kernel large, and of rich flavor. The tree blooms late; valuable for planting in the South.

GANT OR BIJOU WALNUT.—A remarkable variety on account of its extraordinary size. The shell is thin, with rather deep furrows, those of the largest size being made into ladies' companions, where to stow away gloves or handkerchiefs, hence the name "Gant" walnut.

The kernel, though, does not correspond to the size of the shell (Gillet).

GIBBOUS WALNUT (Fig. 92).—This is a very large variety, supposed to be a hybrid, raised in France many years ago. It is of little value, as the shell is very thick and kernel small. Valuable mainly for its immense size.

FIG. 92. GIBBOUS WALNUT.

KAGHAZI.—This is supposed to be a variety of the Persian walnut, of fair size, with a very thin shell. The tree blooms very late in spring, and for this reason is recommended for localities where there is danger from injury by frost. The tree is said to be a very rapid grower, and much more hardy than the general run of varieties of this species. I have been unable to learn its origin, but it has been planted quite extensively in California, and some of our Eastern nurserymen are offering the seedling trees for sale, but whether they will possess the merits of the original or not must be determined by experience.

LARGE-FRUITED PRŒPARTURIENS.—A sub-variety of the Prœparturiens, originating with Mr. Felix Gillet of California.

LATE PRŒPARTURIENS.—Also originated with Mr. Gillet. Valuable because the trees bloom late in spring. Nuts described as of medium size, but with full kernels of excellent quality.

MAYETTE.—Very large (Fig. 93), with a light-colored shell of moderate thickness. Kernel plump, readily extracted whole, as shown in Fig. 94, sweet, and a

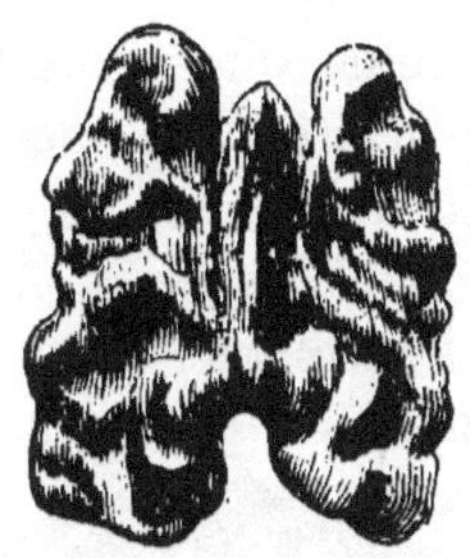

FIG. 93. MAYETTE.　　　　FIG. 94. KERNEL OF WALNUT.

rich, nutty flavor. Tree blooms late and is very productive. An old and standard French variety.

MESANGE OR PAPER-SHELL.—This nut has the thinnest shell of any variety known; it derives its name

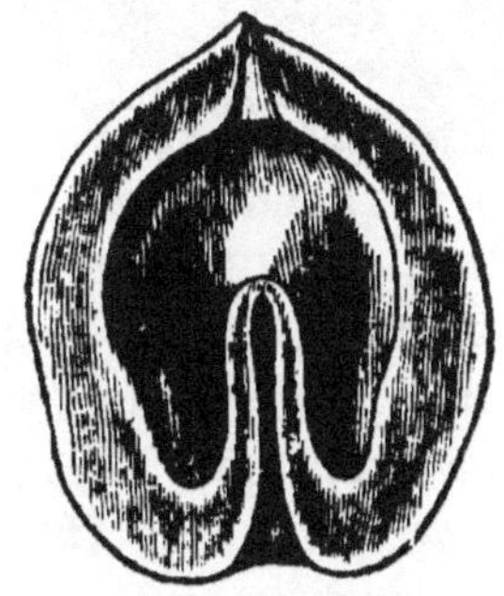

FIG. 95. J. REGIA OCTOGONA.　　FIG. 96. CROSS SECTION.

of Mesange from a little lark of that name, that goes to the kernel through the tender shell. Tree very productive, and the kernel quite rich in oil. We do not, however, recommend the growing of this variety for market, on account of the thinness of the shell, which breaks off too easily in handling the nuts, or even when they drop on the ground (Felix Gillet).

MEYLAN WALNUT.—A French variety that originated near the little village of of Meylan, in the vicinity of which it is quite extensively cultivated for home use and export.

OCTOGONA.—Of uncertain origin, but very much resembles one of the Oriental species in the form and sculpture of the shell (Fig. 95). The shell is also very thick, as shown in the cross section (Fig. 96). Of no special value.

PARISIENNE WALNUT.—Although this was named for the city of Paris it did not originate there, but in the South of France. It is a large and rather broad variety, with a firm but thin shell (Fig. 97) and excellent flavored kernel. It is reported that this variety succeeds in California, also in the South wherever tried. The trees leaf out late in spring and are rarely injured by frosts, and are remarkably productive.

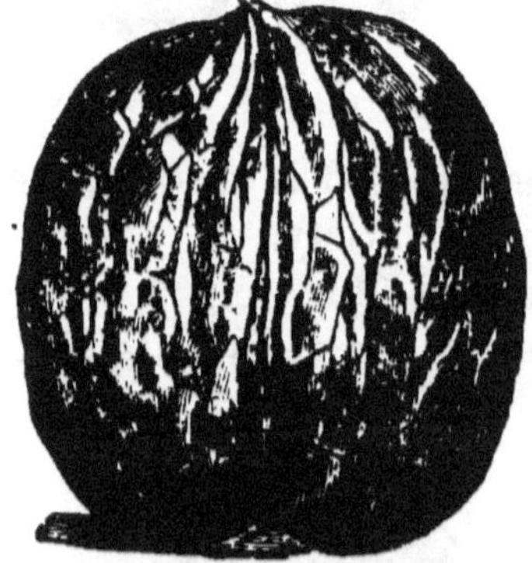

FIG. 97. PARISIENNE.

PRÆPARTURIENS. Precocious Dwarf Prolific.—A French variety of a dwarf habit, and the plants noted for bearing when very young. A correspondent of *The Garden* (London, Eng.), referring to this variety some years ago, says: "It is precocious on account of the singular and exceptional fact that it is born almost an adult; in fact, it is nothing uncommon to see a tree in its third year bearing excellent fruit." He does not say, however, whether he refers to seedlings or grafted plants, but we may presume the latter or those raised from layers, for cultivators who have experimented with seedlings have found that they possess a strong tendency to revert to the original or tree form. This may not show itself very strongly in the first generation if the nuts are obtained from grafted trees of some age, but in the second and third generation the early-fruiting and dwarf are usually entirely lost. The only certain way of securing the true variety is by grafting or layering, but it is to be feared that very few trees propagated by these modes are in cultivation, at least in the Eastern States, although nurserymen have been offering Præparturiens walnut trees in their catalogues during the past fifty years. In one now before me, published in New York city in 1844, trees of this walnut are offered at one dollar each, or about what is charged for seedlings at the present time. As nothing is said in the catalogues about the mode of propagation, we infer that they are seedlings, as grafted trees would be worth more than one

dollar. The nuts of this dwarf walnut are of medium size, thinshelled and of excellent flavor; valuable for gardens of limited extent.

FIG. 98.   SEROTINA OR ST. JOHN.

SEROTINA. Late Walnut, St. John Walnut.—A very peculiar sort, inasmuch as it is the latest of all to bud and bloom in spring, and yet it pushes forward so rapidly that the nuts are ripe with others in the fall. They are of medium size (Fig. 98), with a rather hard shell, but the kernel is plump and good flavored. The tree is very productive, and sure to escape late spring frosts.

VILMORIN.—This is claimed to be a hybrid between some variety of *J. regia* and our native black walnut, *J. nigra*. Scarcely known outside of France.

VOUREY.—A new and splendid variety raised near Vourey, a small town in southeast France. It has much the same shape and qualities of the Parisienne walnut (Gillet).

VARIEGATED WALNUT.—A handsome variety, with young branches covered with dark-green bark spotted with gray, and often striped longitudinally with yellow. The leaves resemble those of the common walnut; the fruit is of a light yellowish-green streaked with darker green, and reminds one closely of certain varieties of pears which, in common with this variety, frequently have their young branches striped in a similar manner. Propagated by grafting or layers. (*The Garden.*)

WEEPING WALNUT.—A tree with pendulous twigs and branches.   Quite ornamental, but not especially valuable for its fruit.   Hardy in England.

In addition to those described, there are a large number of varieties, which may be worth importing and testing in this country, by those who may feel inclined to make experiments with these nuts. Probably some of those highly extolled by earlier writers are now lost, but this cannot be determined until a careful search through the old European gardens has been made.

Among the early-fruiting or precocious varieties we find an account of one raised by Anthony Carlisle, of England, as recorded in a paper read at a meeting of the Horticultural Society of London, March 3, 1812. Mr. Carlisle planted six nuts in March, 1802, these having been received from Mr. Thomas Wedgewood of Blandford. Six years later, or in 1808, one of the seedlings bore and matured ten walnuts, and the next season (1809) upwards of fifty, and in 1810 one hundred and twelve, the tree at that age being nineteen feet seven and one-half inches high. Another variety, under the name of Highflyer walnut, is described in the Transactions of the same society, Vol. IV, 1822, p. 517. The nuts sent to the society were grown in the town of Thetford, and are described as a long oval, with a shell so very thin that the slightest pressure of the fingers crushes it. I find that this Highflyer walnut is mentioned in the recently published "Dictionary of Gardening," but whether obtainable in English nurseries or not we are left in doubt.

I refer to these English varieties mainly to show that some of the very best and thinnest-shelled walnuts have been grown in cool climates, and are not confined entirely to the warm or semi-tropical, as many persons seem to suppose and even claim to be the fact. It is principally from these English walnuts, as they are usually termed, that our hardy old-bearing trees, referred to elsewhere, have been produced, and, doubtless, many more will be, when we begin to pay some attention to this very valuable nut. It is also quite likely that when our horticulturists look about for choice acclimated varieties for propagation, they will be found right here in the grounds of next-door neighbors, and there may be no necessity of sending to Europe or elsewhere for either nuts or trees.

At present there is much confusion and uncertainty in regard to the identity and nomenclature of both species and varieties of the walnut, and it must remain so until they are collected from all countries and climes, of which they are either native or into which they have been introduced, and when so collected, and fruiting specimens produce, it will not be difficult to classify and determine their synonyms. This will be an undertaking scarcely to be expected of the individual nut culturist, but is within the legitimate line of the arboretum, and of public botanical gardens located in both cold and warm climates, thereby securing a division of labor, and at the same time avoiding the uncertainty of trying to produce practical results under uncongenial conditions and surroundings.

Husking Walnuts.—The husks of nearly all the varieties of the Persian and Oriental walnuts part from their shells freely when fully ripened and dried, but in a few varieties the husks are rather persistent, requiring force and friction for their removal. This may be accomplished by placing them in bags and shaking, or in barrels and rolling, until the nuts are scraped clean. But the better way, where there is any considerable quantity of nuts to be operated upon, is to take a strong barrel or cask, and so arrange it on standards that it can be rapidly revolved with a crank attacked to one end. Of course, the cask must have its two heads left in place, and an opening made in the side to admit the nuts and remove them when cleaned. Almost any man handy with tools can make such a cleaner and polisher in a few hours, and if stored in a dry place it will last for several years. With butternuts and black walnuts the husks are much tougher, and they should be thrown into heaps in the open air, and turned over occasionally until the husks become softened sufficiently to permit of their removal, in case they are to be sent to market. Ordinary threshing machines may be used for cleaning the husks from black walnuts, by removing about one-half the teeth, or enough to allow the nuts to pass through without breaking their shells.

Most of the hickories drop from the husk, leaving the nut clean ; but in some varieties of. the pecan the inner part of the husk adheres rather tenaciously, and they sell better if cleaned ; besides, some have rather rough and thick shells, and a little scraping and polishing adds much to their appearance. The revolving cask, either worked by hand or other power, is an excellent implement for preparing these nuts for market, and if the husk is very persistent, a little dry sand thrown in will aid in cleaning and polishing. Sometimes these nuts are subjected to what is called the soapstone polish, leaving the shells very smooth, with a greasy feel. The French walnuts, which are extensively imported under the general name of Grenoble walnuts, are usually bleached with sulphur before they are shipped, and while this adds nothing to the quality of the kernel, the sulphur is an excellent insecticide and fungicide, and may be of some use on that account; but otherwise it is likely to be more injurious than beneficial. As bleaching both walnuts and almonds is often insisted upon by dealers, I give the process suggested by Director Hilgard, of the California Agricultural Experiment Station, which he believes will prove more satisfactory than the one usually employed, and is as follows :

"The nuts, placed in small baskets (such as the Chinese use for carrying), are dipped for about five minutes in a solution containing to every fifty gallons of water six pounds of bleaching powder and twelve pounds of sal soda. They are then rinsed with a hose, and after draining, again dipped into another solution containing one per cent of bisulphite of lime; after the nuts have assumed the desired tint, they are again rinsed with water and then dried. Instead of the second dipping, the nuts may be sulphured (fumigated) for ten or fifteen minutes. The cost of fifty gallons of chlorine dip will be about forty cents; the same bulk of the bisulphite dip, probably considerably less. The time occupied in handling one batch (two dips) is from twelve to fifteen minutes."

Insect Enemies.—The walnut is attacked by the same kinds of insects that infest the hickories, with, perhaps, a few exceptions; as, for instance, the bark beetles and the nut weevils. The leaves appear to be more or less acceptable food for the caterpillars that feed on the hickories, and the same insecticides and means employed for destroying these pests on one will answer for the other.

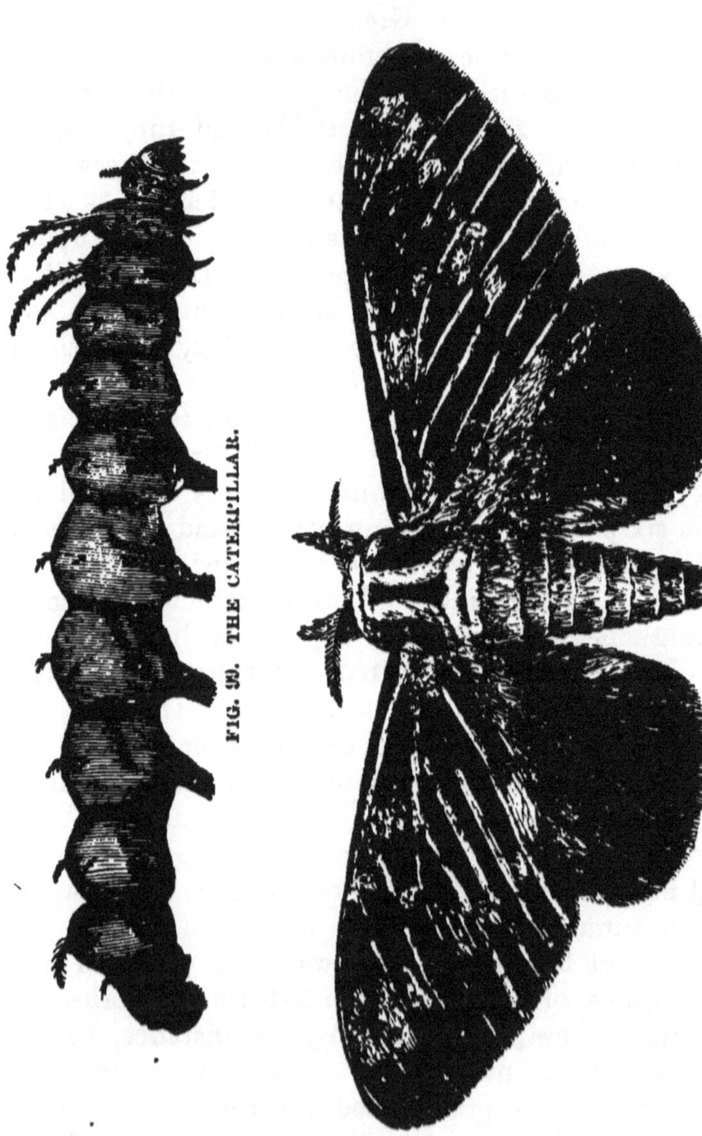

FIG. 99. THE CATERPILLAR.

FIG. 100. THE REGAL WALNUT MOTH—CITHERONIA REGALIS.

The caterpillars of some of the smaller kinds of moths are, as a rule, far more destructive to the leaves than the larger, and their ravages often escape notice until it is too late for the use of preventives, or for their destruction with insecticides.

Ever since I became connected with the New York city press, some thirty odd years ago, scarcely a season has passed during which one or more specimens of the Regal walnut caterpillar (*Citheronia regalis*), shown in Fig. 99, have not been received from some correspondent who had found them crawling down the stem or on the ground near a walnut tree. Such a large caterpillar would naturally attract the attention of almost any person, but to the timid its appearance is exceedingly ferocious and repulsive, while to the entomologist it is a beautiful and interesting creature, and far more likely to be handled with care than injured. This caterpillar is of a green color, and transversely banded across each of the rings with pale blue. The head and legs are of an orange color, also the long spine or horns, with the points tipped with black. It is certainly very formidable in appearance, but perfectly harmless, and may be handled with impunity. The parent moth (Fig. 100) has fore wings of an olive color, ornamented with small yellow spots and veined with red lines. The hind wings are orange-red, with two large irregular yellow patches before, and a row of wedge-shaped olive colored spots between the veins behind. Although this insect appears to be widely distributed over the country, and the caterpillars feed on the walnuts and occasionally on the hickory, it has never been known to be sufficiently numerous to attract any special attention.

CHAPTER IX.

In the following list of plants there are a few that in no way can be considered as related to the true nut-bearing trees and shrubs; but as the word "nut" has been attached as a prefix or affix in commerce, or elsewhere, they are admitted, even if for no other purpose than to designate their true position in the vegetable kingdom. For convenience, they are recorded in alphabetical order, the most familiar of the common names—where there are more than one—being given precedence, the botanical or scientific following, with a brief description, as my limited space will not permit of anything more extended.

It is not claimed that this catalogue of nuts is complete, but it is probably as near it as any heretofore compiled and published, and it may serve as the basis for a better and more extended one at some future time.

ACORN, OR OAK NUT.—The fruit of the oak, Quercus (*Cupuliferæ*), monœcious, evergreen and deciduous trees and shrubs, with alternate and simple straight-veined leaves. A very large genus, of about two hundred and fifty species, mainly in the temperate region of the northern hemisphere. There are some forty species native of the United States. The nuts are, on the whole, rather too harsh and bitter flavored to be esteemed or considered edible by civilized nations at the present day, but in former times some of the oak nuts were often an important article among the garnered food of the household. They were used—and are still, in some countries—boiled, roasted, and even ground and made into bread and cakes. They have also been used as a substitute for coffee, and for malt in making beer. Strabo says that in the mountains of Spain the inhabitants ground their acorns into meal, and Pliny affirms that in his time acorns were brought to the table with the dessert, in Spain. Every student of English history is well aware of the importance of the acorn, not only as food for man, in Great Britain, in the time of the Druids, and later, but also for feeding swine, deer, and other wild and domesticated animals. But with the advance of civilization and the production of better food, the oak nut ceased to be classed among the important culinary supplies. There are, however, a few species of the oak yielding nuts fairly edible in their raw state, and these are much improved by roasting. The best of those among our native species are to be found in the varieties of the white oaks of the North, and in the evergreen (*Quercus virens*) of the Southern States. But with so many far superior species of edible nuts, it is very doubtful if any of the oaks will ever be cultivated for their fruit.

AUSTRALIAN CHESTNUT.—The seeds of a large tree, native of Australia, the *Castanospermum australe*, the name of the genus being derived from *Kastanon*, chestnut, and *sperma*, a seed, because the seeds resemble, in size and taste, the common chestnut. But the tree belongs to the bean family (*Leguminoseæ*), and the seeds are produced in large, long pods. They are about an inch and a half broad, somewhat flattened, and of the color of a chestnut when ripe. They are roasted and eaten by the natives, but are rather unpalatable to those who have been accustomed to something better in the way of edible nuts. These seeds are also known as "Moreton Bay chestnuts."

Australian Hazelnut.—The fruit of *Macadamia ternifolia* (*Proteaceæ*). There are two species, both evergreen trees or tall shrubs confined to eastern Australia. The fruit is a kind of drupe with a fleshy exterior, enclosing a hard shelled nut, not unlike a small walnut. The kernel, when mature, has a rich and agreeable flavor, much like but richer than the hazelnut, hence one of its local names, for it is also known as "Queensland nut." This nut tree would probably thrive in southern Florida, and in the warmer parts of California.

Ben Nut.—Fruit of *Moringa aptera* (*Moringeæ*). Small, unarmed trees; only three species in the order, these inhabiting tropical Asia, northern Africa and the West Indies. The one producing the ben nuts grows from fifteen to twenty feet high, and is found in upper Egypt, Syria and Arabia. The seeds,—or nuts, as they are called,—are produced in capsules or seed-pods about a foot long, and while not edible, an oil is expressed from them which is largely used in the manufacture of perfumery, and known in commerce as ben oil. Another species, the *M. pterygosperma*, or winged-seeded Moringa, is known as the horse-radish tree, the bark of the roots being used as a substitute for horse-radish.

Betel Nut or Pinang.—The fruit of a lofty palm, *Areca Catechu* (*Palmaceæ*). A native of Cochin China, the Malayan Peninsula, and adjacent islands. A slender-stemmed palm, with regular pinnate leaves and long, narrow leaflets. The fruit is produced on an erect, fleshy spike, each fruit about the size of a hen's egg, with a thick, fibrous rind or husk, enclosing a hard nut somewhat like an ordinary nutmeg. These are used by being cut into small pieces or slices, then rolled up in a leaf of the betel pepper (*Piper betel*), a little lime sprinkled over it, and then chewed or held in the mouth, as practiced by those who use tobacco for chewing. This habit of chewing the betel nut is said to be almost universal among the Malayan races, all carrying a box containing the nut leaf and lime. These nuts are shipped in large quantities to countries where they do not grow, and the habit of chewing them has spread enormously, of late years, and is likely to increase, as it has with tobacco; and the effect upon the users is said to be very similar, although some authorities claim that the betel is the most injurious of the two, having a far more deleterious effect upon the teeth and gums. But this may be due to the use of the lime. Travelers in countries where these nuts are in common use tell wonderful tales about the invigorating effects of the betel, and how their assistants and followers are enabled, by its use, to perform the most exhausting labor for days at a time, which, without it, would be impossible. We have no doubt that the users of tobacco will claim just as much for this narcotic weed, and probably could produce as many trustworthy witnesses in support of it. The betel is, like tobacco, a narcotic stimulant, and causes giddiness in persons unaccustomed to it, excoriates the mouth, and is so burning that Western nations will be slow to adopt this Eastern habit.

BLADDER NUT.—A rather inappropriate name for the seed pods and small seeds of one of our common large deciduous shrubs, the *Staphylea trifolia*. It is sometimes planted for ornament. The small white flowers are produced in hanging racemes, succeeded by large bladdery pods, hence its common name.

BRAZIL NUT.—The fruit of *Bertholletia excelsa*, a lofty tree of the myrtle family (*Myrtaceæ*). The tree attains a height of from one hundred to one hundred and fifty feet, with stems three to four feet in diameter. The leaves are broad, smooth, and about two feet long, rather thick, and of the texture of leather. The fruit is produced mainly on the uppermost branches, and is

17

globular, four to six inches in diameter, with a brittle husk on the outside, and within this a hard, tough, woody shell, fully one-half inch thick, containing a large number of the closely packed, three-sided, rough nuts, about an inch and a half to two inches or over in length, as seen in Fig. 101. The kernels are very white, solid and oily. When mature the fruit falls entire, and the natives of the country collect them, splitting the shells to obtain the nuts. An occasional entire fruit is sent to

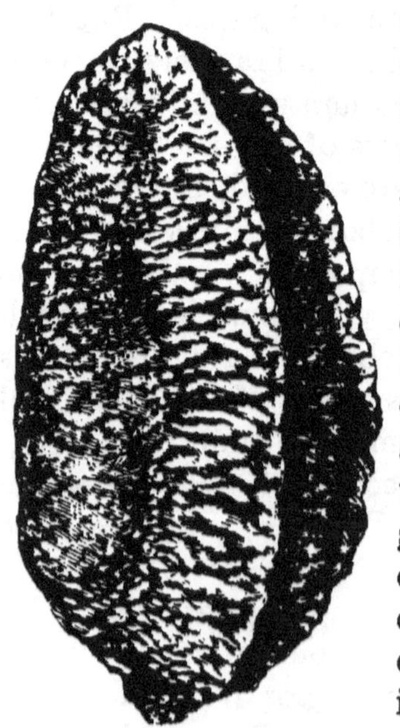

FIG. 101. BRAZIL NUT.

other countries, as a curiosity, or for the cabinet of some botanist. The Brazil nut is not only indigenous to Brazil, but also of Guiana, Venezuela (forming immense forests on the Orinoco, where they are called Juvia), and southward on the Rio Negra and in the valley of the Amazon. In fact, the supply appears to be inexhaustible; the only difficulty is in getting the nuts from the forests to some point where they can be shipped out of the country. The principal export is from Para, but there are many smaller cities and towns where a load of these nuts may be obtained on short notice. A very superior oil may be obtained from the nuts, by pressure, but the principal use for them is for desserts and confectionery. They are always abundant in our city markets.

BREAD NUT.—The fruit of a large tree, the *Brosimum Alicastrum*, of the bread fruit family (*Artocarpaceæ*), native of the West Indies, but best known in Jamaica. The botanical authorities disagree in regard to this species, some claiming that it is a large tree, with wood similar to mahogany; others that it is only a small shrub, only five or six feet high. It has lance-shaped leaves, male and female flowers- in globular heads, and usually on separate trees. The fruit is about the size of a plum, containing one seed or nut,'which is only edible after roasting.

BUFFALO NUT.—See Oil nut.

BUTTERNUT.—See Souari nut.

BYZANTIUM NUT.—See Filberts, Chap. VI.

CANDLE NUTS.—A small evergreen tree, the *Aleurites triloba* of the spurgewort family (*Euphorbiaceæ*). It is a native of most warm countries of the East: India, Malay, southern Japan, and nearly all the islands of the Pacific ocean, and in some of these it is cultivated for the fruit, which is about two inches in diameter. In the center there is a hard nut, very oily, with the flavor of the walnut. The oil obtained from these nuts is in common use among the natives of the Polynesian islands. In the Hawaiian group the kernels are strung on a small, dry stick, which serves the purpose of a wick, and then one end lighted, as with an ordinary tallow or wax candle, hence probably the common name of candle nut. These nuts are said to be used in the same way in India. Large quantities of oil is also expressed from them and used for various purposes, and occasionally small quantities are exported to European countries.

CAPE CHESTNUT.—The name of a beautiful evergreen ornamental tree, native of south Africa, and recently introduced into European gardens from the Cape of Good Hope, hence its common, and its specific scientific name, *Calodendron capense*. It belongs to the Rue family (*Rutaceæ*). The flowers are red, produced in long terminal racemes, the tree growing about forty feet high, and said to be one of the finest trees of that part of Africa. It is now under trial in Florida. Why called a chestnut I have been unable to discover.

CASHEW NUT.—A large shrub or small tree, native of the West Indies, and for this reason often referred to as the "Western Cashew," or *Anacardium occidentale.*

FIG. 102. THE CASHEW NUT.

It belongs to the Terebinth family (*Anacardium*), consequently is closely related to our native poison sumachs (*Rhus*). The tree is an evergreen, with entire featherveined leaves; flowers of a reddish color, very small, sweet-scented, and produced in terminal panicles. The fruit is kidney-shaped, and borne on a fleshy receptacle, and when ripe of reddish or yellow color. The nut proper is enclosed in a leathery covering, consisting of two layers, between which is deposited a thick, caustic, oily substance, exceedingly acrid ; but this is eliminated by heat, so that when the kernels are roasted they have a pleasant flavor and are highly esteemed for dessert. Some care is required in roasting these nuts, as the fumes given off during this operation cause inflammation of the eyes. The nuts also yield an excellent oil, very similar to the best olive oil. Although originally found only in the West Indies, this nut is now widely distributed throughout the tropical countries of the East ; in fact, naturalized in all hot climates, and is also under trial in southern Florida.

CAUCASIAN WALNUT. WINGED WALNUT.—The winged fruit of *Pterocarya fraxinifolia,,* also known as *P. Caucasica* of nurserymen's catalogues. It belongs to the walnut family (*Juglandaceæ*), and is a tree growing thirty to forty feet high, somewhat resembling the common ash (*Fraxinus*). It is a pretty, hardy, ornamental tree, thriving only in moist soils. Seeds on winged nuts produced in long, drooping racemes, but of no special value. Introduced into England from Caucasus in 1800, and now plentiful here in nurseries.

CHESTNUT.—See Chapter V ; also Horse-chestnut, and Moreton Bay, Tahiti and Water chestnuts.

CHOCOLATE NUT OR BEAN.—The seeds of a small tropical tree, *Theobroma Cacao,* of the chocolate nut family (*Sterculiaceæ*). Indigenous to tropical America, but now cultivated more or less extensively in all hot climates. The tree grows from fifteen to twenty feet high, with long, pointed, smooth leaves. The flowers are small, yellow, and produced from the old wood of both stems and branches, succeeded by a pod-like fruit six to ten or more inches long, containing fifty to a hundred seeds, resembling beans more than they do nuts. When the fruit is ripe it is gathered, at which time the seeds are covered with a gum-like substance, and to remove this they are subjected to a slight fermentation, after which they are dried in the sun, this giving them their usual brown color. Chocolate nut trees are extensively cultivated in Brazil, New Grenada, Trinidad, and, in fact, throughout tropical America, and their cultivation is, upon the whole, very profitable, as the demand is almost unlimited.

CLEARING NUT.—This is an East India name for the seeds of *Strychnos potatorum*, a plant belonging to the well-known nux vomica family (*Loganiaceæ*). It is a small tree, native of India, the wood of which is used for various purposes. The fruit is about the size of a cherry, and contains one seed; this is dried, and used for clearing muddy water, this being effected by rubbing one of the little nuts around the sides of the vessel that is to be filled, after which the water is poured in, and then, through some unknown agency, all the foreign matter settles, leaving the liquid perfectly pure, clear and wholesome.

COCOANUT.—One of the most widely-known and largest of edible nuts; the product of *Cocos nucifera*, a lofty, tree-like palm (*Palmæ* or *Palmaceæ*). It is a native of tropical Africa, India, Malay, and of nearly all the islands of the Indian and Pacific oceans. It only thrives near the seacoast or where the sea breezes reach it, requiring no special care after the nuts and young plants once become established in a congenial soil. The coco palm grows from fifty to one hundred feet high, with pinnate leaves from ten to twenty feet long. The nuts are produced in clusters of a dozen or more, and when full grown are somewhat triangular and a foot long, the outer coat or husk composed of a tough fiber.

The nuts, when cleaned of their husks, are too well known to call for a further description here. In countries where these nuts are plentiful, their contents form nearly the entire food of the natives, the milky fluid serving for drink, and the more solid parts as a substitute for meat and bread. The cocoanut is probably utilized in more ways, and for a greater variety of purposes, than any other kind known, and it would require a volume to briefly enumerate them. Of recent years there have been plantations made of this nut on the coast of southern Florida, and one of the most extensive of these is by a man from New Jersey, but 1 have not heard from him of late, or seen any reports as to the results of his experiments. It is reported that there are about 250,000 cocoanut trees now growing in Florida.

Cocoanut, Double.—This is the fruit of another lofty palm, *Lodoicea Sechellarum*, and is usually considered the largest member of the order. It is a native of the Seychelles islands, in the Indian ocean. It is said to reach a hight of a hundred feet, with a stem two feet in diameter. The fruit is a large, oblong nut, with a rather thin rind or husk, and when this is removed the nut appears to be double, or two oblong nuts firmly united, a kind of twin formation, the entire nut weighing from thirty to forty pounds. These immense nuts are produced in bunches of eight to ten, the cluster sometimes weighing from three to four hundred pounds. It is supposed that these nuts require about ten years to grow and mature. They are useless as food, but the shells are manufactured into various useful articles by the natives, and they are also transported to other countries and valued as curiosities. There is a great demand for the leaves of this palm for making hats, baskets, etc., and as the trees have to be cut down to obtain them. they are becoming rather scarce.

COLA NUT, KOLA NUT OR GOORA NUT.—The fruit of a small tree, native of the warmer parts of western Africa, and known to botanists as *Cola acuminata*, and of the Sterculiad family (*Sterculiaceæ*). In its native country it grows thirty to forty feet high. The leaves are oblong-elliptical, six to eight inches long, and pointed (acuminate), and from this it probably derived its specific name. The flowers are yellow, and produced in axillary racemes, and succeeded by simple bean-like pods, each containing several nut-like seeds, which the natives call cola or goora nuts. These nuts have long been an article of trade among the native tribes of Africa, they being valued for their supposed efficacy in allaying thirst, promoting digestion, giving strength, and preventing exhaustion during the performance of hard manual labor. This tree was early introduced into the West Indies and Brazil, but its reputation in Africa does not appear to have been sustained it its Western habitat.

COQUILLA NUT.—The fruit of the Piassaba palm, *Attalea funifera*, a native of Brazil, where it grows about thirty feet high. The fruit is produced in bunches, and are each about three inches long, covered with a thin rind. The nut is very hard, and is used as a substitute for bone and ivory in the manufacture of articles for the household.

COQUITO NUT.—This is the fruit of the wing-leaved palm of Chile, *Jubœa spectabilis*. It is a moderately tall species, and closely resembles, in general habit, the date palm. The nuts are edible, but they are of secondary importance, this palm being valued mainly for the sweet sap issuing from the stem when cut down, this continuing to exude from it for weeks after it is severed from the roots. The sap is gathered and boiled, and when reduced to the consistency of molasses becomes an article of commerce, under the name of Meil de Palma or palm honey.

CREAM NUT.—A local name of Brazil nut.

DAWA NUT.—See Litchi nut.

EARTH NUT, OR EARTH CHESTNUT, ETC.—A small, low-growing, herbaceous plant of the carrot family (*Umbelliferæ*), common in waste or uncultivated grounds in Great Britain and other countries of northern Europe. Formerly botanists supposed there were two species, but of late only one, the *Bunium bulbocastanum*. On the roots there are small, nut-like tubers, of a sweetish taste, and they are eaten by children, either in the raw state or after being roasted. These tubers have various local names, and in addition to the above, they are called kipper nuts, and pig nuts in England, but a familiar local name in Scotland is lousy nuts, because it is said that eating them is sure to breed lice. But this story may have been invented by parents to deter their children from digging and eating the roots of wild plants. Willdenow, in naming this species, certainly recognized its edible qualities, and that children were fond of it, else he would not have called it an earth chestnut,— *bulbo*, bulb, and *castanum* from *castanea*, the chestnut.

ELK NUT.—See Oil nut.

FISTICKE NUT.—See Pistacia nut.

FOX NUT.—The seeds of a floating, annual aquatic plant, the *Euryale ferox*, native of India, and belonging to the water lily family (*Nymphæaceæ*). It is a handsome plant, with leaves about two feet in diameter, of a rich purple on the underside, with thorn-like spines on the veins. Flowers deep violet-red. The seeds of this species are eaten by the natives, the same as the aborigines of this country gathered the seeds of our indigenous *Nelumbium luteum*, under the name of water chinquapin, using them for food in the late fall and winter.

GINKGO NUT.—The large, round, white, somewhat flattened, nut-like seeds of the now common maidenhair tree, or *Ginkgo biloba*, also known as *Salisburia adianti-*

folia of some nurserymen's catalogues and many recent botanical works. The former, however, is the older and correct scientific name. This tree is a native of China and Japan, and of a slender, sparsely branched habit, growing from fifty to eighty feet high in its native countries. It is a deciduous, cone-bearing (*Coniferæ*) tree, with two-lobed, fan-shaped leaves two to three inches broad, divided about halfway down from the top. The male and female flowers are on separate trees, and to secure seed or nuts both sexes must be grown near together. The ginkgo was introduced into European gardens in 1754, and there are now many fruiting specimens, especially in France, from whence the nuts have long been secured for planting, by nurserymen and others interested in tree culture. There are very few bearing trees in this country, and one in Washington, D. C., has been fruiting for a number of years. In China and Japan the seeds or nuts are valued for their edible qualities, but they have a kind of disagreeable, balsamic taste in their raw state, although this is dispelled by roasting, after which they are quite sweet and palatable. As the trees do not begin to bear until of considerable age, and the nuts are inferior to many other kinds, I do not think the ginkgo will ever become very popular in this country as a nut tree.

Goora Nut.—See Cola nut.

Gorgon Nut.—See Fox nut.

Groundnut.—The small, globular tubers of the dwarf three-leaved ginseng, *Aralia trifolia*, are called groundnuts in some of our Northern States, and they are frequently sought for, dug up and eaten by children, as I know from personal experience. The plant belongs to the ginseng family (*Araliaceæ*), and is closely related to the true five-leaved ginseng (*Aralia quinquefolia*), but our groundnut has only three leaves, instead of five; besides, it is a somewhat smaller plant, rarely more than six to eight inches high. When the scattered seed sprout in spring, they send down a long, slender, thread-like rootstock, to a depth of from four to six inches, and at the bottom of this the small tuber is produced. It has a somewhat pungent taste, but this only whets the appetite of a boy when on a hunt for ground nuts.

GROUNDNUT.—The tubers of one of the most widely distributed climbing plants of the Eastern States, and common in low, wet grounds almost everywhere, from Canada to Florida, and westward to the Mississippi. This plant is described in most of the botanical works of the present day under the name of *Apios tuberosa*, and it belongs to the Pulse family (*Leguminosæ*), and is closely related to the common and well-known wistarias, although much smaller and of a more slender habit. It is a smooth, perennial, twining vine, with pinnate leaves, and dense racemes or clusters of small brownish-purple pea-shaped flowers. The subterranean rootstocks bear long strings of edible tubers, from one to two inches long, and from an inch to an inch and a half in diameter, somewhat variable in shape, dark brown on the outside, but white within. When boiled or roasted these tubers have a rich, farinaceous, nutty flavor. This tuber or groundnut is the one described by Mr. Thomas Herriot, the historiographer of Sir Walter Raleigh's expedition to Virginia in 1585, under the Indian name of "Openawk." He says: "These roots are round, some as large as walnuts, others much larger; they grow in damp soil, many hanging together, as fixed on ropes; they are good food, either boiled or roasted." These tubers are to be found in the swamps and damp soils of Virginia at this day, just as they were at the time of Herriot's visit, but many modern historians have tried to make out that Raleigh's colonists found our common potato among the Indians at that time, although I have never been able to find a scrap of trustworthy history to support such a claim, or that Raleigh himself ever planted or cultivated the American potato in Ireland or England, or, in fact, ever tasted one of these tubers.

GROUNDNUT.—See Peanut or Goober.

HAZELNUT, OR CHILE HAZEL.—This is merely a local English name for the fruit of a small evergreen tree, native of Chile, S. A., where it is known as Guevina, and this has been adopted as the name of the genus, adding the specific name of the European hazel, so we have *Guevina Avellana*, although in some botanical works it may be found under the name of *Qudria heterophylla*. It belongs to the Protea family (*Proteaceæ*). It has white, hermaphrodite flowers, in long axillary racemes; these are succeeded by coral-red fruit about the size of a large cherry; the stone or nut-like seeds being edible are largely used by the Chileans. They are said to taste like the hazel, hence the name. Trees are hardy in the southwest of England, and would probably succeed here in the Southern States. It has been planted and found to thrive in California. Readily propagated from seed or green cuttings under glass.

HORSE-CHESTNUT.—The fruit of a genus of deciduous ornamental trees and shrubs, native of Asia and North America. The common horse-chestnut, or *Æsculus Hippocastanum*, is a native of Asia, and was introduced into Europe over three hundred years ago, its large, smooth seeds and prickly husks probably suggesting both its common and scientific names, although these trees do not even belong to the same order as the true edible chestnuts (*Castanea*), but to the soapworts (*Sapindaceæ*). It is supposed that the prefix, "horse," was derived from a custom among the Turks, of giving the nuts to horses as a medicine when these animals were afflicted with a cough or inclined to become wind-broken. In southern Europe they are sometimes fed to cows to increase the flow of milk, and at one time they were employed for making paste for book binders. They are scarcely edible, although containing considerable farinaceous matter, owing to the presence of a bitter narcotic principle. Our native species, better known as Buckeyes, with both smooth and prickly fruit, are equally worthless as food.

IVORY NUT.—There are two species of palms producing nuts hard enough to be employed as a substitute for ivory, in the manufacture of small articles of domestic use. But the one best known to commerce under the name of ivory nut is the fruit of *Phytelephas macrocarpa*, native of New Granada and other parts of Central America. This palm is a low-growing and almost decumbent species, the stem seldom more than six to eight inches in diameter; but the leaves are of immense length, or from fifteen to twenty feet, growing in bundles, or clusters. The fruit consists of about forty nuts, enclosed in a rough, spiny husk, of a globular form, produced on a short footstalk growing from the axis of the leaves, the whole bunch weighing from twenty to thirty pounds. They are two inches long, slightly triangular, and covered with a thin, pulpy coat, which becomes dry, papery and brittle when thoroughly dried, but when in its green state it is sometimes utilized by the natives for making a favorite beverage. The ripe nuts are very solid, hard, and when polished resemble ivory. Immense quantities of these nuts are imported into this country, as well as Europe, and used as a substitute for bone and ivory for making buttons, toys, and similar small articles.

JESUIT CHESTNUT.—See Water chestnut.

JICARA NUT.—A local name, in some of the Central American States for the Calabash (*Crescentia Cujete*). A low-growing, rather rough tree, with simple leaves, usually three growing together on a broad leafstalk.

The fruit is extremely variable, both in size and form, but mainly globose, and two to four inches in diameter. The shell is very hard, and largely used for drinking cups, and these are sometimes highly ornamented on the outside. The kernel is scarcely edible, but is used by the natives as a medicine.

JUBA NUT.—See Coquito nut.

JUVIA NUT.—See Brazil nut.

KIPPER NUT.—See Earth chestnut.

LITCHI NUT OR LEECHEE NUT.—I am inclined to think that the affix of "nut" to this Oriental fruit is an Americanism, and not used elsewhere. There are three distinct species of this fruit known among the Chinese, under the name of Litchi, Longan or Long-yen, and Rambutan, all the product of the Nepheliums, a genus of the soapberry family (*Sapindaceæ*). By some of the earlier botanical works the litchi is placed either in the genus *Dimocarpus* or *Euphoria*. Within the past few years this fruit has appeared in our markets, in consequence

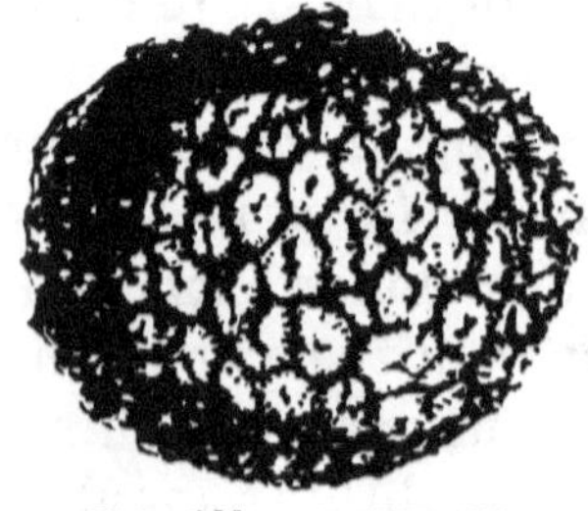

FIG. 103. LITCHI OR LEECHEE NUT.

of the increased trade with Oriental countries, and facilities for rapid transit across the continent. The litchi is a globular fruit, about one inch in diameter (Fig. 103), with a thin, chocolate-brown colored shell covered with wart-like protuberances. When fresh the shell is filled with a white, jelly-like pulp, in the center of which there is one rather large, smooth brown seed. The pulp is of a most delicious sub-acid flavor, but it is often rather dry and stale in the nuts which reach us from China and Japan. The tree producing this fruit is seldom more than twenty-five feet high, with rather sturdy twigs and branches, the leaves composed of about seven oblong pointed leaflets. This is said to be one of the most popular of Oriental fruits, and the trees would probably succeed in many of the Southern States and in California. It is now on trial in Florida, having been introduced there in 1886. It has been fruited in England many times, but always under glass, where the plants receive protection and artificial heat. A full description of this species, accompanied by a superb colored plate of the *Nephelium* or *Dimocarpus Longana*, appeared in the "Transactions of the London Horticultural Society," 1818, p. 402. There are not only a large number of species of the Nepheliums bearing edible fruit, but, as might be expected from their long and extensive cultivation, many local varieties, especially in the southern provinces of China and throughout the islands of tropical Asia. The Dawa of the Fiji islands is the fruit of *N. pinnatum*, a tree growing sixty feet high, and forming extensive forests on those islands. At some future time we may be receiving the dawas under the name of Fiji nuts.

LOUSY NUT.—See Earth chestnut.

MARKING NUT.—The seeds of *Semecarpus Anacardium*, an evergreen tree of the cashew-nut family (*Anacardiaceæ*), native of tropical Asia, and especially Ceylon. It has large, oblong leaves, and grows about fifty feet high, and the fruit is produced on a fleshy receptacle. The natives roast and eat these nuts, and the black juice obtained from the green fruit is used for marking cloth, hence the common name. The juice is also mixed with lime to make an excellent indelible ink, also for a kind of varnish.

MIRITI NUT OR ITA PALM NUT.—These are the Indian names of the fruit of a lofty palm tree, the *Mauritia flexuosa*, of the swamps along the Orinoco river, also in wet soils at higher elevations. This giant palm grows to a hight of a hundred and fifty feet, with an immense crown of large, fan-shaped leaves, and just beneath these the fruit appears in a pendulous cluster eight to ten feet long, containing several bushels, weighing, altogether, from one to three hundred pounds. The individual nuts are about the size of an ordinary apple, with a very smooth shell, somewhat veined or streaked. The natives of the country not only use the farinaceous kernels of these nuts as food, but obtain a saccharine material from the pith, out of which they make wine by fermentation. The petioles of the leaves also furnish them with a strong fiber, used as thread-cord, and for various other purposes.

MORETON BAY CHESTNUT.—See Australian chestnut.

MONKEY-POT NUT.—See Sapucaia nut.

MYROBALAN NUT.—This name is applied rather indiscriminately to the fruits of several species of the genus *Terminalia*, which are, in the main, large trees of the Myrobalan family (*Combretaceæ*). They are native of India, Malay, Fiji, and, in fact, almost all the islands of the Pacific in warm latitudes. The fruits are similar to large plums, but slightly angular, containing a hard, nut-like seed. They are used principally for tanning leather, and also for making ink similar to that made from oak galls. The kernels of all the species are edible, and are eaten by the natives. In the Fiji islands the *Terminalia Catappa* is a favorite tree with the natives, and they plant it near the houses. The kernels of this species have the flavor of the sweet almond.

NICKAR NUT.—The seeds of two species of *Guilandina*, a genus of the bean family (*Leguminosæ*). They are climbing plants, with hard-wooded, prickly stems, forming almost impenetrable thickets near the seacoast in the East Indies and other tropical countries. They have become widely distributed, as the pods readily float when they drop into the water. The pods are about three inches long, very prickly, containing seeds or nuts about the size of small marbles, and exceedingly hard;

but in time the water softens them, after which they
sprout and grow when cast upon the shore by the waves.
The two species are distinguished mainly by the color of
the nuts, those of *G. Bonduc* being yellow, and those of
G. Bonducella gray, or with a reddish tint. Of no value
or use except as botanical curiosities.

NITTA OR NUTTA NUT.—The native African name
of the seeds of *Parkia Africana*, a tree of the sensitive-
tree section of the bean family (*Leguminosæ*). It grows
about forty feet high, and has compound winged leaves.
It has become naturalized in the West Indies. The
pods grow in clusters, the seeds imbedded in a yellowish,
sweet pulp, like the carob or St. John's bread, and the
negroes are very fond of them. In the Soudan the seeds
are roasted, and then allowed to ferment in water until
they are soft and putrid, after which they are washed,
pounded and dried, then made up into cakes to be used
as a sauce for different kinds of food. It is supposed
that the African traveler, Mungo Park, first brought
these seeds or nuts to the notice of Europeans, and
Robert Brown named the genus *Parkia* in his honor.

NUTMEG.—A name applied to the fruits of a large
number of trees, and of different orders of plants. The
true nutmegs of commerce are the fruits of trees belonging to the genus *Myristica*, and of the family *Myristi-
caceæ*. The oldest and best known of these is the *M.
fragrans*, a small, widely branching tree, growing
twenty to twenty-five feet high, and supposed to be
indigenous to the Indian Archipelago. The fruit is
about the size of an ordinary walnut, with a thick rind,
which, upon opening, at maturity, discloses a reddish
aril covering the nut within. This aril or husk is the
mace of commerce, while the true nutmeg is the center
or hard seed (nut). The Brazil nutmeg is longer than
the true species, and is sold under the name of long nutmeg, and is the fruit of *M. fatua*. Another species, the

M. otoba, is cultivated in Madagascar, but is scarcely known in commerce.

Another species, the *M. sebifera*, is a common tree in the forests of Guiana, North Brazil, and up into Panama. It is utilized principally for the oil extracted from the nuts, obtained by macerating them in water, the oil rising to the surface, and as it cools skimmed off.

The seeds of several species of conifers and laurels are known, either locally or in commence, as nutmegs, or are used as a substitute for the true nutmeg. There are three different kinds of trees, native of Guiana, in addition to the one already named, the seeds of which are employed as a spice or medicine. One of these is the *Acrodiclidium camara*. These nuts are known in commerce as "Ackawai nutmegs," and are used mainly as a cure for diarrhœa and colic. Another is the seed of the *Aydendron Cujumary* tree, and they are known in commerce as "Cujumary beans," although they are not, strictly speaking, a bean, and the same is true of the so-called "Puchurim beans," from the same country, for they are the fruit of *Nectandy Puchury*, a small tree of the laurel family. They are used as a tonic, and considered highly stimulating.

Clove Nutmeg, or Madagascar nutmeg of commerce, is the fruit of *Agathophyllum aromaticum*, a small evergreen tree, indigenous to Madagascar.

Brazilian Nutmegs are the highly aromatic seeds of *Cryptocarya moschata*, or *Atherosperma moschata* of some botanists. It is a lofty tree, native of Brazil. The aromatic nuts are used as a substitute for nutmegs, but are very inferior to the genuine.

Peruvian Nutmeg, or Plum Nutmeg.—The seeds of a large evergreen tree with aromatic foliage, like our common sassafras, and for this reason is sometimes called Chilean or Peruvian sassafras. The seeds are of no more economic value than those of our native sassafras. It is known under various botanical names, but *Laurelia sempervirens* is, perhaps, the most familiar.

California Nutmeg, or Stinking Nutmeg, is the nut-like seed of *Torreya Californica,* a small tree of the yew family (*Taxaceæ*). The fruit is from an inch to an inch and a half long, with a fleshy rind enclosing a hard, long nut, which is slightly grooved like a nutmeg. The fruit, leaves and wood are strongly scented, hence the name of "stinking nutmeg," or "stinking yew." Another species, the *T. taxifolia,* is a native of Florida.

OIL NUT.—The fruit of a low-branching, deciduous native shrub, growing three to ten feet high, with alternate leaves and small greenish flowers in terminal spikes. It is the *Pyrularia oleifera* of Gray, and *Hamiltonia oleifera* of Muhlenberg. The fruit is in the form of a pear-shaped drupe, about an inch long, the small seed or nut with an oily kernel of strong acrid taste ; of no value. This shrub is found on shady banks in the mountains of Pennsylvania, and southward into Georgia.

PARADISE NUT.—See Sapucaia nut.

PEANUT, GROUNDNUT, GOOBER.—The well-known fruit of *Arachis hypogæa,* a low-growing annual belonging to the pulse or pea family (*Leguminosæ*), supposed to be a native of South America, but now extensively cultivated in nearly all semi-tropical countries and wherever the summers are long enough to insure the ripening of the seeds. Extensively cultivated in Virginia, south and westward. Too well known to require any further comment or notice here.

PECAN NUT.—See Chap. VII.

PEKEA NUT.—See Souari nut.

PERUVIAN NUT.—See Nutmegs.

PHYSIC NUT.—The seeds of *Jatropha Curcas,* a small tree of the spurgewort family (*Euphorbiaceæ*). It is native of some of the West Indies and warmer parts of South America, but now cultivated in other tropical countries for its seeds, which yield an oil used for the same purposes as castor oil, but rather more powerful and drastic. The seeds have a nutty flavor, but are rather dangerous if eaten in any considerable quantities, and death has been known to follow excess in this direction.

PHYSIC NUT.—In "Bartram's Travels," he refers to a seed or nut of a plant he found growing in Florida under this name, p. 41, as follows: "   .   .   . some very curious new shrubs and plants, particularly the physic nut or Indian olive. The stems arise, many from a root, two or three feet high; the leaves sit opposite, on very short petioles; they are broad, lanceolate, entire and undulated, having a smooth surface, of a deep green color. From the bosom of each leaf is produced a single oval drupe, standing erect on long slender stems; it has a large kernel and thin pulp. The fruit is yellow when ripe, and about the size of an olive. The Indians, when they go in pursuit of deer, carry this fruit with them, supposing that it has the power of charming or drawing that creature to them, from whence, with traders, it has obtained the name of physic nut, which means, with them, charming, conjuring or fascinating."

To what kind of fruit Bartram referred under the name of "physic nut," is not certain, but his description of the plant comes very near that of the American olive (*Olea Americana*), but the fruit of this and other closely allied plants of the same family are not "yellow" when ripe, but purple.

PIGNUT, OR HOGNUT.—See chapter on Hickory.

PINE NUT.—A name applied indiscriminately to the many species of pine trees (*Pinus*) bearing seeds large enough to be conveniently used as food. In southern Europe, and especially in Italy and the south of France, the seeds of the stone pine (*Pinus Pinea*) have been extensively used as food, from the earliest times down to the present day. Nearly all the ancient authors refer to them as among the valuable products of the country. Macrobius, in his story of the *Saturnalia*, speaks of the cones as *Nuces vel Poma Pinea*. These pine nuts are called *Pinocchi* in Italy and Sicily, and occasionally a few reach this country, where the Italian name has been corrupted into *Pinolas*. These seeds or nuts are used for desserts, puddings and cakes, also eaten raw at table, as with almonds. They have a slight taste of turpentine, but it is not strong enough to be at all disagreeable.

In this country we have several native species bearing very large edible seeds, and they are known in the West under the general name of *Piñon*, or nut pines. The best of these nuts, to my taste, are the seeds of *Pinus edulis*, so named

FIG. 104. BRANCH OF NUT PINE.

by the late Dr. Engelmann, because of its large, sweet and edible seeds. It is a small, low-growing tree, more or less common on dry hills and slopes, from Colorado southward through New Mexico, and into western Texas. The seeds of *Pinus Parryana* and *Pinus cembroides*, of Arizona and Lower California, are also called Piñons, and largely gathered by the Indians. Farther east and north we find the one-leaved pine (*Pinus monophylla*), and although the seeds are much smaller than those of *P. edulis*, they were formerly gathered in immense quantities by the Indians, to help eke out their often scanty winter store of food. Occasionally a small quantity of these pine nuts is sent to Eastern markets, but rarely, unless ordered early in the season. The trees of *P. edulis* and *P. monophylla* are perfectly hardy here, and worth cultivating for ornament, as well as their nuts, although their slow growth is a rather severe test of one's patience. Fig. 104 shows a Piñon branch.

PISTACHIO NUT.—Historically, this is a very ancient nut, for Bible commentators claim that it is the one sent by Jacob into Egypt. It is the fruit of a small, deciduous tree of the cashew family (*Anacardiaceæ*), a native of western Asia, but many centuries ago it had become naturalized in Palestine and throughout the Mediterranean regions. It has shining evergreen winged leaves, and the bark on the young twigs is brown, becoming russet-colored with age. There are several different species, but the one producing the nuts of commerce is the *Pistacia vera*, having brownish-green flowers in loose panicles, and these are succeeded by bunches of reddish fruit, about an inch long, with an oblique or bent point. The nuts have a double shell, the outer one usually red, the inner one smooth and brittle; the kernel is pale green, sweet, and of rather pleasant taste. There are a number of varieties, differing only slightly in form and size. This nut has been cultivated sparingly in Great Britain since 1570, but the climate is not quite warm enough to insure its ripening in the open air. It would probably succeed throughout the greater part of California, as well as in the extreme Southern States, but Mr. Berckmans writes me that it is not hardy in his grounds at Augusta, Ga. There is a species of pistacia known as *P. Mexicana*, found in central

Mexico, and extending as far north as San Diego, in California, according to the report of Dr. Cooper (Botany of California, Vol. I, p. 109).

QUANDANG NUT.—A medium size Australian tree, the *Santalum acuminatum*, of the sandalwood family (*Santalaceæ*). It produces a plum-like fruit, which is best known in its native country as the quandang nut. It is used as a preserve, but is little known, except in or near its native habitats.

QUEENSLAND NUT.—See Australian hazelnut.

SAPUCAIA NUT.—The Brazilian name of, at least, two species of large forest trees growing in the valley of the Amazon and its tributaries. The best known of these is the *Lecythis Zabucajo*, a lofty tree of the myrtle family (*Myrtaceæ*). It is closely allied to the more common Brazil nut of commerce. The sapucaia nuts are produced in an urn-shaped, woody capsule, which has received the name of Monkey-pot, because when these capsules ripen the lid at the top is suddenly liberated, emitting a sharp sound, which, as heard by the monkeys, gives them notice that the nuts are falling, and that the first on the ground becomes the fortunate possessor of the largest number. The capsules or pots are about six

FIG. 105.   PARADISE OR SAPUCAIA NUT.

inches in diameter, and the lid opening at the top about two inches. The nuts, which are packed very closely in the shell, are about one inch in diameter, and two to three in length, with a thin, brown, and very much wrinkled and twisted shell (Fig. 105). The kernel is white, sweet, oily, and somewhat more delicate in flavor than that of the common Brazil nut. In New York city these nuts are sold under the name of Paradise nuts. But this is probably only a local name, for I have been unable to find it in any botanical work. These nuts rarely come to this country in any considerable quantities ; a few hundred pounds at a time would be considered a large consignment.

SASSAFRAS NUT.—See Nutmeg, Chilean.

SASSAFRAS NUT.—See Nutmeg, Puchury.

SNAKE NUT.—A large, roundish fruit, about the size of the black walnut, the product of the *Ophiocaryon paradoxum*, a large tree of the soapberry family (*Sapindaceæ*), native of British Guiana. This nut takes its name of "Snake nut," from the peculiar form of the embryo of the seed, which is curled up spirally. The Indians, thinking there must be some virtue in form, use these nuts as an antidote for snake bites, although, so far as known to science, they do not possess any medicinal properties.

SOUARI NUT, OR BUTTERNUT.—This nut, like the last, is a native of British Guiana, and is the fruit of the *Caryocar nuciferum*, a noble tree, growing a hundred feet high, having large, broad, trifoliate leaves, resembling those of our common horse-chestnut, but not quite as broad. The flowers are very large, and, with the tube, fully a foot long, of a deep purple on the outside, and yellow within. They are composed of five thick, fleshy petals, and as showy as some of our best and brightest-colored magnolias. The flowers are produced in terminal clusters or corymbs, succeeded by a large, round, four-celled fleshy fruit five to six inches in diameter; but as some of the embryo nuts usually fail to grow, it changes the form of the fruit as it enlarges towards maturity, and only one or two of the nuts mature and ripen, very much as frequently occurs in both the sweet and horse-chestnuts. The nuts are affixed to

a central axis, and are of a rounded, subreniform shape,
and even flattened to an almost sharp edge on one side,
and broadly truncate at the scar (hilum) where they are
attached to the pericarp or central axis.   The shell is of
a deep brown color, embossed, as it were, with smooth
tubercles.   They are from two to two and a half inches
or more in their broadest diameter, as shown in Fig. 106.
The kernel or meat is pure white, soft, rich and oily,

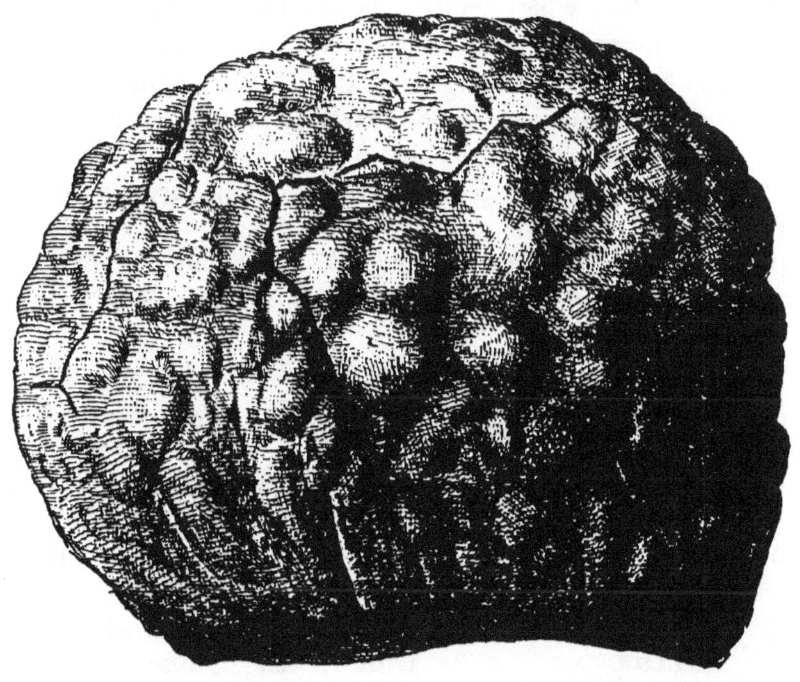

FIG. 106. SOUARI NUT.

with a pleasant flavor.   This nut is a rarity in our markets, and Mr. H. R. Davy of New York, to whom I am
indebted for a specimen, as well as other rare kinds,
assures me that in his forty-five years' experience as a
dealer in foreign fruits and nuts, he has never known of
but one lot, and that one consisted of about one-half
bushel, brought into his store by a sailor, who only knew

their common South American name. These nuts are more frequently seen in European seaports than in those of this country.

SOUTH SEA CHESTNUT.—See Tahitian chestnut.

TAHITIAN CHESTNUT.—The seeds of a tree known in the South Sea islands by the native name of Toi, but to botanists as *Inocarpus edulis*. It belongs to the bean family (*Leguminosæ*). The tree grows sixty to eighty feet high, and when young the stems are fluted like a Grecian column, but as they increase with age the projections extend outward, until they form a kind of buttress all around the lower part, gradually decreasing upward. This so-called chestnut tree has yellow flowers, succeeded by fibrous pods containing one large seed or nut, which, when roasted or boiled, resembles the chestnut in taste. The nuts have a different local name in almost every one of the Pacific islands where it is at all abundant.

TAVOLA NUT.—See Myrobalan nut.

TALLOW NUT.—A local and nearly obsolete name for the fruit of the Ogeechee lime or sour gum tree (*Nyssa capitata*) of the swamps of Florida, Georgia and westward. The fruit is about an inch long, resembling a small plum, the pulp having an agreeable acid taste. Bartram, p. 94, refers to this fruit under the name of "Tallow nut," but why so called is not explained.

TALLOW NUT.—The fruit of the Chinese Tallow tree, *Stillingia sebifera*, of the spurgewort family (*Euphorbiaceæ*), a native of China, where it is, as well as in some of the warmer parts of America, extensively cultivated. It has been planted in a few localities in the Southern States, and appears to thrive. It is a small tree thirty to forty feet high, with rhomboid tapering leaves and a three-celled capsuled fruit, each cell containing only a single seed thickly coated with a yellow, tallow-like substance, hence its common name.

This tallow or grease is used for making soap, burning in lamps, and also for dressing cloth.

TEMPERANCE NUT.—An English name of cola nut.

TORREY NUT.—The hard, nut-like seeds of *Torreya nucifera*, of Siebold, or *Taxus nucifera*, of Kæmpfer, and *Caryotaxus nucifera*, of Zuccarini, a tree native of Japan, where these nuts are eaten by the Japanese, either raw or roasted. An oil is also extracted from the nuts, for use in cooking or for burning in lamps. This Japanese tree belongs to the same genus as the so-called California nutmeg (see Nutmeg) and our Florida stinking cedar (*T. taxifolia*), also the great Chinese cedar (*T. grandis*).

WATER CHESTNUT.—Also known as water caltrops. The seeds of several species of water plants of the genus *Trapa*, of the evening primrose family (*Onagraceæ*). In southern Europe and eastward there is a species found in ponds,

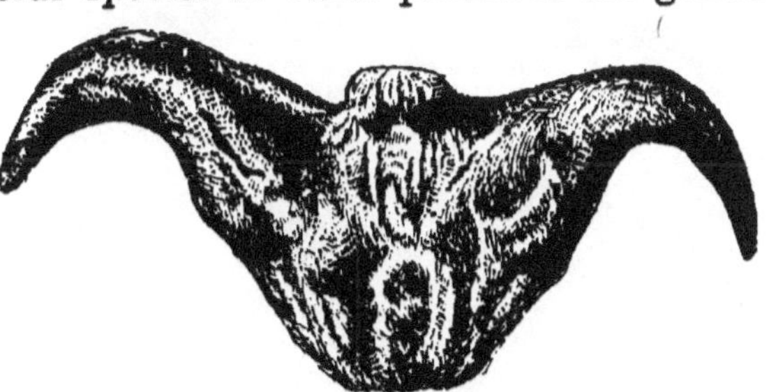

FIG. 107. WATER CHESTNUT.

the seeds of which are called Jesuit chestnuts (*T. natans*), and in India and Ceylon a closely allied one, the Singhara-nut plant (*T. bispinosa*), while in Lago Maggiore there is another (*T. verbanensis*), but all may be varieties of one and the same species, including the *Trapa bicornis*, a two-horned water chestnut, extensively used in China and Japan as food under various local names. In China they are called Ling, and of late years have been occasionally imported and sold, more as curiosities than for eating. These seeds or nuts are of a dark brown color, and of the form and size shown in Fig. 107, resembling, in miniature, the skull of an ox with abbreviated horns. When fresh, the kernel is of an agreeable nutty flavor.

WATER CHESTNUT, OR CHINQUAPIN.—The seeds of the large yellow water lily (*Nelumbium luteum*), a very common plant in small ponds in the West and South, but more rare in the East. The seeds are about the size and shape of small acorns, and produced in a large, top-shaped, fleshy receptacle. They are edible, and are supposed to have been extensively used as food by the aborigines of this country.

INDEX.